THE NEAREST WAY HOME

by the same author

Biography

THE DUCHESS OF JERMYN STREET (ROSA LEWIS)

EMERALD AND NANCY (LADY CUNARD AND HER DAUGHTER)

Autobiography

MERCURY PRESIDES

Fiction

THE ADONIS GARDEN

Daphne and Xan Fielding

THE NEAREST WAY HOME

Daphne Fielding

EYRE & SPOTTISWOODE
LONDON

First published 1970

Printed in Great Britain for
Eyre & Spottiswoode (Publishers) Ltd
11 New Fetter Lane, EC4
by Western Printing Services Ltd, Bristol
SBN 413 27490 X

to

Dirk Bogarde

Contents

Illustrations

The longest way round is the nearest way home

Seventeenth-century proverb

1

Cornwall

Xan was roaring in the kitchen:

'If you don't come down at once and eat this bloody lobster bisque, I'm going to chuck it over the cliff!'

His voice rose over the slap and surge of the waves.

We had been married that morning. It was July 11, 1953, and my birthday.

I was upstairs with my friends, Oonagh Oranmore who had come over from Ireland for the wedding, and John Strachey (the painter, not the politician) who kept insisting that he had given me away. But, in the register office at Liskeard, there had been no such ceremony. Oonagh and I had subsequently fallen into a nettle patch and John was now applying calomine lotion to the stings.

The lobsters for Xan's bisque were a present from the Looe fishermen who had been our wedding guests. One of them, Nibs, had passed out in the drawing-room as a result of confusing cherry brandy with red wine on top of champagne. He had been laid to rest on the floor by his ship-mates, with a cushion propped under his head 'to make him more comfortable' and his new hat pulled over his forehead 'to make him more decent'. 'We'll come back for him later,' they said.

Another roar came from the kitchen.

'Oh dear, this isn't a very auspicious beginning,' I said to myself, and started to weep.

'Never mind,' said Oonagh, 'it's not the first time you've cried on your birthday. With you, over-excitement always ends in tears.'

'Now then,' John broke in, 'you'd better both pull your socks up and face the Major's bisque. It smells as if it's burning.'

It *was* burning, but lashings of rum eventually helped to conceal the taste of carbonisation.

After dinner the wedding party embarked in two 'gondolas' for a trip round St George's Island and up the Looe River. These gondolas were in fact a couple of old cockleshells which had been tarted up for the summer tourists. Luckily the sea was calm, for their elaborate superstructure made the vessels alarmingly top-heavy.

Another feast had been prepared for us in an isolated cottage on the far side of the estuary: the home of a couple who helped behind the bar at our favourite pub, the Fisherman's Arms. In the parlour a table was spread with Cornish pasties, crab sandwiches, saffron buns and flagons of 'scrumpy', the rough local cider that goes to one's legs and has one tumbling into the nettles before one can say, 'And shall Trelawney die?'

The door leading from the parlour into the bedroom had been left open, deliberately, to disclose a vast double bed to which, in the almost impossible event of our failing to notice it, our two hosts now drew our attention.

'It's comfy enough, m'dears, I guarantee. Maybe not quite long enough for you, but you won't be worrying about that, will you?'

'And the floor's close enough if you happen to fall out . . .'

'Pity we couldn't find you any upstairs fish for supper. Still, the crab ought to do the trick . . .'

By 'upstairs fish' they meant skate or ray, locally believed to be endowed with the properties which the term all too clearly suggests. Only then did it dawn on me that Xan and I were being invited to consummate our marriage then and there.

'Go on, m'dears, make yourselves at home. We'll see your guests get back safely, then we'll doss down in the pub ourselves.'

And finally, as though to clinch the argument:

'Dozens of couples have spent the first night of their honeymoon in that bed. No need to be shy with us, you know.'

True, there was no need to be shy. We managed, however – not too ungraciously, I hoped – to decline this hospitality and, when the time came to leave, Xan and I left too.

By now the tide was out and the gondolas were aground, embedded in the mud-flats like a couple of overpainted hippopotami. We set out on foot, by the light of a full moon, guided by our hosts who showed us where to tread in order not to sink waist-deep into the seemingly boundless morass. With their help we sank no deeper than our ankles.

'The men ought to carry the women on their backs,' they suggested. 'That's what all the honeymooners do,' they added, as though this form of locomotion was decreed, like the usage of their bed, by some long-hallowed tradition.

To humour them, I clambered on to Xan's shoulders, thereby driving him several inches deeper into the slime, jeopardising his precarious foot-hold and almost bringing him to his knees. Understandably, he objected. So I dismounted.

John, however, declared he was all in favour of the suggestion – providing the respective roles of the sexes were reversed. He eyed the sturdy, besweatered and betrousered frame of our hostess. He knew she was the local skittles champion who had recently won the pig at Looe Fair for her prowess at bowls; he had also once seen her frog-march a customer out of the bar.

Without another word he gallantly relieved her of the heavy sea-boots she was carrying in her hand (for, like all of us, she was walking barefoot) then lowered himself (for he stood a good ten inches taller than she did) on to her back and, using one of the boots as a whip, urged her forward.

Cowrie, the house we lived in, stood on the edge of a cliff above Plaidy Beach, a couple of miles east of Looe. It was a modern, strictly functional building, but its lack of distinction was redeemed by the view: a noble seascape with St George's Island in the middle distance and Eddystone Lighthouse on the far horizon. The garden, sloping gently to the sea, was ingeniously terraced with banks of blue hydrangeas and hedges of fuchsias in every shade of red and purple. Mesembryanthemums trailed over the slate paths and tamarisks waved their dusty-pink plumes in the wind. At the bottom, over a sheer drop of twenty feet, a ship's ladder led down to a deeply indented cove and a cave which was once used by smugglers, inaccessible except from the sea or from straight above and therefore inviolate. Here rock pools provided shrimps, and the shingle yielded marine treasure in the shape of cowrie shells, salt-frosted sea-glass, mermaids' fans, bleached cuttlefish, and driftwood pickled by the salt water into snowy antlers and coral bones. The sea seemed to be in our ears, in our eyes and noses, all day and all night long; and from one end of the year to the other we were conscious of the tang of salt on our skin.

On the top terrace, just outside the french windows of the drawing-room, we had installed an old ship's bell: a dome of resonant brass supported by a pair of lead dolphins. This was a useful as well as decorative feature; for in foggy weather we could ring it to warn any fishing craft that had lost its bearings of the dangerous proximity of the Limmicks, a formation of hull-shattering rocks which at high tide lie just below the water a few furlongs off shore.

One November evening, when Ed Stanley was staying with us and a couple of other friends had come to dine, a particularly thick mist materialised, reducing visibility along the coast to a matter of feet. The five of us were playing poker and we had agreed that after each hand the heaviest loser should go and ring the bell. As the evening wore on, Xan and I noticed it was almost always he or I and scarcely ever Ed who was assigned to this chore. We therefore doubly regretted the game, which was presently interrupted by voices hailing from out at sea.

This time all of us went on to the terrace and rang the bell more vigorously than ever. To our relief, the voices almost immediately grew more distant, then faded away altogether.

'Well, we've kept them off the rocks,' said Ed. 'Better notify the coastguards all the same.'

Xan and I tried to explain that the coastguards were continually and pointlessly pestered by alarmists and hoaxers. But Ed was adamant, picked up the telephone, asked for the required number and, as soon as he was put through, announced in his most official voice:

'This is Lord Stanley of Alderley, peer of the realm, owner-skipper of *The Gables*, a sea-going yacht, and lieutenant-commander in the Royal Naval Reserve. It's murky weather outside and some mariners seem to have drifted dangerously close to the Limmicks. That's all I have to report. And now that I've made my number I'll bid you a very good night and return to the more pleasant and profitable business of fleecing my host and hostess. The fog seems to have dulled their wits and they're not holding very good cards. With any luck I'll be buying myself a bigger and better boat on the proceeds of this evening's game of cards.'

What action the coastguards took after receiving this message, we never discovered. But we did find out next morning that a fishing vessel had indeed lost its way in the fog and that the crew had heard our bell, which had enabled them to pinpoint their position, steer clear of the rocks and head for Banjo Pier, where again they were enabled to get an accurate bearing; for most of the inhabitants of Looe, knowing that one of their boats was missing, had dutifully assembled there with pots and pans and various other items of kitchen equipment to create an ear-splitting but fog-piercing din and thus signal the harbour entrance.

The granite cliffs stretching in an unbroken ridge all the way to Looe from our house, were tufted with cushions of sea-pinks and pranked with the vivid green and yellow of samphire. Here a pair of kestrels built their nest in the spring and I was able to observe through binoculars the whole of the young birds' life cycle. Most of all I enjoyed watching their flying lessons. As a preliminary exercise, the parents would encourage the fledglings to flap their wings and thus develop their strength. When at last the time came to take to the air, the young birds behaved like bathers faced with the first plunge into cold water, hovering on the edge of the precipice until they were gently nudged into the void. Fluttering uncertainly at first, they soon gained confidence and could presently be seen swooping and darting past our windows like a flight of russet arrows.

The cliff-top path was honeycombed with rabbit burrows and provided an exciting walk for our two Pekinese bitches, Sunflower and her daughter Salote. But when the myxomatosis epidemic was at its height, this walk was transformed from joy into nightmare as we came across increasing numbers of victims in every stage of affliction. One day I found a tiny orphaned rabbit in the hedgerow. It looked healthy, so I took it home and made it a nest from a cardboard shoe-box upholstered with hay and lined with red flannel. For some days I fed it from a fountain-pen filler but it preferred the bread and milk I sometimes gave Sunflower and Salote, who in time grudgingly accepted the interloper and even allowed it to nibble from their own plates. Not being able to decide whether the foundling was a male or female, we gave it the ambiguous name of Coney.

One evening, soon after Coney's adoption, Walter Greenwood came to dinner, which in itself was an unusual event; for although he had lived several years in Cornwall – ever since the production of his highly successful *Love on the Dole* – he still clung to the habits of his native Lancashire and preferred high tea as his last meal of the day. Suddenly, half way through the soup, he fell silent for a moment while a look of mild perplexity crept into his shrewd blue eyes. Then he clapped his hand to his vicuna-clad thigh and, in a voice which betrayed only a hint of alarm, announced:

'Stone the crows, I believe I've got a rabbit up me bags!'

I admired his composure no less than his ability to identify the trespasser without having seen it (for at that time he did not even know of Coney's existence). Had I been in his trousers I should have smelt a rat, or at least a mouse.

In addition to the intrusions of this baby rabbit, our guests – and indeed ourselves – also had to tolerate those of a blue budgerigar that Nibs had given me, knowing that I was an admirer of 'Fruity Metcalfe', the brilliant bird of the same species which recited nursery rhymes on the wireless. But mine never rose to the heights of the B.B.C. prodigy in spite of Nibs's confident assertion, 'Just you wait, m'dear, he'll be making sermons like a parson after I've finished with him.' He never made a sermon of any sort. By the time Nibs had 'finished with him' all he could utter was my Christian name (contracted to one syllable) preceded by a mild expletive used locally as a term of endearment, so that his total vocabulary to begin with was limited to the single phrase, 'Dirty bugger Daph'. To give him his due, however, he eventually extended this to include the words, 'Good boy', followed by his own name, 'Bumpy'.

How did I come to christen him so obscurely? Simply because I happened just then to be reading about Black John, the last of the West Country jesters – 'his height is under four feet, hump-backed and misshapen; his head, with tangled elfy hair falling wildly on his shoulders, droops upon his chest' – who had a narrow escape from being buried alive. He had been found in a snowdrift, apparently dead, but, as his body was being committed to the earth, a loud thump came from inside the coffin. As he later explained to the astonished mourners, at the sound of the words, 'dust to dust', he felt 'it was high time to bumpy'.

This was the only connection between Black John and Bumpy, but, for all his paucity of speech, the bird proved as entertaining as any jester. He spent most of his life at liberty, flying about the drawing-room, skidding across the dining-room table at meals, using his cage simply as an hotel and restaurant. From time to time he would alight on our heads or shoulders, or make a daring pancake landing on one of the Pekinese, whose superciliousness or native inscrutability prevailed over their annoyance even when he tweaked their whiskers.

It was presumably inquisitiveness rather than a bent for literature which prompted his interest in books and manuscripts. When I was writing he would take up a position by my right hand and try to pick up the hieroglyphs as they appeared on the sheet of paper, as though they were as three-dimensional as seeds; while the mere sight of a book being read induced him to perch on the binding and peck away at the pages. In time almost every volume in the house appeared to be deckle-edged. Nor did he spare the property of our guests. Even the equanimity of Paddy Leigh Fermor, who had come to stay for a few days to work on the proofs of his latest book, was put to the test by Bumpy's behaviour – 'Look here, this bird of yours is eating his way through my galleys faster than I can correct them. These misprints can't be good for his digestion.'

Paddy had come down from London by train and we had gone to the station to meet him. Looe stands at the end of a single-track branch line meandering down the valley from Liskeard, so I suppose it can accurately be called a terminus. But to insist on such a grandiose word for it would give a misleading picture, for it was scarcely noticeable even as a wayside halt. In fact most of our friends arriving here for the first time never realised they had reached their destination, unless they happened to notice the name LOOE spelt out in flowering plants on a patch of grass facing the diminutive platform.

Paddy was no exception. Long after the train had disgorged its passengers there was still no sign of him.

'The same old routine, damn it,' Xan muttered irritably, although by now he should have been used to wandering through the three carriages in search of our quarry, whom we would usually find, if it was dark, a trifle puzzled by this unexpected halt in what appeared to be the middle of nowhere, or, if it was in the daytime, gazing in admiration at the wood-fringed estuary which gave no hint of any town in the vicinity and wondering when the train was going to move on – unaware that if it did it would be in the sea a minute later. This time, however, just as we were about to embark on our usual procedure, Paddy's head and shoulders appeared at one of the carriage windows.

'You're here!' we yelled at him.

'I know I'm here,' he yelled back. 'I was waiting for you to help me. Hop in and give me a hand, will you?'

Paddy always travels light, so what possible help could he need, we wondered? As soon as we entered his compartment we found out. His suitcase had fallen (burst? been broken?) open and its contents scattered. The floor and seats were littered with his clothes, a dispersed ream of foolscap paper, a ship's compass, several boxes of Swan Vestas, the remainder of a bag of toffee and a score or so of loose cigarettes which had escaped from the big blue box of fifty Players constituting his minimum daily nicotine ration.

'I was looking for my sand-shoes,' he explained. 'I couldn't very well start off from Paddington wearing them – ah, good, here they are – but I wanted to arrive at the seaside appropriately shod.'

He beamed with pleasure at the rubber-soled white canvas plimsolls for which he had by now discarded a pair of hand-made black leather brogues, then bundled his possessions back into the suitcase, slammed down the lid, picked up the case and moved towards the carriage door. There was a slight check before he reached it. In the process of repacking he had overlooked a shirt, one cuff of which had somehow hooked itself on to the luggage rack while the other remained trapped under the suitcase lid, so that both sleeves were now stretched to rending point. But he noticed nothing until, with the sound of an ogre sneezing, the shirt split from hem to collar-band.

'Never mind,' he murmured unconcernedly, as he moved on with several square feet of Sea Island cotton trailing from his case. 'The main thing was my sand-shoes. I'm so pleased I found them.' He turned his head in the direction of the sea and inhaled deeply. 'I now feel I'm an integral part of this salty marine scene.'

Cornish folk are suspicious of foreigners, and by 'foreigners' they mean anyone who is not Cornish. To them a North-countryman is as alien as a native of Calabria or Montenegro. It therefore says much for Walter Greenwood's personal qualities that he was promptly and universally accepted at Looe.

I might have been considered a foreigner myself, for I was born in London and had spent all my adult life outside the Duchy. But people remembered – and if they didn't, I reminded them – that my childhood home was in the Glynn Valley, only fifteen miles away, and that I was a Vivian, 'one of those mad Vivians from Bodmin'. (Bodmin had always been noted for its gaol and its asylum. 'Took to Bodmin' was the local way of saying 'sent to prison', 'put to Bodmin' – another constantly recurring phrase – was the lunatic's fate.) So now that I was back I was straightaway regarded and treated as though I had never crossed the border of the Tamar.

I could almost persuade myself that this was so, for in spite of the lapse of years nothing seemed to have changed. Up on the moors near Dozmary Pool, into which Sir Bedivere flung Excalibur and from which the hand of samite rose to receive it, my 'secret place' – a deserted cottage – looked just as secret as when my brother and I, in our teens, used it as a hideout for meeting such friends of ours as were banned from Glynn by paternal decree. The sense of mystery exuded by the landscape (quaking bogs; skylines broken by ivy-clad chimney-stacks, isolated columns marking the position of long-abandoned and half-flooded tin-mines; the stone circles, Celtic crosses and burial chambers which gave Walter de la Mare such an impression of darkness and dread that he vowed never to return to Cornwall) seemed just as overpowering; but whereas this spot used to be connected in my mind with the Hound of the Baskervilles – how easy to imagine the beast baying and slavering, in full cry under the moon! – I now found myself picturing it as a potential landing-ground for flying saucers.

I also rediscovered another nearby pool, bounded on one side by milk-white pyramids of powdered china clay, on the other by a man-made landslide of cuttings from a disused granite quarry. The water was still as fathomless, and still as icy-cold, as I had always remembered it. Naturally so. But less naturally, almost miraculously indeed since it was accessible by motor-car, it still appeared to be unused. Whenever Xan and I drove up here for a picnic, even in the height of summer when the more adventurous or less gregarious trippers would sometimes abandon sand and sea for relatively uncrowded moorland, we had this perfect bathing place entirely to ourselves.

Even the coastline west of Looe, which now looked dangerously like ideal building land to me, had remained mercifully unchanged. We would often walk all the way to Polperro, across the fields and along the cliffs, and from the moment Looe Harbour dropped out of sight until we approached the slope down to the little fishing village five miles further on, we rarely saw anyone. And Polperro itself was unaltered – the incongruous and unfortunate pisky souvenir shops were already there when I was a girl – except for a new and welcome addition: a small restaurant where the lobsters were so choice and succulent that even Xan, not notorious as a trencherman, could eat two at a sitting.

Another childhood joy, now renewed, was the annual week-long Looe Fair which was held, as of old, on the quayside. Here again no concession had been made to modernity. Brass had not changed to chromium, nor solid wood to trashy plastic. Above all, there was no loudspeaker. The barkers relied on their vocal cords, and the music of the roundabout was provided by a mechanical organ. It was delightful to be whirled round and round, mounted on a heaving dragon or ostrich and clinging to a burnished barley-sugar column, without having one's ear-drums tortured by electrically produced decibels.

Yet the atmosphere was by no means staid or genteel, for Nibs was not alone among the local inhabitants in increasing his normal intake of scrumpy during fair week. In fact I was always surprised, considering their rowdiness, that none of them ever fell over the quayside into the river. It could so easily have happened. Indeed I had seen it happen. But not to a local inhabitant; and not during fair week; and not in the dark; and not on a bellyful of scrumpy. It was in winter, in broad day-light, and long before opening time, that a guest of ours – Wynne Godley – absent-mindedly took a step backwards and went over the edge.

When I say, 'I saw it happen', this is not strictly true; for I had my back turned to Wynne at the time and was talking to his wife Kitty, the daughter of Jacob Epstein. All I heard behind me were the words, 'I say, I'm off,' spoken in an almost con-versational tone which gave no hint as to their true meaning. But I saw the accident reflected on Kitty's lovely face. Her eyes widened with incredulous horror. And no wonder: the tide was out, the river bed was exposed, and the drop was over twenty feet. We rushed to the edge of the quay together, dreading what we would see below.

Wynne was half sitting, half lying in eighteen inches of muddy water, looking up at us with a rather pained expression. He resembled more than ever at that moment his father-in-law's statue of St Michael, for which he had in fact been the model. Kitty and I were so relieved to find he had nothing more than a twisted ankle that we failed at first to realise what an escape he had had: the spot where he had landed was a mere puddle fringed by jagged rocks. It was not until we were home, and

Wynne had had a mustard bath and been put to bed, that Kitty said, 'Think what would have happened if . . .'

Cowrie was ideally designed for a married couple who were both writers. We each had our own work room. Xan's was a monkish cell, with a high window which gave him light but – and this was the reason why he chose it – no distracting view. The furniture was reduced to a functional minimum: bookshelves, an office chair, and a built-in desk running the whole length of one wall. Here his typewriter sat enthroned, ancient and majestic, kept in a caul of silk when not in use.

The old-fashioned Remington had a special attraction for Bumpy. He loved its noisy chatter, prelude to a joy-ride. As soon as he heard Xan at work he would fly in and perch on its carriage, dodging the little hammers as they struck the paper, delighted by the ping of the bell at the end of each line which heralded an exciting struggle to maintain balance as the roller rotated and the carriage whizzed back to its starting point. Apart from its owner, Bumpy was the only creature in the house who was allowed to touch this sacrosanct object. A girl friend of one of my sons, who thoughtlessly left a half-eaten apple on the keyboard, was not asked to Cowrie again.

My own requirements were different. Unlike Xan, I need a vista to encourage me and so I used to work in the bay of the dining-room, a semi-circular platform almost independent of the room itself, at a table looking out through a bow window on to the expanse of sea and cliff. Here, with the gulls crying like starving children outside, I wrote most of *Mercury Presides*.

Yet I never managed to maintain regular working hours and would sometimes find myself hankering after an hotel bedroom with the bare essentials, no clutter of personal possessions, meals appearing magically when required, no animals to feed or exercise – in short, no household chores. Not that Cowrie made too many demands on my time – it was an easy house to run – but I did not have the necessary discipline or organisation to be both an efficient housewife and a writer. Besides, I wasted too much of every day playing with the animals.

It soon became apparent that we could not carry on without some sort of domestic help. Since we preferred to employ someone local, we inserted an advertisement in the West Country papers. This elicited only one reply in three weeks, from a man in Devonshire who stated that he '*thought* he could fulfil all our requirements'. Hopefully we sent him his fare to come for an interview. When he arrived our hearts sank. He was mild-mannered and soft-spoken but extremely elderly, with an auburn wig and a facial twitch. There was something disturbingly ecclesiastical about him and indeed the only reference he produced was from a parson, stating that he was a proficient church organist. This did not sound particularly promising, but we engaged him on the spot. After all, he was the only applicant.

Three days later, when we were expecting our 'butler' to assume his duties, we received instead a letter from him confessing that he 'thought he could *not*, after all, fulfil our requirements'.

Since there seemed to be such little response from the locals, we decided next to try Ireland. Oonagh eventually sent us a couple of girls from the Wicklow Mountains, and the Cinderella-like beauty of the younger one compensated for the Ugly-Sister appearance of the other. That they were completely untrained was a minor disadvantage in view of their willingness and cheerfulness; and we were prepared to put up with a staple diet of bacon and eggs and sausages – the only food with which they seemed familiar or could cook without assistance and guidance – since they got on so well with us, with the animals and with each other.

They continued to get on well with us and with the animals, but we soon noticed that between themselves some difference of opinion had arisen. In a short time they ceased to be on speaking terms. Then one morning we woke up to find that Cinderella had done a midnight flit. 'She only came here,' the Ugly Sister explained, 'to save enough money for her bridal dress. She's gone off to marry her boy. He's a black man, but they're having a white wedding.'

Shortly afterwards she too left, a victim not of romance but home-sickness. So for us it was back to the kitchen stove.

Xan and I took it in turns to do the cooking – an arrangement which not only ensured a fair division of labour but should also have provided a certain variety in our meals and even an element of surprise, since we were both keen on culinary experiments. Unfortunately I was too heavy-handed with the scrumpy – I had recently read somewhere that rough cider could be used in cooking in much the same manner as wine – so that every dish I produced had a high alcoholic content and an identical taste; while Xan, whose use of curry-powder was equally over-enthusiastic, turned out concoctions which, however diverse their ingredients, were indistinguishable to the palate except in their degree of pungency.

We were eventually saved by Walter Greenwood. 'Look,' he told us, 'there's a couple from Salford, Danny and Beryl Owens. They're on holiday here but want to settle permanently. Mind you, I don't know if they'll suit. Beryl has never done any skivvying, she's been a hairdresser and a secretary. But Danny was a cook in the army. Anyway, why not give them a try?'

Why not indeed? We promptly arranged an interview, at which Beryl did most of the talking. She was neat and tidy, almost frail in appearance, and in spite of her assurance that she 'could turn her hand to anything' it was hard to imagine her doing housework. Danny's sole contribution to the conversation was, 'I expect the Major likes a nice plate of cornflakes for breakfast'. But from the moment they took over the running of Cowrie, our lives were changed.

From then on meals – and what meals! – appeared at regular intervals. We did not even have to plan the menus unless there was a special dish we wanted, which Danny invariably mastered at the first attempt, but for the most part we relied on, and revelled in, his own North-country specialities. What could be better than Lancashire hot pot followed by Yorkshire pudding served as a sweet course with golden syrup? Our pre-luncheon and evening drinks would be automatically accompanied, as in Greece and the Middle East where Danny had been an Officers Mess sergeant, by home-made cheese straws and other appetisers. And at tea-time we were able to surprise our guests by offering them 'one of Beryl's melting moments' or a 'Chinese chew-chew,' another of her confections, suitably as popular with the Pekinese as with us humans.

It was no idle boast that she could 'turn her hand to anything'. She not only kept the house spotless but was also ever-ready with scissors and comb should Xan or any of our visitors want a haircut. 'And don't forget,' she insisted, 'I can always find time for a bit of typing as well.' She even found time to feed and groom the dogs when we were particularly busy, while Danny volunteered to take Bumpy off our hands for at least part of the day. Until they grew accustomed to the sight – for a chef's cap was not a common form of headgear in Looe – the tradesmen calling at the back door were somewhat abashed to find themselves greeted by a man crowned with a two-foot tall cylinder of starched white linen surmounted by a bright blue bird squeaking, 'Dirty bugger!'

2

The Dark Continent

Perhaps it was living on the Cornish coast, with a pirates' cave just below us, that prompted Xan's interest in the history of piracy. For several months his reading seemed devoted exclusively to the activities of Buccaneers and Marooners; and his conversation was peppered with references to Lamarck's Sea Beggars and Condé's Rochellois, to the sailor geniuses of Cornwall and Devon and the great captains of the Spanish Main. Finally he announced that he wanted to write a book about the Barbary Corsairs and suggested we both drive out to North Africa and visit their former lairs. Once again I was to be his photographer, as I had been in Crete before we were married.

'Bring me back a parrot!' Nibs shouted as I waved goodbye.

Not knowing what to expect on our travels – Africa was still 'the Dark Continent' to us – we had prepared as though for a full-scale safari. Our Land Rover was piled high with tents and camping equipment, jerrycans for water and extra petrol, medicine chests and tin trunks, suit-cases and map-cases, cameras and binoculars, picnic baskets and thermos flasks, tropical kit and emergency rations. But we drew the line, just, at solar topees. Since the car had a canvas hood and could not be locked, Xan had devised a Heath-Robinson anti-burglar system to protect all this gear from possible robbers: lengths of heavy chain passed through handles or wrapped round bundles and fastened together with a big brass padlock.

On our way through France we stopped at Chantilly to spend a couple of days with Diana Cooper, who greeted us with the announcement that we were going that very evening to a charity ball at the Château de Compiègne for which she had taken tickets.

'But I have nothing to wear!' I moaned.

'Never mind,' she said. 'I'm not wearing anything special myself.'

So Xan started unloading the car to see what we could rustle up in the way of clothes that would not be too unsuitable. 'Whew!' he gasped when he had finished and staggered inside with the last bundle. 'I pity anyone who tries pinching this lot.'

The nearest to an evening dress that I could produce was a Marks & Spencer cotton frock, over which I flaunted an embroidered Cretan cloak which had belonged to one of Xan's war-time guerrillas. Though slightly the worse for wear, it could be taken, I hoped, at a pinch, at a distance, for one of Christian Dior's more eccentric creations.

Xan's sartorial problem was less acute. He did at least have a dark suit. 'With a black bow-tie,' he said hopefully, 'it would look almost like a dinner jacket.' But he had no bow-tie, black or otherwise, and had to make do with a velvet hair ribbon of mine. It was a pity, though, that his only choice of footwear was between a pair of sandals and desert boots.

Diana was true to her word. She did not put on anything special. In fact her dress would have been inconspicuous had it not been worn with an astrakhan kalpak and a fringed shawl, in keeping with my own unavoidably exotic and fanciful garb.

Thus accoutred, the three of us set off for Compiègne in the Land Rover.

'It's not very comfortable, I'm afraid,' Xan apologised, as we rattled over the cobbles, with the wind whistling through the gaps in the canvas hood and the loose chains clanking dolefully against the metal floor in the back.

'Discomfort's not the sort of thing I mind,' said Diana, who sat wedged between us on the hard front seat. 'In fact I rather enjoy it.'

'It's not very elegant either,' Xan remarked, as the floodlit château sprang into view round a bend in the road and we joined the procession of gleaming limousines purring their way into the forecourt. 'I feel rather like a mongrel trying to get into Crufts.'

Crowds of onlookers had gathered to enjoy this free display of opulence and fashion, and we could hear 'Oohs' and 'Ahs' of admiration as each vehicle disgorged its complement of elaborate coiffures crowned with tiaras, deep *décolletés* glittering with diamonds, bare shoulders sprinkled with shimmering *grains de beauté*, glowing draperies, mink stoles, opera hats, tail coats and stiff white shirtfronts adorned with the multi-coloured ribbons of various orders and decorations. As we drew up at the entrance and disembarked, there was a gasp of astonishment followed by a round of applause and a roar of laughter.

Diana seemed genuinely surprised by this outburst of merriment. 'But why are they laughing?' she asked one of the gendarmes on duty. He himself was too overcome to reply and merely motioned us up the flight of stairs leading to the front door, lined for this occasion by a guard of honour drawn from a regiment of Spahis. 'Too beautiful,' Diana murmured, as we slowly ascended between the white-robed figures, the drawn swords, the turbans framing fierce hawk-like countenances which reminded me of Xan's. At the top of the stairs she popped a large boiled sweet into her mouth, then offered one to each of us from the paper bag she was carrying.

1 *top* Daphne and Xan at Cowrie, Looe, the day before their wedding

2 *above* Nibs

3 *left* Kitty Godley with the bell

4 Camping out on the Barbary Coast

5 Filming *Ill Met by Moonlight* at Villefranche, from left to right Tony Forwood, Daphne, Dirk Bogarde, Xan

'Better have one,' she said, oblivious of the consequent bulge on one side of her face. 'The château is owned by the State, and if I know anything about French officialdom there'll be *No Smoking* notices plastered all over the place.'

We had not worked out a detailed itinerary through France. Our only decision was to avoid main roads as much as possible, while heading in a southerly direction, and stop for as long or as short a time as we liked wherever chance or our fancy led us. Thus we found ourselves, two days after leaving Chantilly, on the banks of the Dordogne, at Carrenac, in an old château that had once belonged to Fénelon and had since been converted into a comfortable hotel. Here we lingered for over a week while I corrected the page proofs of *Mercury Presides*, working in a little tower connected to our bedroom by a winding stone staircase.

Many years later, while researching the life of Nancy Cunard for the book I was planning about her and her mother, I came across a description of this very same tower in one of her letters. She too had stayed here and she too had been correcting the page proofs of one of her own books at the time – the sort of coincidence (or, to use her own word, 'circle') which would have pleased her as much as it did me.

I was very reluctant to leave Carrenac, for I had quickly grown to love the soft green melancholy of the Dordogne and its atmosphere of mystery which reminded me of Cornwall. Besides, I had begun to dread the thought of Africa and was filled with a sense of foreboding which I was unable to explain or analyse but also unable to shed. 'You'll get over it,' Xan assured me. But I didn't. It persisted all the way through Spain and intensified as we approached Algeciras, from where the mountains of Morocco loomed across the narrow straits between the Pillars of Hercules. Here we lingered even longer than at Carrenac before I could steel myself for the final plunge.

'There now,' Xan exclaimed triumphantly, as we entered Tangier harbour. 'It's not so bad after all, is it?'

During the short crossing on the car ferry he had tried to restore my spirits by describing the delights in store for us: '. . . a free port . . . no customs, no taxes . . . no government even, just an international administration . . . the nearest approach to freedom you can get in the modern world . . . smugglers galore, which ought to appeal to your Cornish instincts . . . delightful riff-raff of every race and creed and colour . . . no conventions, no inhibitions . . . and we'll get to know the Arabs through Peter Mayne.'

We had both revelled in *The Alleys of Marrakesh*, which had been published earlier that year – compulsory reading for anyone about to visit North Africa – but knew nothing about its author, though we had a letter of introduction to him. From a short passage at the beginning of the book, in which he mentions hiring a bicycle as a means of transport, we had formed a mental picture of a tall, gangling, languid student figure. This picture was at once dispelled by the voice that replied to our telephone call with a brisk 'Peter Mayne here', followed by an invitation to lunch on the following day and precise instructions as to how to find our way. Suitably, he was living in an Arab house right at the top of the kasbah.

He proved to be what his voice had suggested: neat, trim, taut, as compact as a hazel-nut. He also proved to be a very good cook. The meal he had prepared was unusual and delicious: grilled swordfish, followed by a Moorish speciality of thinly-sliced oranges spiced and sugared and stewed until they were almost caramelised. We were enchanted, too, by the house, as compact as its occupant, tiny in fact, but with an air of spaciousness due to open archways instead of doors leading from one room to the next. From outside it had looked unprepossessing, merely one of a row in a narrow whitewashed lane, but now we could see how it was built into the ancient battlements, where it clung like an eagle's eyrie, dominating the whole medina, the old Arab town, and affording a magnificent view of the modern city and the sand-fringed bay beyond.

'I don't own it, alas,' Peter told us, giving his characteristic laugh, a sound reminiscent of the mating call of some exotic game-bird. 'I don't own anything. I'm just living here for the moment. It belongs to a friend of mine. As a matter of fact he wants to sell it.'

Xan pricked up his ears at this and glanced across at me. Then he turned back to Peter and casually enquired: 'Do you happen to know how much he's asking for it?'

'But you *must* buy it,' David Herbert insisted at dinner that evening when we told him the price that Peter had mentioned. 'It's going for a song. And just think what fun it will be to have your own house here for holidays.'

David, a very old friend of mine, had been living in Tangier for a number of years. He loved the place and expected everyone he knew to share in his enjoyment. 'There's never a dull moment here,' he assured us, 'but of course you have to know the right people. I'll see that you do.'

And so he did. Every morning he would ring us up at our hotel and outline our programme for the day: drinks at Dean's Bar or at The Parade, a picnic at Robinson's Beach or in the Diplomatic Forest, a luncheon party at his own villa up on the Mountain or with one of his friends nearby, tea with another friend, a cocktail party followed by a dinner party with yet another and another . . . By the end of a fortnight we must have met almost every member of the large colony of foreign residents. But, apart from their servants, we never saw an Arab in any of their houses.

'Nor are you likely to,' affirmed Paul Bowles, the American writer. 'There's an element of make-believe in the native life as seen from without – which is the only viewpoint from which you ever see it, no matter how many years you remain.' He and his wife Jane had lived in Tangier even longer than David and were the only foreigners we met who had really tried to participate in the native life. But I felt less and less inclined to get to know the Arabs after coming across the following passage in one of Xan's notebooks:

> 'The Emperor Moulay Ismail had eighty-three brothers . . . One of them used to fill the imperial coffers by enticing the richest women in the Empire to place their breasts under a box; he would then jump on the lid till they agreed to part with their money . . . He himself, suspecting one of his concubines of infidelity, had her stuffed with gunpowder and then set alight . . . He forced seven of his daughters-in-law to eat their own breasts, cut off piecemeal and placed in their mouths . . . One of his wives – an English girl, abducted at the age of fifteen from her home in Cornwall – was made to place her feet in a basin of boiling oil to persuade her to adopt the "only true religion" . . .'

At this point I stopped reading, feeling more than ever like Ruth among the alien corn. I tried to persuade myself that the Arabs were now more civilised and less fanatical than in the days of Moulay Ismail, but that very afternoon my nerves were shattered again by an encounter with a native funeral procession. We met it head-on, as we were climbing up the lane to our hotel in the medina and, judging by his subsequent description of it in *Corsair Country*, Xan was as alarmed as I was by the experience:

'The sound of screaming preceded it by at least two minutes, striking our ear-drums in that confined space with the effect of a jet of icy water on warm bare flesh. A crippled beggar tapping his way along the gutter seemed to reel under the blast and, as though bowled over by a fireman's hose, tumbled back into the nearest doorway. We dived in after him. Just in time. For as the din rose to an almost unbearable pitch, reverberating from the echo-chamber of our hollow refuge, the view of the wall facing us – little more than two yards away – was blotted out by a human mass which swept past not so slowly but as relentlessly as a flow of volcanic lava.

'Had these men been marching in step, they might have been taken for the remnants of a rather tattered regiment in retreat, even though the noise they made was anything but martial. But shod as they inevitably were in flapping babouches, they could only shuffle forward; and this inexorable surge seemed all the more sinister for its utter lack of precision. Each man had his head thrown back, his mouth locked open in an endless screech, his eyes staring wide as though begging the sun to sear them from their sockets; and each upturned face, distorted by vocal effort and by the unnatural position of the jaw-bones in relation to the neck, looked as unfeeling as a zombie's ... They were all as sightless as they looked, blinded not by the sun's rays but by the branding-irons of bigotry.'

David, however, kept reassuring me that the Arabs were the sweetest people in the world. No matter what they did, he always had an excuse for them. If he heard of any foreigner having his pocket picked (an almost hourly occurrence) he would sympathise not with the victim but with the culprit – 'the poor dear was obviously hungry and didn't have the price of a meal'. Even when his own flower beds were robbed of a large quantity of daffodils, and the thief was eventually identified by the footprints he left on the ground – footprints made by a pair of shoes which David had given to a boy whom he had once employed in the garden – he merely showed the utmost understanding: 'I don't blame him, the poor dear just can't resist spring flowers'. And one evening, when he was driving me in his car just outside the town and we saw three young Arabs savagely beating up an older one by the side of the road, he drove on heedless of my concern – 'it's none of our business. You don't want to meddle like a missionary, do you?' – adding, as an afterthought, 'He must be a very nasty old man for three of the poor dears to be attacking him like that.'

I was not completely convinced on this particular score, but David's enthusiasm for Tangier in general was so infectious that by the time we were due to leave on our journey along the coast we had arranged to buy the little house in the kasbah.

To repay him and his friends for all the hospitality we had received, we decided to give a party on the eve of our departure. We were not subject to the usual currency regulations, since Xan had obtained a special Treasury allowance for the research on his book; but this was barely sufficient to cover our travelling expenses, so we could not afford to be lavish. A midnight feast on the beach, where we pitched our tent, was the best we could do. This also gave us an opportunity to test our camping equipment and safari expertise.

Vodka sprinkled with Cayenne seemed an appropriate apéritif for the main course which – inevitably, since Xan was doing the cooking – consisted of a vast cauldron of curry. This was followed (we must have been out of our minds) by a dish of Mexican tamales drenched in Tabasco. Fortunately, we had laid in several demijohns of the local wine; unfortunately, someone had advised us to make it more palatable by flavouring it with pepper. Using this mixture to quench our internal fires was equivalent to adding fuel to the flames. Eyes watered, noses ran, brows glistened, and conversation was punctuated by hiccoughs. One of our guests, a bald Argentinian painter called Jorge Jantus, kept passing his hand over the egg-smooth dome of his skull and murmuring: 'I can feel each individual hair sprouting from my head like a blade of young corn.'

Our friends still looked rather overheated when they came to see us off next day. 'A most memorable meal,' said Jorge. 'Last night I dreamt I was a Rhine Maiden, a great big blonde with long golden tresses. But, alas, when I woke up this morning . . .'

'You British are so *intrepid*,' Jane Bowles gasped, as she watched Xan fix a small Union Jack on the bonnet of the Land Rover.

He had insisted on this precaution 'just in case we run into any trouble'. But he did not specify what sort of trouble he had in mind. Nor did I see, whatever it might be, how a flag could help us. And even if it could, this particular one did not look very firmly attached and would probably be blown away before we had gone a few miles.* With Janey's words echoing in my ears, however, I did my best to assume the demeanour of Lady Hester Stanhope coolly entering Damascus clad in velvet pantaloons and tasselled burnous or Gertrude Bell casually donning a pair of clean white gloves to ride across the desert.

David, however, sensed my poltroonery. 'Here,' he said. 'Whenever you feel nervous, just clench this.' And he slipped into my hand a lump of jade, its almond-green surface carved

* It was.

in the shape of a pomegranate. This comforting talisman lay cradled in my palm as we drove off.

It did not protect me, however, from a hazard I had not even envisaged – illness. I was struck down in the middle of nowhere, half way between Tangier and the Algerian border. We had spent the previous night in a fly-blown Spanish Legion outpost on the coast, where the food was atrocious even by Spanish colonial standards. There was no bread available for breakfast, which consisted instead of some peculiarly repulsive buns: coils of orange-coloured batter streaked with tallow-white grease. Xan wisely declined them, but I took a tentative nibble so as not to offend the old Arab watchman who had gone out specially to buy them.

'Are they as nasty as they look?' Xan asked.

'Much nastier.' But I went on eating, even giving a hypocritical smile of enjoyment, for the old man was still hovering by our table, clearly awaiting our approval.

An hour later, as we were negotiating the hairpin bends of a road aptly named The Toboggan, I began to feel distinctly queazy.

'You're looking a bit green,' said Xan. 'Are you all right?'

'Very much *not* all right,' I told him. 'In fact I'm going to be sick. Please stop . . . now, at once!'

We stopped. We stopped again a little further on. We stopped several times more in the course of the morning. At one of these halts Xan took my temperature, then muttered grimly: 'You need a doctor. We'd better push on into Algeria.' This was all we could do, for, short of driving all the way back to Tangier, there was no hope of finding a doctor elsewhere.

At the frontier we had to stop again in any case, but this was little consolation to me, for, on the Spanish side, there was not so much as a lavatory and the passport formalities seemed endless. But, aware of my obvious need, the officials were sympathetic. 'The French are better equipped than we are,' they said. 'If the lady cares to step across at once, we have no objection. And our colleagues on the other side will understand.'

I stumbled across the border, more grateful than ever for the amenities of French civilization.

By the time we reached the nearest town I was in a state of near-delirium, conscious only of uncontrollable shudders and agonising gastric spasms, and unaware of my surroundings except in intermittent and incoherent flashes: a darkened room (in an hotel, I presumed) . . . Xan sitting by my bedside (just sitting, not smoking, so I knew I was really ill) . . . Then another figure standing over me (a doctor? Surely not. No doctor would be wearing such abbreviated khaki shorts . . .)

But it *was* a doctor, and a good one. The antibiotics he prescribed had an almost immediate effect and two days later we were on the road again.

As we drove slowly along the coast, stopping for a day or two, or occasionally even a week, at each of the former corsair harbours which Xan needed to visit, we kept running across a travelling circus which must have set out on tour at about the same time as ourselves and was now following the same itinerary. I thus developed a new fear – earthquakes (a serious one had occurred in this area only two years before) – and the consequent hazard of the lions and tigers escaping. Yet we became very attached to this circus – the long convoy of caravans was a reassuring sight on the lonely roads – and never missed a performance whenever we found it encamped close by. Though the acts were very soon all too familiar, and so were the fleas which infested the Big Top, it was with genuine regret that we parted company on the Tunisian border.

There was an armoured car drawn up outside the frontier post, and inside we noticed three young Arabs manacled together and under guard.

'Who are they?' we asked one of the French officials.

'*Fellagha*,' he replied.

'*Fellagha*?'

'Terrorists,' he explained. 'Members of the anti-French independence movement. They're more and more active these days, so I advise you to keep to the main roads and never travel by night.'

Needless to say, we took this advice and I clutched my jade talisman more tightly than ever. We had no means of telling how serious the situation was and, though we kept hearing about *fellagha* activity, we saw no sign of it ourselves. There was an atmosphere of apprehension wherever we went, however, and I was relieved when Xan's research in Tunisia was completed and we drove across the frontier into Libya where independence had already been achieved and there was so far no political unrest. My spirits soared as we entered Tripoli, the last port of call on the Barbary Coast. Our journey was over.

The joy of arrival was enhanced by the prospect of seeing a familiar face again after six months spent among total strangers. We had been told that Hugh Cruddas was now living in Tripoli, engaged in selling *Tatlers* to the Arabs – a peculiar and surely not very profitable occupation. We had visions of poor Hugh standing at a street corner with a large pile of glossy magazines beside him, and with about as much chance of selling them as a Protestant missionary would have of making converts in the Vatican City. But we soon discovered that he dealt not in *Tatlers* but in tractors, which were much in demand to boost Libya's agriculture. He was therefore doing very well for himself. His office was in Tripoli itself, but he lived in a villa on the coast just outside the town and here he invited us to stay.

It was delightful to live in a private house again instead of in hotel bedrooms or in our tent, to be pampered by Hugh's smiling servant Magic Touch (so christened because of his ability to mend anything from an electric fuse to a motor-car engine – an unusual gift among Arabs whose general attitude to anything mechanical is that it should *not* work). Delightful, too, to discover a hitherto unknown and unimagined experience – underwater swimming, equipped with an aqualung. Just as the patina of grime adhering to my talisman, and the sand that had invaded all our luggage, soon disappeared under the administration of Magic Touch, so were all my fears and apprehensions washed away in the gravity-free depths off the Libyan coast.

We had planned to go home by the inland route across Algeria and Morocco, but by this time the political situation had deteriorated in those two countries as well and we were warned that the roads were no longer safe. There were no regular sailings from Tripoli direct to Europe, but we eventually found a small Italian cargo vessel which was willing to take us and the Land Rover to Naples by way of Malta: a welcome port of call for us since the new Governor there, Bob Laycock, was an old friend of ours.

There was no means of cashing a traveller's cheque on the scruffy little tramp steamer and, by an oversight, we had no Italian currency. In fact we had little ready money of any kind and, when we offered to pay for our drinks in Moroccan and Algerian francs or Libyan piastres, we were treated as though we were trying to fob off counterfeit coins. Our prestige rose, however, when we put in at Valletta and Bob called for us in the Governor's launch, accompanied by his ADC in naval uniform. For the rest of the voyage I felt we could have used chocolate coins and got away with it.

But more money trouble awaited us at Naples. Since we arrived on a Sunday and all the banks were shut, we decided to stay just for the night at one of the most expensive hotels where traveller's cheques would be accepted.

'Can you cash me £20?' Xan asked, after registering and handing in our passports.

'Certainly, *signor*,' said the receptionist, a young man with a prominent Adam's apple and a pursed face that reminded me of an anaemic prune. He also seemed to me unnaturally tall; no doubt he was standing on a platform behind the counter so as to add to his supercilious and would-be intimidating manner. From this vantage point he carefully examined the cheque which Xan had just signed, turned it over to read the wording on the back, then triumphantly announced: 'No good.'

Unfortunately he was right. Since we had not intended to come home via Italy, we had omitted to ask for our cheques to be made valid for that country.

'But they're the only cheques we have!' Xan exclaimed. 'Two hundred pounds' worth too!'

'I'm sorry,' said Prune-face, the delight in his eyes belying his words. 'Perhaps another hotel would suit you better,' he added with a barely concealed sneer, for he had just caught sight of the two battered suitcases we had extracted from the back of the car. What would he have said, I wondered, had he seen the rest of our travel-stained safari gear?

'Certainly not,' Xan replied. 'We're staying here. We'll go round to Thomas Cook's in the morning; they'll soon settle this business.'

But at Thomas Cook's we were told it would take several days to settle; telegrams would have to be sent to Head Office in London, to the Bank of England, and we would have to wait for the replies. And we didn't have enough money even for the telegrams.

'I'll stake you for them out of my own salary,' said the helpful young clerk, who, we subsequently learnt, was aptly named Angelo. 'You can pay me back when your money arrives.' Then, with a gesture which acted like a dock-leaf on the sting we still felt from Prune-face's nettle-like behaviour, he shyly handed us a few banknotes. 'You can pay this back at the same time. It's not much, I'm afraid, but I can't afford any more.'

Small though it was, this generous loan was a godsend and enabled us to while away the time sight-seeing, which we would otherwise not have been able to afford. We visited Pompeii almost every day and one afternoon we climbed Vesuvius. Our guide demonstrated how an egg could be boiled in the clouds of steam rising from the volcano and, as I gazed at the smoking crater, I felt this was symbolic of my own volcanic anxiety, which seemed to produce a hard-boiled egg in the pit of my stomach each time I thought of our mounting hotel bill.

Angelo's money also enabled us to get our own back on Prune-face, by keeping him guessing as to how we were managing to survive. He had obviously expected us, since we had no ready cash, to eat in the hotel restaurant and sign for our meals. We might indeed have done so, had I not discovered that the glass of orange juice I ordered for breakfast one morning (which, moreover, came out of a tin) cost the equivalent of ten shillings. Rather than pay such prices, and also to increase Prune-face's bewilderment, we preferred to eke out our small resources by dining in the cheapest pizzeria or trattoria.

One evening, after our usual plate of spaghetti or shared

pizza, we found that the Land Rover had been robbed. Xan's anti-burglar device, which had worked perfectly in North Africa for month after month, had failed within the space of a few days in the more sophisticated *milieu* of Naples. The chains and padlock still stood firm, but the thieves had made off with several pieces of our luggage by the simple expedient of sawing through the handles – and under the very nose of the police too, for we had left the car parked outside the local *questura.* I gave thanks, however, to Mercury (who presides over travellers as well as thieves) that at least I had been left one of my most precious possessions – my Cretan cloak, which I happened to be wearing.

Our passports were still at the hotel, so the police to whom we reported the theft had to ring up there to check our particulars. We gave a complete inventory of what had been stolen and, on hearing that this consisted mostly of clothing, the pleasant young man who had volunteered to interpret for us said, 'Then perhaps I can be of further service to you,' and handed us his card which denoted him as a tailor by profession.

When we got back to the hotel we found Prune-face more bewildered than ever. Why were we back here and not under arrest for trying to pass dud cheques? – for this was clearly what he thought we must have been up to on receiving the telephone call from the police. His bewilderment turned to disgust when he saw the gilt and marble hall in which he presided littered with our tent and camping equipment, for Xan had ordered what remained of our luggage to be removed for safe keeping. This precaution was of course tantamount to shutting the stable door after the horse had departed, especially since all our gear had to be bundled back into the car the very next day.

For, early in the morning, we heard our cheque problem had at last been solved. We rushed down to thank and reimburse angelic Angelo, hurried back to settle our bill – at which even Prune-face unpursed his cheeks for a moment into two fairly smooth Victoria plums – and by midday we were on the road to England.

3

Farewell to Glynn

On our return to Cornwall we found a great pile of mail waiting for us. It was months since we had received any letters, and several weeks since we had seen an English newspaper. Now, as I tore open envelopes, a complexity of troubles was released, splintering the joy of home-coming.

It was a shock to learn that my brother Tony had been shot with a revolver by a girl friend, who was charged with maliciously wounding him and had been sentenced to six months' imprisonment.

Equally alarming was the news contained in a telegram and letter from my solicitor Raymond Gardner who, among other friends, had received an advance copy of my autobiography *Mercury Presides* which had been published during our absence. The book had reached him just as he was sailing to New York, so that it was only while reading it in mid-Atlantic that he learnt to his amazement and concern that Henry Weymouth and I had been married secretly in 1926, a year before our 'official' wedding in 1927:

> A month before Henry was due to leave England [I had written] we made the bold decision to get married secretly, for we could not see our parents' attitude towards the

6 *left* The Arab house in the walls of the kasbah

7 *below* Paul Lund (in background) with Cameron Rougvie

a Casita, the house on
ιe cliff edge looking
ver the sea to Spain

l Rocio, Spain, from
to right: Jaime Par-
, Daphne, Jay
elwood, Annie Davis,
ɔo Devonshire

10 *left* Sunflower and Salote in the Land Ro

11 *right* The Cerrado, Valley of the Wolves, Portugal: dining terrace and Judy

12 *left* Trubshawe at the Cerrado

13 *right* Piggy (formerly Princess Precious Pearl) at the Cerrado

14 *left* Maids and animals, from left to right Lourdes with Judy, Maria-Elena with the blonde half-wit, Maria with Salote, Salome with Piggy

marriage softening, even after a year. We decided that we would tell them we were married when Henry returned and face the music then.

To this day I cannot imagine how this wedding has never been discovered. We took out an ordinary licence and the banns were read out for three Sundays running at St Paul's, Knightsbridge. Henry gave his name as Frederick Thynne, which was quite correct. I used my second name, Winifred.

When Henry returned after nine months abroad all opposition to our marriage had surprisingly caved in and our engagement was announced. Everyone suddenly became so understanding that we had not the heart or the nerve to say, 'Thank you very much, but we're already married,' so we decided to risk the possibility of the quiet secret ceremony being discovered and go ahead in the grand style with the marriage which was being planned for us at St Martin-in-the-Fields, with a reception afterwards at Dorchester House.

When I wrote the book my father and both of Henry's parents were dead and I felt there was no one left who could be affected by this disclosure. But, when Henry and I were divorced in 1953, I had declared only the date of the second marriage, which I had always looked upon as the valid one. As Raymond now pointed out to me, this was a serious inadvertency on my part, for, although the 1927 marriage had been dissolved, the previous one was still valid and I was therefore still legally married to Henry. But meanwhile Henry had remarried, and so had I. We therefore both appeared to be bigamists!

On his return to England, Raymond advised me that this irregularity would have to be straightened out as soon as possible, and in May 1955 I requested the court for a ruling that the divorce I obtained should apply also to the secret wedding. My application was rejected by Lord Merriman (whose name, in the circumstances, I could not help considering inappropriate) who pointed out that the information relating to Henry's and my 'status' was incorrect since we were described as 'bachelor' and 'spinster' respectively, and this description had been repeated in my affidavit given in the divorce petition and again at the hearing. Lord Merriman added that 'some points arising from the case might be for consideration by others' – a phrase which rang ominously in my ears – but he granted me leave to appeal.

The story was naturally seized upon by the press and at Cowrie we were pestered by reporters. Xan dealt with the daily series of telephone calls from Fleet Street by simply saying, 'No comment,' and replacing the receiver. He also refused to admit any journalist who called at the house, but an unusually persistent one did manage to slip in through the back door, and although Xan bundled him out again in a matter of minutes, the report of 'a long interview' with us appeared next morning in a London daily.

A lighter touch was provided by one of Osbert Lancaster's pocket cartoons in the *Daily Express*, depicting Maudie Littlehampton saying to her husband, 'Darling, do you remember betting me a fiver that it was going to prove a lot easier to unite the Germans than to separate the Baths?'

It was a harassing time, but Xan did his best to allay my anxiety by appearing unperturbed. 'Why should I worry?' he said facetiously, '*I* can't be charged with bigamy.' Not that he believed I could, either. 'The law is an ass,' he added, 'but surely not *such* an ass.' Yet how could we be sure? We could only wait and see.

There were two months to wait before my appeal was due to

be heard. Meanwhile my brother came to stay with us. He too was waiting – for his girl friend's release from prison – so that we were both saddled with demons of disquiet, though each of us reacted to them differently. Tony felt an obsessive urge to discuss his drama, while I shied away from any mention of the horrid imbroglio I had brought upon myself, so his worries were almost a relief to me since they took my mind off my own.

I was glad that I did not have to be present at the hearing, which occupied three judges and lasted five days. To my intense relief, it was found that there had been no fraud and the tangle was duly sorted out. But it was a close thing, for one of the judges considered that my appeal should be dismissed. Luckily he was in the minority. The successful conclusion was undoubtedly due to the brilliant representation of my case by Mr Geoffrey Lawrence, who was later to prove equally successful in defending Dr Bodkin Adams on a charge of murder.

Once again Cowrie was besieged by the press, but this time no intruder managed to force an entry. The journalists appeared to draw a similar blank with Henry, for one paper reported, in an unconsciously poetical vein, that 'the only sign of life at the Marquess of Bath's mill house in Wiltshire was a black-coated butler walking through the daffodils.'

The expense of all this litigation was a heavy drain on our finances, which were already depleted by the rising cost of living in England. Though we did not live extravagantly, even the upkeep of Cowrie was proving too costly for us. We might have economised by doing without the services of Danny and Beryl, but they were now such an integral part of the household that we could not envisage it without them. Yet they were not to remain with us much longer. Shortly afterwards Beryl's father died, and she and Danny had to leave us to help her mother run the lodging house she owned.

We knew we would never find another couple who suited us so perfectly, so we decided to abandon Cowrie altogether, leave England and settle somewhere abroad. This idea had already occurred to us from time to time – it seemed the only solution to our financial problem – but so far we had been unable to steel ourselves to act upon it. Our minds were now made up. After all, we already had somewhere to live – the little kasbah house in Tangier – and though I knew Morocco could never replace Cornwall in my heart, I consoled myself with the thought that at least Tangier was on the sea.

I dreaded moving again, for I still had sad memories of packing up the house in which Henry and I had lived and where our children had grown up. Belongings seem to accumulate like an organic growth of moss or lichen and I remembered how, when dismantling my previous home, some long-forgotten object – a garment from the dressing-up box, a dog's collar or a letter – would turn up unexpectedly, almost shaking my resolve and disarming me.

To spare me a repetition of this experience, Xan kindly volunteered to supervise the packing up of Cowrie, while I went to Ireland to stay with Oonagh. But before this final leave-taking, there was another farewell visit which I felt impelled to make. With my two younger sons Christopher and Valentine, who were steeped in my Vivian mythology, I went to have a last look at Glynn.

The house had been empty for many years. The drive had become a jungle path invaded by rhododendrons which interlaced their branches above us. It was a sultry afternoon, the sky was swollen with dark cumulus clouds, and presently heavy raindrops began to splash down on the leaves. As a Macbeth-like storm broke overhead, we sheltered under a green tunnel of ponticum, watching the lightning flashing on the hills and listening to the thunder rolling round the valley. When the rain stopped we made our way up to the house. The ghostly grey stone façade looked as noble as the ruins of a Greek temple. We found a broken ground-floor window and, as we climbed through it, were startled by some chickens scuttling through the hall. Rainwater dripped through a hole in the roof and the warped floorboards creaked beneath our feet. . . .

I have never gone back to Glynn.

4

The Kasbah

We set out for Tangier in the Land Rover, with our two Pekinese, Sunflower and Salote, sitting between us in the front seat, and Bumpy swinging to and fro like a bell in his travelling cage suspended from the roof. He delighted in the rocking movement and chattered softly to himself all the way.

Once again we broke our journey at Chantilly and stayed a couple of days with Diana, who fell in love with Bumpy at first sight and begged us to bring him down to the *salon* after dinner. We had put a record of *Swan Lake* on the gramophone and no sooner was Bumpy released from his cage than he alighted on Diana's head. 'He wants you to dance,' I told her. And like an Edwardian headdress, his plumage matching her eyes and swirling blue dress, he nestled happily among the silvery-gold feathers of her hair as she waltzed beneath the crystal chandelier.

On landing at Tangier we drove straight up to the kasbah and let ourselves into the tiny house with a disproportionately massive iron key. The interior seemed as dark as the bottom of a well and looked smaller than I had remembered. Our furniture had not yet arrived from England and there were only a few bits and pieces left behind by the previous owner: a rough kitchen table, a small cooking stove, and a refrigerator of doll's house dimensions which produced half a dozen ice cubes no larger than poker dice.

We climbed up the narrow winding staircase on to the landing which, with its glass roof and glass-tiled floor, resembled a big cucumber frame and at once suggested itself as an ideal site for an indoor garden, a prospect which cheered me up considerably and compensated to a certain extent for the meagreness of the bathroom equipment (impossible to lie full length in the short tub which had a raised seat at one end on which to sit) for the absence, so far, of a proper bedroom and for the bareness of the living-room. One wall, however, was lined with a narrow built-in banquette, on which there was just enough space for us to sleep if we stretched out foot to foot.

But sleep, for me at least, was barely possible on account of the invisible army of bugs which crept out of the upholstery to regale themselves on my fresh Cornish blood. Envying Xan's apparent immunity to them, I watched dawn break over the flat white roofs below us and listened to the alien sounds of the kasbah's awakening: the muezzin calling the faithful to prayer from the minaret of a nearby mosque, echoed by the alarum of the household cocks answering from all over the town in ever-increasing numbers, until the sun itself seemed to burst forth in the sky crowing like a great golden cockerel. Later came the tinkle of the hand bells rung by the water-carriers, the miniature fanfare of small brass trumpets blown by the garbage-collectors, and finally the clatter of goat hooves on the paving-stones as the early-morning herds were driven through the narrow alleyways, exuding a pagan smell as they waited to be milked outside the front doors of the neighbouring houses.

Sunflower and Salote found these foreign sounds and strange smells perplexing and kept glancing at me reproachfully. But

Bumpy was bird-happy and delighted that the world should be stirring at such an early hour. I had fears for his safety, however, for in the dark I had seen sinister feline silhouettes slinking along the battlements, framed for a moment in the archway giving on to our terrace, and I realised that I would never be able to risk leaving the windows open at night.

Later in the morning, as we were planning how we were going to furnish and arrange the house, I noticed a small snake gliding across the floor.

'Let's hope it's only a baby grass snake,' Xan said, trying to introduce a note of confidence into his voice.

'It looks more like Cleopatra's asp,' I replied, as I watched the gun-metal coils winding themselves round one of my bedroom slippers.

We felt it would be unlucky to kill anything on our first day in the house, so Xan tried to pick it up on a sheet of foolscap to remove it from the room. But at each attempt it writhed and lashed about so menacingly that he finally had to bash it on the head with the heel of his shoe before dropping it over the battlements.

Had I known then, as I discovered a little later, that this type of snake was extremely venomous and hatched out in the old town walls on which our house was perched, I would have felt less guilty about killing it. For the time being I merely took the precaution of buying a mosquito net, hoping it would keep out snakes as well, closing my eyes to the nightmarish picture of getting into bed and carefully drawing the curtains only to find a gun-metal coil on my pillow. This picture subsequently almost came true. But it was not after drawing the curtains (by this time I had abandoned the net which proved too hot and stuffy to be used) nor was it on my pillow. It was on getting up one morning that I found the lifeless form of one of these little reptiles on the bottom sheet. It must have fallen from the roof before I had got into bed and I had slept on it all night and squashed it flat.

A considerable amount of repainting and refurbishing had to be done to make the house decently habitable. New upholstery for the banquette was essential. So was a full-length bath. A bedroom would somehow have to be contrived from a largish recessed space on the landing, and a windowless alcove in the well-like hall converted into a dining-room. Meanwhile we continued to camp out in the sitting-room in order to supervise the work.

We were fortunate in finding a jack-of-all-trades, by the name of Mohammed, who spoke English. He had learnt the language as a boy and had once worked as a guide at one of the smart hotels. We wondered why he had ever given up this job, in which his good looks and charm must have proved valuable assets, for he was certainly not very proficient as a handyman. On some days he would not turn up for work at all, but subsequently compensated for this by an almost fanatical outburst of activity; plaster and paint would fly in all directions and for several weeks Sunflower, Salote, Bumpy and a tortoise we had acquired were all dappled with the Pompeian pink which was meant to be on our sitting-room walls. He himself was often the victim of his own slapdash methods. The ladder would collapse under him when he was perched on the top rung; he would forget to turn off the current before changing a light switch and an electric shock was the inevitable result; he would fail to turn off the water before renewing the washer on a tap and a shower-bath was the unexpected but obvious outcome. But the pleasure he derived from these unintentional comic performances and the laughter they provoked were so infectious that we always welcomed his presence in the house.

At the end of each working day he would join us over a glass or two of wine which, being forbidden by Koranic law, he appeared to enjoy all the more and, since pork was likewise forbidden, he would cheerfully devour a ham sandwich with an appetite sharpened by a sense of sin.

Gradually we became acquainted with our neighbourhood. Next door to us was a private braid-manufacturer: a bare shed with a long bench, on which three cloaked and hooded figures sat cross-legged all day, each tethered by a long silken thread to a child standing outside in the street, his tiny hands performing cat's-cradle figures to make the necessary crosses and loops in the braid. One of these little slaveys was a butter-ball of a boy with a flat Esquimo face and a grin like a Hallowe'en pumpkin which disclosed a row of teeth like pointed seeds. His head was clean-shaven but for one lock sprouting from the crown (by which Allah would be able to drag him up to heaven). He could not have been more than five years old, yet he and his two equally juvenile companions seemed perfectly content to work all day providing they could knock off for a minute or two every now and then and frisk around the nearby alleys, like colts released from a stable into a grass field.

At times this part of the kasbah seemed to be one vast playground, full of ragged but completely happy urchins who, since they had no toys, devised their own amusement and games. Sunflower and Salote at once provided them with additional entertainment. Never before had such strange animals been seen in the neighbourhood. What were they? A rare kind of monkey? With their domed heads, furrowed brows, bulging eyes and practically non-existent noses, they caused gales of laughter whenever they appeared, and each time we took them out for a walk we were followed by a hilarious crowd who imitated them, snuffling, screwing up their faces and putting out their tongues. Xan and I did not mind this much, but the dogs did. Unnerved by the alien commotion, they began to bark and growl neurotically and no longer wagged their tails at the sight of their leads and collars.

The situation improved, however, as soon as Khemo came to work for us.

Our first glimpse of Khemo, in a friend's house, was of a brightly clad figure coming a cropper down a flight of stairs and landing with a thud at our feet, grazing her knees but saving the tray of drinks she was carrying. Not a single glass was broken, scarcely a drop of liquid was spilt. With a cat-like bound she was back on her feet in a trice, while a broad grin spread across her coffee-coloured face. Clearly, a remarkable woman.

We learnt from our host that she was the grand-daughter of one of El Glaoui's black slaves (hence her features, which were more Negroid than Semitic), that she had been married to a drunken taxi-driver, had given birth to a daughter, had left her husband and become the mistress of a rich American (we were later to see some photographs of her, dolled up in a picture hat trimmed with ostrich feathers, presiding over a smart beach picnic) but had left him on discovering that he too was a drunkard, since when she had come down in the world. We learnt, moreover, that she was a good cook, was only temporarily employed and wanted a permanent job. We engaged her at once.

She would arrive at our house every morning clad in an elegant caramel-coloured robe, sailing up the narrow street like a galleon, her great kohl-rimmed eyes sparkling above her black veil, gold ear-rings (and one or two gold teeth too) gleaming inside her hood. Once indoors she went through the reverse process of a butterfly emerging from the drab chrysalis, as she unveiled and shed several layers of colourful gossamer until she was finally stripped to her working clothes: a man's sweater and a pair of baggy bloomers reaching down to her knees.

Sunflower and Salote took to her immediately. She always spoke to them in Arabic and they were as enchanted as we were by the sound of her voice, which was deep and gurgling. Escorted and protected by her, they were no longer provoked by derisive crowds when they went for a walk in the kasbah.

Sometimes, however, she failed to turn up in the morning and would send her little daughter to tell us that she was unwell, having eaten something that had disagreed with her. But we knew what the trouble really was, for, as far as wine was concerned (she drew the line at pork) she was as emancipated and unbigoted as Mohammed. On the following day she would arrive still suffering from a hangover, as green in the face as the leaves she had inserted under her turban and plastered over her brow: the traditional Arab remedy for what she euphemistically called 'food poisoning'.

When our furniture eventually arrived from England we found we could not get the large wooden crates through the front door, so we had to unpack them out in the street. It seemed as though the whole population of the kasbah turned up to watch this operation and presently we realised why. The discarded cases, packing paper, cardboard, wadding and string were eagerly pounced upon and sold round the corner. Children crammed themselves into the largest crate, which could not be immediately removed, recalling the numerous offspring of the old woman who lived in a shoe. Fights broke out over the sharing of this plunder and Khemo had to disperse the crowd again and again, laying about her with a broom.

I was moved by the sight of my familiar objects exposed in this foreign environment. A collection of white china pussy-cats with turquoise-blue ribbons round their necks and baskets of flowers in their paws, looked all the more prissy and insular as the live lean alley-cats of the neighbourhood slunk past on their prowl for food; while my stuffed boar's head was greeted by the local populace with shrieks of horror. Khemo told us later that everyone had thought it was the Devil.

By the time we had unpacked the last crate there was barely room to move inside the house. It was impossible to get some of our larger pieces of furniture up the spiral staircase, but fortunately we managed to farm these out on various friends and were no longer faced with an obstacle race every time we entered the front door. By Christmas we had cleared the decks sufficiently to be able to give a house-warming party and even to have friends (or rather one friend at a time, there was no room for two) to stay. Our first guest was my eldest son Alexander, then an undergraduate at Oxford.

One afternoon he returned from sight-seeing in the town, looking flushed and angry. 'An old Arab sitting on a bench patted my behind as I walked past him,' he exclaimed indignantly.

'Just an old Arab custom,' I told him. 'You mustn't mind.'

'But I *do* mind! I couldn't believe it. I walked past him again, just to make sure. And he patted my behind a second time!'

'No wonder. He must have thought you were encouraging him.'

But my light-hearted attempts to placate him were of no avail.

'I should have knocked his fez off, damn him!' he exploded.

'Well, that's one way of starting a riot,' Xan said. 'You're lucky, though. No one pats *my* behind when I go for a walk.'

But Xan's attempts at soothing him were as useless as my own and Alexander continued to simmer.

The prospect of our party delighted Khemo, who forthwith summoned various friends of hers to help with the preparations. For several days our diminutive kitchen was packed with her cronies engaged on the mysterious rites which accompany the making of *cous-cous.* The huge copper cauldron we had borrowed gradually filled with pellets of semolina deftly rolled by a succession of practised fingers and presently it was time to buy the chickens.

Khemo insisted on coming with me to the poultry market – just as well, since I now discovered that I was expected to bring the birds back alive and have them killed on the premises in Moorish fashion by Mohammed. The poultry stalls were festooned with clucking, fluttering bodies strung up in bundles by their legs. To my inexperienced eye they were indistinguishable, but Khemo urged me to probe and pinch every feathery backside before making a choice. To please her (for this procedure left me none the wiser) I did so, and we carried home our victims in half a dozen baskets. They were penned in the kitchen for the night, and each cluck and squawk of protest from them prompted Bumpy to squeak, 'Dirty bugger Daph' – a description which, in the circumstances, I felt to be not entirely inappropriate. In the morning, to my guilty relief, Mohammed neatly slit their throats and left them to bleed to death according to custom.

Mohammed, who was also looking forward to the party, suggested we should have music for our guests and promised to bring along a friend of his who played the *raita.* (His friend proved to be a doleful mannikin vaguely connected with the neighbouring mosque, whose instrument – a cross between a zither and a banjo – produced a limited number of twangs, each as plaintive and melancholy as his expression.)

Not to be outdone, Khemo declared that she too had friends

in show business. There was a dancer she knew, a *belly* dancer indeed, who would be delighted to perform for us. She rushed out at once to make the necessary arrangements.

Half an hour later she was back. 'I left a message,' she told us, 'My friend will be here in a few minutes to look at the house and see if there's enough room for the performance.'

'Is she really as big as all that?' we asked. How big could a belly be, we wondered, for its owner to require a preliminary reconnaissance? But Khemo merely laughed and said, 'You'll see.'

Shortly afterwards there was a knock at the door and she rushed down to let her friend in. But instead of the voluptuous houri we were expecting, we saw only a young Arab boy, a rather plain young Arab boy in fact, dressed in faded blue jeans, tattered canvas shoes and an old mackintosh. But for his dyed hair (his thick curly locks were bright orange) he would have been indistinguishable from any of the other kasbah youths. After a cursory glance round the hall he gave a nod of approval and left.

Khemo's face split into an extra-broad gold-and-ivory grin as she saw the disappointment on ours. 'Don't worry,' she said, 'you'll see.'

'What a let-down,' Xan complained. 'Not only the wrong sex, but even the wrong size. The fellow's as thin as a rake. The party's bound to be a flop.'

But it wasn't. The house was crammed to bursting point and our guests overflowed from the hall and the dining-room, up the stairs, on to the landing, into the sitting-room and even into the bedroom. (We slept that night in wine-stained sheets, after picking our way across a floor littered with plates, glasses and chicken bones.) The skinny youth arrived during dinner, still dressed in his shabby clothes but carrying a suitcase. After half an hour in the bathroom he reappeared transformed, unrecognisable in a black veil and heavy make-up, resplendent in appropriately padded bodice and low-waisted pantaloons which revealed a midriff as burnished as the skin of a pomegranate. What it lacked in size it made up for in agility, expanding and contracting, coiling and uncoiling, undulating and gyrating, as though with an independent life of its own, while he himself, balancing on his head a tray laden with glasses of mint tea, circumambulated the house in a series of exaggeratedly mincing steps, miraculously avoiding the countless obstacles and hazards.

I had made a habit of giving the three little braid-makers next door a handful of sweets each time I passed them. When Khemo heard of this she rolled her eyes in alarm. 'You will have trouble,' was all she said.

She was right. Within a few days there were half a dozen other children picketing our front door, who would only disperse on being given what they considered their due. The half dozen soon increased to a score and eventually to such numbers that it would have needed a whole shop to satisfy all their demands. I began to see what Khemo meant.

'A kind act never goes unpunished,' Xan murmured in a maddeningly righteous tone. 'You'll have to stop this daily dole.'

But stopping it brought no immediate solution. For some time, in fact, it only made matters worse. The children, on seeing me emerge empty-handed, would follow me down the street, clamouring. When I came back they would be waiting for me, still clamouring. When I did not leave the house all morning they would bang at the door, clamouring as usual, until Khemo chased them away. And when they were chased away we would be interrupted for the rest of the day by visits from their parents, or grandparents, or great-uncles and aunts – old crones and ancient greybeards who politely but firmly explained that they had come to collect the children's rations.

This experience should have taught me a lesson, but only a few weeks later I thoughtlessly made another mistake.

On our first night in the kasbah we had left the car in the nearest parking place we could find: a little square just up the hill. Next morning we had found the tyres punctured, the hood slashed, the windscreen-wipers and driving mirrors wrenched off, the paintwork scratched and scraped. The Spanish mechanic to whom we took it to be repaired was amazed at our good fortune. 'You've got off lightly,' he told us. 'You left it out all night? Usually they do more damage than this in five minutes. You were lucky to find the wheels still on it. *Never* leave your car unattended in the kasbah.'

But where else could we leave it since that was where we lived? We continued to park it in the little square, which a gang of teen-age Arabs also used as their playground. But, in the belief that a poacher makes the best gamekeeper, we engaged the toughest member of the gang – another Mohammed – to act as watchman. In return for his services we bought him a proper football to replace the bundle of rags which he and his friends used to boot about all day.

The arrangement worked perfectly. The Land Rover remained unscathed. And Mohammed and his pals seemed delighted with the football. But not for long. A few weeks later they had once again reverted to their bundle of rags.

'Where's the ball, Mohammed?' we asked.

'Gone,' was his ambiguous reply.

Was his tone disconsolate or sheepish? Hard to tell. Had the ball been stolen or had he sold it? Impossible to decide. But I felt we ought to give him the benefit of the doubt.

'Never mind,' I told him, 'we'll get you another.'

We did. But two days later the second ball had also 'gone'.

We were not going to repeat our mistake, as Mohammed evidently expected us to do. He looked frankly puzzled when we drove away without promising him a third football. His bewilderment turned to anger when he saw us return empty-handed on foot (for we had taken the precaution of parking the car, inconveniently but more securely, outside the kasbah and next to a police station).

That evening an English friend of ours dropped in for a drink and remarked on the absence of the Land Rover from the little square where, as usual, he had just left his own car, since Mohammed's protection had so far extended to our visitors as well. But no longer, as we now explained. Our friend moved fast. 'I hope it's not too late,' he muttered, as he rushed out of the house.

He was just in time. The gang had not yet done the usual damage. To his relief, his car appeared to be untouched. It was only as he was about to drive it off to a safer place that he found all the door handles had been smeared with human excrement.

Occurrences of this sort were surprising, to say the least, yet I soon found myself almost taking them for granted, accepting them as the normal hazards of Tangier life. It was an exception to go out shopping *without* having my pocket, or rather my satchel or basket, picked. I dislike women's bags, especially those made of crocodile skin, and preferred to carry something I could sling over my shoulder or swing in my hand. But a satchel or a basket, as I found to my cost, is as tempting to an Arab as an unlocked door or an unattended car, and on coming home I would find that my purse, and sometimes even some of my purchases, had vanished on the way. After this had happened half a dozen times Xan calculated how much money I had lost. 'Just think what we could have bought with it,' he added, knowing that this argument was bound to convince me. From then on I took to carrying my purse on me, in the pocket of my skirt which, at the risk of appearing unduly coy and chaste, I could at least protect with my hand whenever I found myself jostled in a crowd.

This method proved successful for quite a time. One morning, however, on emerging from the bank where I had just cashed a cheque, I was almost knocked over by a young thug barging into me. Instinctively my hand went to my pocket, but it was too late. My purse was gone and the robber was already bolting down the street.

Xan, who was walking just ahead of me and had not realised what had happened, was surprised to see me rush past him shouting and waving my arms. 'I thought you were greeting a friend,' he told me later. 'That's just how you behaved when you caught sight of those pals of yours on the piazza at Capri.' I remembered the Capri incident; I had indeed rushed across the piazza waving my arms and shouting. But I had not shouted, 'Stop, thief!' in several languages while dodging through heavy traffic, which is what I proceeded to do now.

A policeman on point duty joined me in the chase and we eventually cornered our quarry at the end of a cul-de-sac into which he had dived for refuge. Vehemently he denied ever having seen me before. And of course he knew nothing about a stolen purse.

'Are you sure this is the boy?' the policeman asked me.

'Absolutely,' I replied. 'I kept him in sight the whole time until he vanished round the corner. I remember his black woolly cap and navy-blue jacket.'

But the boy we had cornered, though wearing a black

woolly cap, was in shirt sleeves, as he now triumphantly pointed out. 'You can search me if you like,' he added.

Just then Xan appeared with a second policeman who, much to my relief, carried a navy-blue jacket in his hand. 'We picked it up on the pavement,' he said. 'I think you'll find a red leather purse in one of the pockets,' I told him. Sure enough, the purse was found.

Having recovered the housekeeping money, I had no wish to pursue the matter any further. Nor, clearly, did the young thug. But the two policemen were adamant: 'How do we know this boy was wearing this jacket? How do we know this purse belongs to you? We'll have to sort it out at the police station.'

I was painfully conscious of the effect we created as we made our way through the crowd that had gathered: a couple of self-satisfied Europeans (self-satisfied, that is, in the eye of the prejudiced onlooker, but in reality less self-satisfied than sheepish) supported by two policemen (symbols of fascist and racialist injustice) dragging off a defenceless and innocent native youth (the expression and attitude he had now assumed were indeed exaggeratedly defenceless and innocent) on mere suspicion, if not on a false charge. I could well understand the hisses and hostile gestures (at one point, while passing a café, we were pelted with some small metal caps marked 'Coca-Cola') that accompanied our progress.

At the police station, however, the suspect was immediately identified as a notorious *voleur à la tire* by the name of Mohammed (yet another!) ben Absolam, more commonly known as Habibi or 'Darling'. Darling to whom, I wondered. Certainly not to me.

5

Well Met by Sunlight

Long before leaving England, long before our journey along the Barbary Coast, long before our marriage in fact, Xan had been asked by the film director Michael Powell to act as technical adviser on the production of *Ill Met by Moonlight*, the story of the abduction of the German General Kreipe by Paddy Leigh Fermor in enemy-occupied Crete. Afterwards the project had been postponed until Xan had almost forgotten it. Now, five years later, he was summoned by telegram to the south of France where work on the film was due to begin in a few days' time.

I was determined to get there too if I could, for I had no wish to spend the whole summer alone in the kasbah. Yet how intrude on the film unit as an unofficial camp follower? Besides, there were the dogs. Who would look after them? In the end Xan agreed to take Salote with him, leaving me to follow with Sunflower as soon as I had arranged with a newspaper to write a series of articles on the making of the film, which would give me a valid reason for joining the unit.

Xan wrote to me a few days later from Nice to say that in spite of the urgency of his summons there was no sign of Michael Powell or of any film unit in the vicinity. Meanwhile he was enjoying the luxury of the Hotel Negresco, where rooms had been booked for him, and Salote had fortunately recovered from her first experience of air travel which had been absolutely horrid. He had been told at the airport that providing she was put in a basket she would be allowed to stay with him in the passengers' compartment, but on boarding the aircraft she had been taken away and placed in the luggage hold from where he had heard her pathetic barks throughout the flight.

Rather than subject Sunflower to such an ordeal, I decided to travel by sea. But she was likewise separated from me on the voyage, as dogs were not allowed in the passengers' quarters, and housed in a special kennel barred with iron like a prisoner's cell. I was allowed to visit her whenever I liked, but she was terrified by the ship's siren and during my absences kept trying to force her way out. By the time we docked at Cannes, where Xan and Salote met us, her nose was rubbed raw by her attempts to escape.

I arrived just in time. On the very next morning a car turned up at the Negresco to take us to Draguignan, which had been chosen as the unit headquarters. Here we learnt that the actor cast for the role of Paddy was Dirk Bogarde. He was not staying at Draguignan, however – there was no proper place for a star in a little market town already overcrowded with the production staff, camera crews, sound engineers, minor actors and lesser fry like ourselves – but in St Raphael, on the coast, where Xan was to meet him before shooting started.

Though I looked forward to meeting him too, I was rather nervous about it, for in spite of my newspaper commission I still felt like an interloper. I was almost relieved when our repeated attempts to reach him were in vain: Mr Bogarde was busy, had just gone out, was not available. Eventually, in the bar of his hotel, we ran to earth his manager Tony Forwood whose blue eyes sized us up in a wary glance, then suddenly twinkled. 'So you're the Fieldings, are you?' he said. 'Dirk's upstairs in his room. I'll go and fetch him.'

When he reappeared with him a few minutes later they both seemed to be enjoying some private joke, which added to my confusion, especially as I happened at that moment to be trying to extricate myself from the dogs' leads which had wound themselves round my legs. Dirk's smile turned to a broad grin as he watched my antics. 'Just how many legs have you got?' he asked.

After the ice was broken, at ease with him, I said, 'You seemed to be avoiding us on purpose.'

'I was,' he admitted. 'Mickey had told me about Xan's war record and I'd conjured up a dreadful picture of you both – "The Major and his Wife," a sort of Osbert Lancaster cartoon. I couldn't bear the idea of meeting you. If it hadn't been for Tony . . .'

'Yes,' said Tony, 'I told him Xan didn't have a clipped moustache and you weren't wearing a regimental brooch, so we took the plunge.'

'Anyway, now we've met,' Dirk concluded.

'Well Met by Sunlight,' I said to myself.

Two days later, after the cast had assembled, there was a final reading of the script followed by a wardrobe meeting. Though some of the costumes did not meet with Xan's approval – 'they look more Ruritanian than Cretan,' I heard him complain – Dirk at least could not have been dressed more authentically, for I lent him my Cretan guerrilla's cloak, and Xan had brought with him a black silk headkerchief which had been part of his own wartime disguise and which he now taught Dirk to bind over his brow in the proper Cretan fashion.

Dirk was rather alarmed by this unfamiliar headgear. 'What on earth do I look like?' he asked.

'The genuine article,' Xan truthfully assured him. 'Very dashing. Just like Paddy.'

Next morning the whole unit was up before dawn, ready to move off for the first day's shooting and, as the sun rose, the long convoy of char-à-bancs, headed by the director's yellow Land Rover, was on its way to the chosen location up in the hills.

I had been slightly worried about my unofficial position. Was I entitled to a seat on one of the buses? And what about Sunflower and Salote? With characteristic thoughtfulness, Dirk solved the problem for me. 'There's plenty of room in my car,' he said, 'for you and Xan *and* the two dogs. I'll call for you.' And so we set off, in undeservedly grand style, in the star's Bentley.

This was to be our daily programme for several weeks and I never tired of it. Each early-morning start recalled the thrill I used to feel as a child when getting up in the dark and dressing by candle-light to go cub-hunting. Only now it was followed, not by autumnal Cornish mists, but by the unremitting sunshine of Mediterranean midsummer. The locations had of course been chosen for their suitability, but to me they seemed to have been specially selected for their beauty and variety. Small rocky coves on the coast, the banks of mountain streams, forest glades and lavender fields – all these were perfect sites for what to me was a protracted picnic accompanied by an open-air floor show.

It was also fascinating to watch the various members of the cast at such close quarters, to see each one's interpretation of his role. For the first time I realised what an exacting and exhausting job film-acting must be, especially for anyone as meticulous as Dirk Bogarde. Before each take he would sit by himself, so withdrawn that his nervous tension was contagious. Throughout working hours he remained apart and abstracted, hardly reverting to his own character even when off the set. But once the strain was over – during the luncheon break, for instance, or when packing up for the day – he resumed his normal personality and the relief from his intense concentration would lead to an outburst of high spirits and gaiety which usually took the form of teasing me.

Knowing that I was in awe of the director, and knowing too that shyness makes me clumsier than usual, he would score off me by suddenly saying, 'Look out, Daphne, those dogs of yours are eating Mickey's sandwiches,' or, 'I didn't like to tell you at the time, but during that last take one of your six legs was almost in shot.' I became so apprehensive lest Salote or Sunflower, or indeed myself, might unconsciously stray within the range of the camera (a constantly recurring nightmare of mine) that I took exaggerated measures of precaution, hiding behind bushes and repeatedly checking the dogs' leads, and would almost take to my heels at the sight of Michael Powell for fear of a reprimand.

Dirk was naturally delighted by the effect his banter had on me. 'That's better,' he said one day, as we unpacked our luncheon baskets in a clearing outside a cave which had been the scene of that morning's shooting. 'You've been very good and you deserve a present. Open your hand and shut your eyes.'

I did so, hoping to receive an orchis or some other floral token, for Dirk shared my passion for collecting wild flowers and used to pick them almost absent-mindedly as he strolled about the set. But what I felt in my palm was something warm and furry and fluttering, which I dropped at once with a shriek of disgust, having identified it without needing to look.

'But it's only a baby!' Dirk exclaimed, genuinely puzzled by my reaction since he was unaware of my phobia of bats.

This one – a baby, admittedly – must have been alarmed by the unusual activity in the cave and had taken refuge in the pocket of his jacket. That at least was where he had found it, much to his own surprise, before offering it to me.

During the last stages of the production we all moved from Draguignan up to Peira Cava, a skiing resort close to the Italian border, and here Paddy Leigh Fermor joined us for a few days.

Paddy's impending visit had been dreaded by Dirk as much as the prospect of meeting Xan and me. I sympathised with him, realising how awkward it must be for an actor to play a living character when that character is watching him at it. Xan tried to reassure him:

'Don't worry, Paddy's not a typical army officer or guerrilla leader. He's not a typical anything, he's himself, a romantic figure, in the Byron tradition. Very erudite, a sort of Gypsy Scholar, with an inexhaustible fund of incidental knowledge. He can talk to you for hours about hagiography or heraldry or . . .'

'He sounds too damned intellectual for me.'

But Paddy's charm and adroitness immediately overcame Dirk's prejudices, in spite of an incident on the night of his arrival which might have affected their future friendship.

One of Paddy's wartime henchmen, Michali Akoumianakis, who had played a leading part in the abduction of the general, was also attached to the unit as a technical adviser and had brought with him from Crete a demijohn of *tsikoudia*, the potent local spirit, which he had been saving for just such an occasion as this. 'We'll have a proper Cretan *glendi*,' he said but, since no other member of the unit would touch the stuff, it remained for Paddy, Xan and myself to help him celebrate in the appropriate fashion – with some trepidation on my part, for I knew from personal experience that a *glendi* involves a great deal of noisy singing and dancing and is likely to last all night.

By midnight, long after everyone else in the hotel had gone to bed, the *tsikoudia* was beginning to take effect and Paddy and Xan had broken into song. Soon the bar, empty but for the four of us, was resounding with *mantinades* punctuated by the thump of feet performing the *pentozali*.

'Please stop it,' I begged them. 'You're keeping everyone awake.'

'But we've only just begun,' they objected, 'and the bottle's still half- full.'

'In that case I'm going to bed,' I announced, foreseeing, as I fled, an irate Michael Powell appearing in the bar like Christ in the temple.

Even from upstairs the sound of revelry, though not quite so deafening, continued for some time, unabated. I was on the point of going back to make one last attempt at stopping it, when it came to an end. A few minutes later Xan stumbled in.

'Dirk came down,' he announced.

'No wonder. Was he furious?'

'He *looked* a bit angry. But all he said was, "Some people have to work in the morning and want to get to sleep." He's right, of course. I don't blame him. Anyway, Paddy and I have just slipped a note under his door to say we're sorry.'

In the morning Dirk did not even mention the matter, nor did anyone else in the unit. But Paddy did. At breakfast he casually remarked to Michael Powell: 'Who the devil was making that fiendish din last night? I couldn't sleep a wink.'

Such frivolity and exuberance endeared him to everyone, though these qualities did not accord with the preconceived idea of him which some members of the unit had formed. 'I just can't see him capturing a German general,' Dirk's dresser said. 'He's not the strong, silent type at all.'

'What about Major Fielding?' Dirk asked.

'Major Fielding? Oh, yes. He looks a fucking little killer.'

Whether this was meant as a compliment or not, from then on Xan was referred to on the set as F.L.K.

To me it was like school holidays coming to an end when the last shot was 'in the can' and the unit began packing up to return to England for further work in the studios. Xan's assignment was now over and we too prepared to leave. We had planned to go back by sea, on account of the dogs, but there was no ship immediately available. After Salote's recent experience of flying it was hateful to have to subject her to it again. But all direct flights from Nice were booked for several weeks to come. Dirk therefore offered to drive us up to Paris, where we were more likely to find a plane.

We stopped overnight at the Hermitage in Digne, one of Dirk's favourite hotels in France. For Xan, however, Digne had other associations. It was here, while working as a secret agent during the occupation, that he had been arrested by the Gestapo and sentenced to death.* In fact the house in which he had been imprisoned was next door and we could see it from our bedroom window. Dirk was extremely upset when Xan mentioned this to him over dinner.

'You should have told me at once,' he said. 'We could easily have stayed somewhere else. We'll move out now if you like, it must be horrid for you . . .'

'Not at all,' Xan told him. 'I don't mind a bit. In fact I'm glad to be back here in such different circumstances. After all this time. Twelve years . . . Good heavens, it's twelve years exactly, to the very day!'

'This calls for a bottle of champagne,' said Dirk.

* For a fuller account of this adventure, see Xan Fielding: *Hide and Seek*. Secker & Warburg, 1954.

6

The House on the Mountain

We had already noticed signs of unrest in Tangier, reflecting the crisis through which Morocco was passing. The French protectorate was about to come to an end and the country was to be granted independence. The International Zone had so far been spared the disorder and violence accompanying the creation of the new nation, but on our return from the south of France we were immediately aware of an increased tension in the atmosphere and even of certain changes in the appearance of the town. The harbour, for instance, looked emptier than before. I pointed this out to Xan.

'You realise what's happened, don't you,' he said. 'All the smugglers' boats have gone, they're no longer operating from here. That's not a good sign.'

Soon the demonstrations and riots in the rest of the country spread to Tangier, fomented by political agitators from outside. These thugs were to be seen all over the town, organising strikes and, in the name of 'Freedom' and 'Independence', ordering shops and cafés to close. For good measure, they also closed the brothels and banned the smoking of kif. They had no authority to do this, but the local police seemed unwilling or unable to stop them.

Though it was hateful to see the free-and-easy international regime replaced by the puritanical 'reforms' of the new Moroccan government, Xan and I were not particularly affected by this activity. Neither of us was addicted to kif, so that the sight of thousands of kif pipes strung up by their stems on the kasbah gates, like birds of prey shot by a gamekeeper, was less painful to us than to the Arabs. And from what I saw of the women who still loitered disconsolately in the lane of curtained cubicles behind the Little Socco where they previously plied their trade, the closing of the brothels could have frustrated only the most sex-starved Ancient Mariner.

Living in the Arab quarter, we were also more isolated from the sound and fury of the European city where most of the disturbances took place. It was only when the local garbagemen were ordered to strike that the situation was brought home to us personally. Hemmed in by the narrow lanes, the stench from the unemptied dustbins and overflowing refuse became daily more unbearable.

'There'll be a plague next,' I said to Xan, not entirely in jest.

'We'll have to go,' he agreed.

We could have moved provisionally into an hotel and then come back once the crisis was over. But – though neither of us would admit it – the charms of the kasbah, even at the best of times, were beginning to pall. We longed for less claustrophobic surroundings where the dogs, and indeed ourselves, would be able to step outside the front door without being pestered. And so we rented La Casita, a little bungalow in the grounds of a larger house up on the Mountain.

The Mountain (in reality little more than a hill) was where the more well-to-do members of the foreign community lived. But, in spite of the international composition of these rarefied upper reaches, the atmosphere was parochial rather than cosmopolitan, for each national group tended to keep to itself. The

British colony was centred round the Country Club and the English Church, Dean's Bar (where the latest copy of the *Illustrated London News* was always available) and the amateur dramatic society. Dainty little tea parties, croquet on the lawn, and more or less harmless and harmful gossip contributed to the creation of a Cranford in Africa tinged with the cantonment heartiness of an Indian hill station in the palmy days of the Raj. Metaphorically, the smell of saddle-soap, damp tweed and pipe tobacco was permanently in the air. This was preferable, however, to the smell of garbage.

Compared to all the other houses on the Mountain, La Casita was more than modest. Compared to our house in the kasbah, it was palatial. It must originally have been built as a gardener's cottage, to which had been added a vast studio room giving on to a broad terrace on the edge of a steep cliff. The situation reminded me of Cowrie, so did the view. Only here everything was on a larger scale. Instead of Eddystone Lighthouse, the huge mass of Jebel Mousa was visible in the distance; and in the foreground, in place of Looe island, stretched the coast of Spain. Here, too, a rough path zig-zagged down to a small private beach lapped by waters that were bluer and warmer, however, than in Cornwall.

Sunflower and Salote were as delighted as ourselves to be back in marine surroundings. They had always swum as naturally as young seals, which, in the water, they closely resembled. But their greatest joy was the overgrown parkland belonging to the big house, where we were allowed to roam at will. Avenues of giant eucalyptus trees stretched in all directions, and the dogs' paws soon became impregnated with the scent of the leaves and seed pods that covered the ground.

From the previous tenants we inherited a first-rate cook, Ayesha, to replace Khemo who did not care for rural life but whom we kept on to look after the kasbah house. Our lease also included the services of a night watchman, with which we would have preferred to dispense since we were not sure whether this elderly dwarf, stone-deaf, excitable and armed with a musket, could be relied upon to distinguish friend from foe. But as he was employed by the owners of the big house, we had to put up with him. Fortunately he always fell asleep on duty and we were careful not to rouse him when we came in late, for we noticed that he slept with one finger curled round the trigger of his gun. From time to time during the night this finger would involuntary twitch and the consequent detonation was followed by further shots as the old dwarf fired at random into the surrounding bushes at a host of imaginary assailants.

Salote was now over two years old and had never been mated. We decided it was time for her to have a litter, and Rupert Croft-Cooke who lived nearby suggested that his champion male Pekinese should be the father of her puppies. At the appropriate moment, therefore, he left the dog to spend the night with us at La Casita.

During her previous heats Salote had never shown the slightest sign of false modesty or inhibition. In fact we had had to protect her from several fortuitous encounters which she would have willingly exploited, irrespective of the aspect, size or shape of the suitor. So we hardly expected her to reject the advances of Rupert's canine Adonis. Yet she did, immediately, persistently, continuously, with all the outraged dignity of a professional old maid. The big white beauty resorted to every flirtatious ploy of which a dog is capable – winsomeness, caveman tactics, downright plaintiveness – all in vain. By two o'clock in the morning his repertoire was exhausted, and so were we.

'Maybe it's because we're looking on,' Xan suggested. 'After all, how would *you* like an audience? Come on, let's go to bed and leave them to it.'

So we did.

Next morning Xan got up before me to see how the dogs had fared. As he opened the door of the room where we had left them, I heard him give an agonised cry: 'Oh, no!'

'What's the matter?' I shouted.

'Bumpy has been torn to pieces!'

The words were blurted out in shock. I immediately pictured with horrid clarity what Xan had actually seen: scattered blue feathers and a small broken body on the tiled floor.

The pretty bamboo cage I had just bought for Bumpy had proved too frail to protect him from Rupert's dog who, in his frustration, had pulled it down from the low table on which it was kept and had then gnawed through the bars.

Uselessly, I blamed myself for buying such a cage. Uselessly, I blamed the cage itself. I could not bear the thought of ever seeing it again and told Ayesha to throw it over the cliff. She did so, but it caught on the branch of a tree and hung there, inaccessible yet painfully visible. Each time we made our way down to the beach we had to pass beneath it. But even without this reminder I could never forget the savage fate that had befallen my blithe and trusting bird.

Next time Salote came on heat she was successfully mated to David Herbert's dog. True to form, she took at once to this engaging little mongrel (his Pekinese pedigree was tarnished by a strain of chihuahua blood) and was only too pleased to grant him what she had refused Rupert's thoroughbred.

The puppies were born in our bedroom in the middle of the night, and for once I was glad I sleep so lightly for otherwise I might have missed the whole process. How clean and silent, how effortless it seemed! Salote looked almost unconcerned as her offspring emerged, each neatly enveloped in a transparent membrane and accompanied by a whiff of ozone. The sixth, and last, of these naturally antiseptic packets was surprisingly different in colour. 'It's a white one!' I exclaimed out loud.

This was the one I wanted to keep, but it was a female and Xan was reluctant to add to our exclusively bitch pack. I therefore chose one of the black males, which I christened Trubshawe, and found suitable homes for the rest of the litter. To my relief, the white one was adopted by a close friend, Phyllis Della Faille.

I had met Phyllis during our first visit to Tangier and had fallen straight away under her spell, enchanted by her appearance. The large, round, tortoiseshell-rimmed spectacles perched on her small, beak-like nose made her look like a perky little owl. Her fine-boned wrists were hung with various amulets, including a tiger's claw, charms to ward off the evil eye, articulated fishes of gold and silver, and doll's eyes set in diamonds. The heels of her shoes were studded with gold and silver nails. I found her conversation equally eccentric and delighted in the fantasies and superstitions which she expressed in an incongruously deep voice and with an authority which lent verisimilitude to the most extravagant statements.

She and her husband Charles lived just outside Tangier, in a large house surrounded by extensive grounds. Even so they were overcrowded, for they shared their living space with one hundred and fifty dogs, thirty-seven horses, countless cats, dozens of parrots and other birds, one chimpanzee and a number of smaller monkeys. This was their average animal population. The exact figures fluctuated from day to day, decreasing with the death of the oldest pensioners and increasing with fresh acquisitions, for Phyllis could never hear of a lost dog or a horse doomed to destruction without adding it to her collection.

A visit to the Della Failles was always fraught with hazards. One evening, in the middle of dinner, the chimpanzee climbed on to my lap and helped himself from my plate. Later, on going to the gentlemen's cloakroom, Xan found the lavatory-pan occupied by a school of goldfish. Not wishing to disturb them, he hurried out into the garden but scarcely had he unbuttoned his trousers than a couple of ravens advanced on him. 'There was a predatory look in their eyes,' he told me afterwards.

The grounds were patrolled at night by a pack of fierce watchdogs. When leaving the house, it was advisable to sprint from the front door to one's car. The other dogs were lodged in spacious kennels, tended and exercised by a troop of Arab boys, inspected weekly by a vet, and given a daily ration of vitamin pills. From time to time they also received a stimulant or tranquilliser since Phyllis was apt to confuse the animals' supplies with the contents of her own medicine chest. Her keys too sometimes turned up in a dog's dinner, after being buried for safe-keeping in a sack of hound-meal and then forgotten.

None of her dogs was identified by a name. They were almost as anonymous as the inmates of a concentration camp and I could not help regarding them as such. I was therefore relieved when she told me she planned to make an exception of the white puppy. 'I'm going to call her Princess Precious Pearl,' she said.

In exchange for Princess Precious Pearl, she offered me a baby donkey which I had always longed to own. The little beast was driven up to La Casita in the back of one of the Della Faille cars and carried inside like a babe in arms by the driver. I called her Antoinette and in a short time she was thoroughly domesticated, wandering in and out of the house, wearing garlands and straw hats. As she grew older, however, she abandoned these demure habits and developed into a hoyden, galloping from room to room, playfully nipping the dogs, and not so playfully kicking out at Xan for whom she had taken a strong dislike which he reciprocated.

'Can't you control your ass?' he would complain.

I couldn't, though I wouldn't admit it. But Antoinette soon became too much of a handful and I eventually gave her away to a friend who had started a riding school, where, as though to spite us and prove us wrong, she behaved with the utmost decorum and was regarded as a paragon of virtue.

After Antoinette, I decided not to have any more large animals and turned my attention to the humble hedgehogs in the garden. Before going to bed I used to leave saucers of milk for them on the front doorstep; in the morning I would find the saucers empty. When one of these milk-fed hedgehogs presently ventured into the house I resolved to keep it, for I knew what its fate might be. I had seen hedgehog skins on sale in the market and been told that Arab women in labour bind these prickly pelts to their stomachs in the belief that the resultant discomfort mitigates the birth pangs.

I housed my new acquisition inside the windjammer I was wearing, to accustom him to a human environment. After an initial exploration of my torso he settled down and went to sleep so soundly that I would have been unaware of his presence but for the mushroomy odour he exhaled and the number of fleas he released. That evening I put him to bed in a basket lined with one of my shawls.

Like Antoinette, he soon made himself at home and would wander about from room to room quite happily, regardless of the dogs, at whose approach he merely curled himself up into a ball until they lost interest in him. In the autumn, however, he grew less sociable. Though I knew he was somewhere in the house – for his saucer of milk was regularly emptied – I would lose track of him for days on end, until Xan or I or one of our guests rose quickly from an armchair or sofa where the hedgehog had somehow infiltrated into the upholstery. In the end, to avoid being punctured (though I persuaded myself it was really to save him from being squashed) I took him outside and left him to hibernate in a thick drift of eucalyptus leaves.

'Just as well,' said Xan. 'We can't have this house transformed into another Della Faille menagerie.'

He was right. We had neither the space nor the means to indulge in Phyllis's passion, and so I resolved in future to limit the animal population of La Casita to the three dogs. But I woke up one morning to find that a pair of baby owls had been deposited on our doorstep. Attached to their cage was a note in a friend's handwriting: 'You can't resist these, can you?'

Of course I couldn't. They looked so pathetic, like a couple of starved foundlings dressed in second-hand fur coats. I took them inside. They glared at me with furious sulphur-yellow eyes and bobbed up and down angrily, but grew calmer when I offered them some raw meat which they snatched from my fingers. They too were eventually given the freedom of the house. To begin with, they merely perched side by side on a beam, clicking their beaks apprehensively and swivelling their heads round in a full circle, but after a few days they gained confidence, found their bearings and took to the air, drifting on silent wings through the twilit rooms like flakes of burnt paper.

As they grew older they lost their fluffy owlet feathers and developed handsome plumage, their rust-red and smoky-grey morning-coats contrasting elegantly with their buff-coloured waistcoats patterned with Maltese crosses. Adulthood, however, was accompanied by disease. They began to sicken and refused all food. There were no more flights at twilight. Instead, they huddled in their cage, wheezing and yawning as though in the throes of asthma. The vet diagnosed the gapes, an affliction common to chickens and pheasants and caused by some parasite or other. He prescribed several medicines and advised me to paint the inside of their throats with paraffin twice a day.

This was easier said than done but, with the aid of a feather and at the cost of repeated pecks on the hand, I managed to perform this operation. Alas, the treatment proved ineffective. Very soon the patients were too weak even to peck and simply sat like Cock Robin, 'with his head tucked under his wing, poor thing.' They reminded me of those two French princelings, devoted brothers, who were kept imprisoned in a cage. The two little captives slowly died, one after the other. So did my two little owls.

Only a few days after their death another calamity occurred.

We were taking the three dogs for a walk in the Diplomatic Forest, some miles outside the town, when we noticed Salote had lagged behind. We looked back and saw her in the distance, apparently convulsed, rolling in the grass and clawing the air as though wrestling with some invisible enemy.

'My God, she's been bitten by a snake!'

I voiced this thought out loud, and Xan rushed back towards her. When he had almost reached her he stopped dead, then shouted over his shoulder to me:

'Wasps! She's swarming with them!'

Instinctively I picked up Sunflower and Trubshawe. Meanwhile Xan had taken off his shirt and was waving it round his head, at the same time calling to Salote. Since she was evidently unable to move, he darted forward, wrapped the shirt round her and picked her up, beating the air frenziedly with his free hand.

'I'm going back to the car,' he shouted, but he took no more than a dozen steps before he put Salote down again and tore off his trousers to use as a flail. 'Keep clear!' he yelled, seeing me move towards him still carrying a dog under each arm.

But it was too late. The buzzing cloud was already round my head and simultaneously I felt the stings, on my face and arms, round my neck, then all over my body. Xan snatched Salote up again and together we stumbled forward. By the time we reached the car I felt my blood was on fire, the pain so general and all-consuming that I was no longer conscious of the dagger-like thrusts that continued. In a desperate bid to get rid of the swarm, we dumped our loads on the ground and clutched alternately at the dogs' coats and at our own scalps, removing wasps by the handful, squeezing them to death in our fists. Then we flung Sunflower, Salote and Trubshawe into the back, climbed in ourselves, slammed the doors and drove off, still swatting the rearguard of the enemy that had followed us inside.

By this time my blood seemed to be not only incandescent but also at the point of ebullition. Xan glanced at me and exclaimed, 'Good heavens, your eyes! They're bright red.' It was then I noticed that the whites of his own eyes had turned scarlet. We gazed at each other and, in the driving mirror, at ourselves, then burst into hysterical laughter.

But by the time we got home I was no longer laughing. A burning rash had covered me from head to foot, and my face was so swollen that I could hardly see through the slits of my puffy eyelids. Xan, less allergic to bites and stings, recovered almost at once. So did Sunflower and Trubshawe, who had not been exposed to the full fury of the wasps. But Salote and I had to be given injections for shock and, for two days the poor little dog lay in a coma before she rallied.

This incident, however, was overshadowed by what occurred shortly afterwards.

I was puzzled one morning by the length of time Xan was spending over his bath. Rattling on the bathroom door and calling out to him produced no reply. All I could hear was the sound of heavy breathing, something between a snore and a groan. I tried the door and found it was bolted on the inside (for otherwise it could not be closed, since the lock was broken). Terrified, I shouted for Ayesha. Luckily our combined weight was sufficient to force the flimsy bolt and we stumbled into the room to find Xan lying unconscious on the bath-mat.

We carried him to bed and I rang up for the doctor. By the time he arrived Xan had recovered consciousness and was mumbling more or less coherently, though his voice seemed to be coming from the back of his head, his words were slurred, his teeth were chattering and he was shivering uncontrollably.

'Carbon dioxide poisoning,' said the doctor. 'There must be a leak in your geyser. The worst thing he could have done was lie down on the floor. He must have been inhaling pure gas.'

But Xan did not remember lying down on the floor. He did not even remember getting out of the bath-tub. He had been unaware of any poisonous fumes. 'I just had a vague sensation of claustrophobia,' he said, 'which reminded me of Tripoli, going under water with an aqualung.' This was his last recollection before he passed out.

'You're lucky,' the doctor told him. 'You might have drowned, or else suffocated to death.'

'If I had, it would have been quite painless,' Xan replied.

With his usual resilience, he recovered almost at once. By the evening he was up and about again, apparently none the worse for this experience. But I remembered what the doctor had said, and could not help reflecting that Tangier was becoming an unlucky place for us.

7

El Rocio

While living at La Casita we used to call in once or twice a week at our kasbah house, where Khemo would greet us each time as though we had been absent for several years. She hated solitude and inactivity and always contrived to prolong our visits by cooking us one of our favourite dishes. From time to time we lent the house to various friends, and her delight at seeing it occupied again was reflected in the care she lavished on them.

When I told her my god-daughter Nell Dunn and her husband Jeremy Sandford would be spending their honeymoon here, she hugged me like a child who has just been promised a special treat. On the eve of their arrival she bought armfuls of flowers in the market and spent all night wiring jasmine heads on to fillets of bamboo and studding the flat leaves of prickly pears with camellia blossoms. In the morning every room was decorated with scented posies and miniature flowered lawns.

A few days later Nell rang me up to say that Jeremy was ill. The symptoms she described pointed to appendicitis. I told her I would come at once and sent for the doctor. But by the time I arrived the patient was already in Khemo's hands, or rather under her feet, lying flat on his back while she lovingly kneaded his stomach with her bare heels. He made a rapid recovery, which she believed was entirely due to her 'Moorish massage'.

Archie Lyall was another recipient of her special attentions. 'I've travelled all over the world,' he told us, 'and I'm used to being treated like a pasha. I *expect* to have my back scrubbed in the bath every morning. . . . Seriously, though, I've never had it done so well.'

Not all our friends were as appreciative as Archie. A later occupant of the house, whom Xan and I had both known for years, was attracted to Tangier mainly by its lurid reputation. We told him that the 'Wicked International City' no longer lived up to its name and warned him in particular to steer clear of one of the kasbah boys, nicknamed Sticky Jumbo, who was known to supplement his income from touting by serving as a police informer.

Early one morning, less than ten days after his arrival, our friend rang us up. 'I'm rather worried, my dears,' he said. 'I've just had a summons from the police.'

'You'd better answer it,' Xan advised him. 'Nothing to do with Sticky Jumbo, I hope?'

'My conscience is quite clear,' was the ambiguous reply, 'but to be on the safe side I'd like to know where I can contact you in case there's any trouble.'

So we gave him the telephone number of the people with whom we were lunching.

Half-way through the meal Xan was interrupted by the call which by then we were fully expecting:

I'm afraid you'll have to leave your smart luncheon, my dear, and meet me at once in the little Socco. I hope you have a lot of money on you, because I shall be needing it. I'm in serious trouble.'

Xan went off at once and found our friend in the Café Central. 'Was he under sixteen?' was his first question.

'Considerably, my dear,' was the answer.

'Then you really are in trouble. Tell me what happened.'

'When I went to the police station I was confronted by the boy . . .'

'One of Sticky Jumbo's?'

'I'm afraid so, my dear. . . . Of course I denied ever having seen him before, so it was his word against mine. But now they're looking for the taxi-driver who took us back to the house. A rather inconvenient witness. I don't fancy the inside of an Arab jail, my dear. You'll have to get me out of the country.'

Luckily we knew the one person in Tangier who could help in a case like this. Xan got in touch with him at once and our friend was safely smuggled out on the next boat, in disguise and under a different name.

Three days later he sent us a postcard depicting a Gibraltar ape and bearing the inscription, 'Not unlike His Nastiness who shopped me.'

Meanwhile the police had taken action. Furious at having been given the slip, they tore up the floorboards of the kasbah house on the pretext of searching the premises. They also arrested Khemo and her little daughter, from whom they tried to extract a statement accusing our friend of assaulting them both. Xan and I made a strong protest, pointing out the manifest absurdity of this charge, and the two prisoners were eventually released. To make up for the inconvenience they had been caused, the police came to the house next day bearing gifts of milk and honey and a large bowl of *cous-cous*. But for months afterwards our telephone continued to be tapped, with as much lack of skill as of purpose; for whenever we lifted the receiver we would be greeted by a fanfare of Arab music (presumably from the police station radio) before the call was put through.

In these circumstances the atmosphere of Tangier seemed more suffocating than ever. So far, whenever we had felt the urge for broader horizons and less alien surroundings, we had simply crossed the Straits and spent a few days in Spain or Portugal. But now this urge was becoming more pressing and more frequent, and we found ourselves staying for weeks on end with our friends Bill and Annie Davis, who lived in feudal splendour in Churriana, a little village a few miles inland from Torremolinos.

Churriana had an additional attraction for us in the person of Gerald Brenan, whose house was within walking distance of the Davises. But although he lived so near, we had to plan our day with care to make sure of seeing him. Not that he was elusive. In fact, for a busy writer, he was singularly approachable. But his timetable differed radically from ours. In spite of over fifty years spent in Spain he resolutely eschewed Spanish hours, so that by the time we had finished lunch and were ready for a siesta, he would already have had his afternoon nap and be receiving his first evening visitors. When Xan and I strolled down a little later, while everyone at the Davises was still fast asleep, we would find him surrounded by old friends, young admirers and even perfect strangers, self-invited literary pilgrims, all drinking up his wine and drinking in his words.

It was Gerald who first told us about Las Marismas, a vast uninhabited area of mudflats and marshland south-west of Seville, where a fiesta is held every year in honour of a miracle-working Virgin. My appetite was whetted by his description of the landscape, a wilderness reserved for wild bulls, wild horses, wild cats, foxes, lynxes and various birds and reptiles that are found nowhere else in Europe. 'It must be as primitive and remote as the Cretan highlands,' he said. This was enough to win Xan over. We decided to come back to Spain in the spring and attend the fiesta.

Meanwhile we learnt more about it.

Some five or six hundred years ago a shepherd fom Almonte, a village on the edge of the marshland, was led by his dog into the midst of a dense thicket where he came upon a cavernous hollow tree-trunk. Here, half-hidden, lay an exquisite carved figure of Our Lady (no doubt one of the many sacred relics concealed during the Moorish occupation of Spain and subsequently mislaid). Delighted by his find, the shepherd set out for his village with the figure on his shoulders, but on the way he lay down to rest, fell asleep, and on waking found that the statue had crept back to its original hiding-place.

Filled with fear, he proceeded alone to Almonte and reported his discovery to the authorities, who made a solemn vow to erect a shrine on the very spot. This was done and a hamlet of thatch-roofed adobe buildings subsequently cropped up to house the annual influx of pilgrims to *Nuestra Señora del Rocio* (Our Lady of the Dew). 'Or rather, to house a small part of them,' Gerald explained. 'To accommodate them all, a full-size town would be needed. So most people sleep out in the open. That's what you'll have to do. El Rocio doesn't cater for tourists.'

But we did not have to sleep out. Thanks to Jaime Parladé, an influential young Spanish friend, we arranged to rent the last available house in the little hamlet. The Davises agreed to share expenses with us. So did Jay Haselwood, the American owner of the Parade Bar in Tangier, who had a passion for Spanish folklore. 'Our court jester must come too,' said Jaime, meaning Rafaelito Nevill, the leader of the Torremolinos 'fast' set. And at the last moment Debo Devonshire and Paddy Leigh Fermor flew out from London to join the party.

We set off from Churriana in a long convoy preceded by a truck laden with barrels of wine, crates of whisky, hampers of food, bedding and kitchen equipment. By the time we reached Almonte our progress had been reduced to a snail's pace by the traffic: wagons decorated like carnival floats, their canvas roofs foaming with paper flowers, drawn by cream-coloured oxen with lyre-shaped horns caparisoned like maypoles; four-in-hand brakes driven by caballeros in full fig and occupied by Carmen-like figures in polka-dotted, parrot-coloured dresses, their glossy chignons pranked with carnations and crested with tortoiseshell combs; columns of mule-teams and donkey carts; gypsy caravans by the score; all converging for the final trek along the dead-straight carriageway across the plain to El Rocio.

Dusk was falling as we rolled into the little hamlet, which already was pulsating to the sound of drums, pipes and castanets. Tents and booths sprouted like giant mushrooms at the foot of the eucalyptus trees on the main square, and every other open space seethed with groups of drinkers and dancers in traditional Andalusian dress.

'And the fiesta doesn't really begin until tomorrow,' Jaime told us. 'There'll be still more people then.'

Meanwhile, from other directions, more processions were arriving: members of the various brotherhoods affiliated to the shrine. Some of these fraternities from the more distant villages had been on the road three days. Each group was headed by leather-chapped cavaliers carrying silver-pointed staves, followed by an ox-drawn waggon embossed in silver bearing the local replica of the Virgin to pay its annual homage to the carved wooden original.

The house we had rented turned out to be even smaller and more primitive than we had expected. It consisted simply of one main room, earth-floored and furnished with a plain deal table and a couple of benches, and a smaller room already occupied as a kitchen and sleeping quarters by Jaime's butler and a potboy who had driven on ahead of us to make the place habitable.

'It's going to be really hugger-mugger,' said Debo, selecting a suitable corner for her camp-bed.

'I'll be your squire and keep vigil at your feet,' said Paddy, unrolling his sleeping-bag, while Jaime, Jay and Rafaelito laid their respective claims to floor space in various other parts of the room.

Xan and I still had the tent we had used on the Barbary Coast: a canvas igloo supported by ribs of rubber tubing inflated with compressed air. Bill and Annie had a similar brand-new model, which they pitched next to ours in the yard outside the house. These were luxury quarters compared to the house itself. But in the middle of the night we were woken by a sinister hiss and we saw our rigid structure start to sag as the air continued to leak out through some faulty valve or unsuspected puncture. A minute later we were struggling like twin Laocoöns in innumerable coils of twisting canvas, out of which we eventually and ignominiously crawled to join our companions in the dormitory.

Here we found everyone asleep except Debo, who was sitting upright in her camp-bed with a pile of fir-cones beside her. 'My ammunition,' she explained. . . . 'And here's another target,' she added, as one of the recumbent figures near her began to snore. Deftly she lobbed a fir-cone at the culprit's head. Promptly and without waking, he fell silent. 'It never fails,' she said. Thanks to her marksmanship, our sleep was only intermittently disturbed.

Sanitary arrangements at El Rocio were as rudimentary as the accommodation. In fact they were non-existent, but Jaime's butler had devised a makeshift substitute in the yard, consisting of a bucket surmounted by a wooden plank and surrounded by a screen of sacking with a slit in it through which any occupant could thrust his hand to indicate his presence. The device was never used, however, except by its designer and his assistant. The rest of us preferred to drive right out into the wilderness in search of a convenient coppice.

By the time we got back from the first of these after-breakfast excursions the fiesta was in full swing. Rockets exploded overhead in an almost continuous salvo, punctuated by fervent cries of '*Viva la Virgen! Viva la Blanca Paloma!* (Long live the White Dove).' In the bludgeoning sunshine the chatter of castanets seemed to harbour the ear-splitting stridency of a million cicadas. The wine-stalls were doing a roaring trade and cavalcades of gallants, their girls mounted pillion behind them, surged from house to house and from one stirrup-cup to another.

I envied them. We should all have been in the saddle ourselves. But the horses we had ordered from Seville had failed to materialise. We managed to rustle up some donkeys, however, and joined in the procession, turning a deaf ear to the cries of derision provoked by our Sancho-Panza-like appearance.

One of our first ports of call was the biggest house in El Rocio, rented every year by our friend Doña Matilda Union de Cuba, a lady from Madrid, with a character and bearing appropriate to her resonant name. It was a far cry from our humble cabin. A gleaming landau stood outside the front door, and half a dozen Arab thoroughbreds were tethered to a post nearby. Under the porch sat a number of Doña Matilda's guests, impeccably turned out and giving the impression of the elegance and affluence suggested by a *New Yorker* advertisement for some millionaires' playground.

To enter the forecourt, we had to urge our steeds up a short flight of stairs. Debo's little donkey resolutely refused to negotiate this obstacle; whereupon it was lifted off its feet by a couple of local stalwarts and, with Debo still mounted, carried bodily over the threshold.

By the end of the day all of us – with the exception of Debo, still spick and span in sand-coloured bush-shirt and skirt – looked as though we had emerged from a chalk-pit or been rolled in flour. The dust seemed to have been sucked through our clothing and carefully spread all over our skin. And, of course, there was no question of a bath. We did, however, have some plastic bowls and buckets, which we filled from the well outside, and our communal ablutions in our one and only room would not have seemed in the least comical or squalid had we not been surprised in the midst of them by Doña Matilda and her party who, smelling of scent and bath salts, chose this very moment to pay us a return call.

Next morning Rafaelito announced that he would not be taking part in the festivities. 'I'm going to stay at home,' he told us. 'I'll be your little maid and wash all your dirty clothes.' He was already dressed for the part, in a pale blue slumber-suit bought from the lingerie department in the Tangier Monoprix. In one hand he held a small travelling iron, in the other a plastic fan operated by batteries. 'Madame Butterfly,' he murmured, setting the fan in motion and bursting into falsetto song.

When we got home that evening we found he had indeed washed some clothes – a pair of pants and a couple of handkerchiefs of his own. 'But I've had a very busy day,' he assured us. 'I've prepared a surprise for dinner.'

Towards the end of the meal there was a loud report, a flash of flame, and a demijohn of wine standing in one corner of the room shattered, leaking its contents. A split-second later came a second explosion, more flames, and the curtains caught fire. Further detonations occurred in quick succession, each followed by a short blaze and accompanied by a whiff of gunpowder.

By this time we were all on our feet and diving for cover as though in an air raid – all except myself, still pinned to my chair by six-foot-four of not so very upright American manhood, since Jay who was sitting beside me had leapt into my lap at the first sign of alarm and buried his head in my bosom.

Xan, who had taken refuge under the table, was the first to discover the network of fuses that had been cunningly camouflaged in the earth floor. 'The crackers were stronger than I thought,' Rafaelito admitted, extinguishing the curtains by sprinkling them with the spilled wine which he scooped up in a tin mug. 'It was a nice surprise, though, wasn't it? Now we're all in the right mood for the Rosario.'

The Rosario, an open-air candle-lit procession, started about midnight. All the village fraternities lined up one after another, each carrying the banner of the Virgin. Slowly the long serpentine column coiled across the sand, while fireworks sparkled and crackled overhead and wave after wave of Bengal lights drifted gently down in a shower of golden rain round a set-piece of the Blanca Paloma encircled by silver doves.

But the climax of the festival was yet to come – the procession of the original wooden statue. This was reserved for the following morning.

It was due to start at eight o'clock. But it was well past nine before the gold-robed figure appeared, swaying dangerously on its heavy silver-canopied litter as its bearers, striving to push their way through the close-packed multitude, chanted in unison:

'*Nadie toque a la Virgen . . .*'

'What are they singing?' I asked Jaime.

He explained that since the discoverer of the statue came from Almonte, only the male citizens of that village now had the honour of carrying it round El Rocio. So I was able to translate the words of the song for myself:

> 'Let none other touch the Virgin,
> Let none other dare,
> Only men of Almonte
> Her burden shall bear . . .'

Slowly the litter advanced, the men beneath it staggering along, their features contorted with fatigue, drink and religious fervour. The crowd surged round them, tears of ecstasy pouring down their cheeks, and struggled to try to touch the hem of the Virgin's robe.

The tussle lasted all morning. It was two o'clock when the litter once more appeared before the door of the shrine, heralded by a peal of bells and loud cries. A regular battle ensued just outside the entrance as the crowd tried to hold back the men of Almonte in their anxiety to keep the statue with them a moment longer before it disappeared inside. Then, with a final thrust, the litter was past the door and the effigy was restored for another year to its place above the altar.

The festival of El Rocio was over.

That evening, while we were packing in readiness for an early-morning departure, there was a knock at our front door. I opened it to reveal two figures standing side by side in the gloaming. The taller one was draped in a threadbare blanket and wore a handkerchief knotted round his head. I would have taken him for an Arab had it not been for his brick-red complexion. His cheeks glowed almost phosphorescently through their coating of dust and his features were so distorted by sun and wind and mosquito bites that I could not tell if his teeth were bared in a smile or a rictus.

His companion had a scarlet mane of hair sprinkled with confetti and decked with paper carnations. Her face, too, looked blurred and incongruously tinted, like a badly focussed close-up in a Technicolor film. The shawl round her shoulders was of silk and beautifully embroidered, but in tatters.

'Beggars,' I said to myself, and was about to turn back for my purse when the female figure, bouncing with exuberance, exclaimed, '*Viva la Blanca Paloma!*'

Then the man gently remarked, 'We spent last night in a cork grove with some gypsies. Have you got a corner to spare?'

Only then did I recognise Gerald Brenan and Hetty McGee, a young admirer of his from Torremolinos.

When we got back to Tangier we were given an alarming report by the friend with whom we had left the dogs.

In our absence Salote had gone off her food, though she seemed to be growing fatter. Sensing something was wrong, our friend took her to the vet, who diagnosed dropsy and tried to draw off the adipose matter by puncturing the poor little dog with a hollow needle. But there was nothing to draw off.

Shortly afterwards our friend was woken in the middle of the night by heavy panting from Salote's basket, which he kept by his bed. As he reached down in the dark to pat her head and comfort her, his hand encountered several moist objects squirming round her. He switched on the light and saw she was suckling five new-born puppies.

'If only I'd known she was in pup,' he told us, 'I would never have taken her to the vet.'

But we had not known ourselves. During Salote's last heat we had made sure that no strange dog approached her. It was inconceivable that she should have conceived, unless immaculately. Her only companions had been Sunflower and Trubshawe . . . Trubshawe! I had not reckoned with him, of course. After all, he was still a puppy himself and had never shown any signs of precocity. Yet the resemblance between him and the new litter was unmistakable.

By this time he had grown into something more like a mythical beast than any imaginable breed of dog. His coat, once as soft as gollywog hair, was now sparse and bristling; stroking him was like running one's hand along the spine of a wild boar. His teeth, too, were like a wild boar's tusks, projecting from an underslung jaw and transforming his face into a Japanese war mask. In a crowded street his muzzle would inadvertently rake the shins and ankles of strangers, who drew back in alarm at the sight of an unidentifiable jet-black quadruped with the fangs and smouldering eyes of a dragon.

But his appearance belied his character. No dog ever had a sweeter nature or friendlier disposition. His only vice was chasing the chickens which occasionally strayed into our garden from the poultry farm belonging to our Arab neighbours. Not that he ever caught any, for his legs were too short to enable him to compete even with the doziest old hen, but he enjoyed putting them to flight and would wag his tail and bark with delight as they scattered through the eucalyptus trees.

This spectacle seemed to entertain the neighbours themselves, for they often witnessed it and their laughter used to echo the cackling of the birds. While appealing to their sense of humour, however, it also encouraged their mercenary leanings. One morning they turned up on our doorstep with several paper bags full of feathers, claiming that Trubshawe had plucked them out and demanding compensation. When we refused to pay they showed no sign of surprise or annoyance but merely gave a fatalistic shrug at the failure of their ruse and took their leave, still carrying their trumped-up evidence. But the next time the chickens strayed within Trubshawe's range Xan gave him a warning clout before he gave chase. This one admonishment was enough to cure him of his vice for ever.

One of the dogs' favourite outings, and ours too, was to Robinson's Beach a few miles outside the town. Bathing here was dangerous, for the sea was almost always rough and there was a fearsome undertow, but the sand which stretched for several miles in both directions was so inviting that even Xan who prefers rocky coastlines could not resist it. There was no question of trudging like Foreign Legionaries as we skirted the water's edge; the surface underfoot was firm and compact but at the same time miraculously soft and buoyant. Sunflower and Salote especially enjoyed scampering in and out of the foam, dodging the breakers, and Trubshawe did his best to emulate them.

One day, when an exceptionally heavy sea was running, a wave as high as a cottage wall came thundering in. The two older dogs promptly scuttled for safety. Trubshawe, less experienced and slower off the mark, was engulfed. As his head emerged from the foam, he was swept off his feet by the undertow and once more disappeared. The following wave flung him back again; through the spray I could just distinguish a black form that appeared as inert as a piece of driftwood. I grabbed him as he was being washed away once more and barely had time to pick him up before being knocked off my feet myself by the next breaker. Still clutching him, however, I managed to struggle ashore.

He looked even more limp than I felt as I laid him down beside me in the sand. But in a minute he was on his feet, wagging his tail and licking the water trickling down my face.

At that moment I knew a special bond had been forged between me and this grotesque little creature which I had helped to deliver into the world and had now saved from the sea.

8

Memory

One of the most colourful of the foreign residents in Tangier was an Englishman by the name of Paul Lund, a fair-haired shortish figure with a Van Dyke beard, sea-blue eyes and a loping gait that contrasted oddly with his swashbuckling manner and buccaneer features. We had known him by sight ever since our arrival but had never met him. We knew only that he was a smuggler.

Now that Tangier was no longer a contraband centre, he had opened a small bar which catered for the few remaining raffish characters in town. Of course this establishment was disdained by the rest of the British colony, and Xan and I were frowned upon for frequenting it; but such disapproval as we incurred was amply compensated by the pleasure we found in Paul's company.

To begin with, he was a first-rate raconteur and spoke in a curiously earnest voice punctuated by a slight impediment of speech which was more like a hiccough than a stammer. This unconsciously donnish manner of his was all the more humorous in view of his vocabulary which was peppered with prison slang, for, as we now learnt, he had had a long criminal career in England. This had come to an abrupt end a few years before, when he was implicated in the manslaughter of a coppers' nark called Wobbler Johnson. 'For once I was completely innocent,' he told us. 'When those friends of mine borrowed my truck to cart away an oil drum, I didn't know old Wobbler was inside it. And I didn't know they were going to tip him over a cliff. I was innocent, I tell you, but with a record like mine I wasn't taking any chances. I skipped. That's how I turned up here.'

He was neither proud nor ashamed of this, he merely acknowledged it as a fact (while also exploiting it as a conversational gambit) and this attitude of his lent all his other stories of skulduggery the same quality of authenticity. However improbable they sounded, I felt they were essentially true. At any rate they were entertaining.

Through Paul we came to know Cameron Rougvie, a Canadian friend of his, who had so far been something of a mystery to us. He was a tough, burly figure with the rolling gait of a seaman, dressed invariably in an open-necked shirt and rather shabby flannel trousers. There was something in his expression that reminded me of a plump bullfinch about to nip the blossom off a cherry-tree. At first we had mistaken him for a beachcomber or one of the smugglers, for he always seemed to be in their company and never associated with the staid denizens of the Mountain. Then, in Paul's bar where he was a regular customer, we discovered that he was a journalist, owned the largest liquor store in Tangier, and lived in a comfortable bourgeois house with a lovely wife and two little fair-haired daughters. A thoroughly domesticated man in fact, though he might not have liked being described as such. A relatively rich man, too, for he owned a yacht. We had already noticed it in the harbour – a ketch called *Memory* – but did not know it belonged to him.

'I'm going on a short cruise,' he told us one night. 'To the south of France and back. Why not join me? My wife's having a baby, so I'm afraid you'll be the only woman on board,

Daphne. No objection? Good. Do either of you know anything about sailing? No? Never mind. My crew's not up to much, but Paul will be with us and he's a master mariner as well as . . . all the other things he's been.'

On the evening of our departure the wind was whistling through the Pillars of Hercules with the strength of a giant blow-lamp. 'We'll be sailing right into the teeth of a gale,' Cameron informed us delightedly, as we stepped on board.

When we went below, we were surprised to find two old Arab women swabbing the deck and dusting the furniture. They looked singularly maladroit and landlubberly. Cameron had told us his crew was not up to much, admittedly, but we hardly expected it to be quite so meagre and unsuitable. Reading our thoughts, he hastened to explain:

'I've just had a mutiny. My three Spanish boys walked out on me. Without a word of warning. And leaving the boat in a filthy mess. So I had to get a couple of maids down from the house. Don't worry, they'll soon have everything ship-shape. Meanwhile Paul's rustling up another crew. Let's have a drink till they arrive.'

We had had several drinks by the time Paul turned up and announced, 'All I could find was a trio of apes,' by which he meant three Arabs. 'I don't know about the other two, but I can vouch for Mustapha. He's been on several runs with me and we were in clink together after those Eyetie coastguards nabbed us.'

'They'll have to do,' said Cameron. 'Come on, let's get going.'

Not wishing to be in the way while they weighed anchor, Xan and I remained below and inspected our quarters. We had a small double cabin to ourselves which, if not luxurious, was more than adequate; and there was a lavatory on the other side of the saloon. Xan tested it by pumping the handle up and down a couple of times. There was a gurgle, a rumble, then a sudden gush of water which filled the pan without draining away. The boat gave a lurch and the water overflowed on to the floor. Xan hastily closed the door. 'Better forget about it for the moment,' he said.

As soon as we were out of the harbour, the boat began to plunge about like a mad porpoise. We took to our bunks. But sleep was impossible, what with the roaring of the wind, the battering of the sea and the creaking and groaning of *Memory*'s old timbers. My previous experience of yachting had been limited to large well-appointed ships with a qualified captain, a trained crew and white-coated stewards. No vessel I had travelled on before had ever behaved like this. The discomfort I could bear, but what alarmed me was the prospect of danger.

'Is it *meant* to be like this?' I shouted to Xan who was in the bunk above me.

Before he could reply there was a thundering crash, as though we had been hit broadside-on by a battering-ram, the boat keeled over, shuddering, and we were both deposited on the floor in a tangle of bedsheets and blankets.

'I'm getting out of here,' I yelled, pulling on the smart sky-blue sailing suit I had bought specially for the voyage. We stumbled out into the saloon.

Water from the wave which had just swept over us was still dripping down the walls. The table, which had been bolted to the floor, had come adrift and smashed into a cupboard, revealing a cataract of broken crockery and glasses. In one corner Rubio, Paul's marmalade cat, was being copiously and noisily sick.

From this chaos we managed to unearth a bottle of vodka, still miraculously intact, a badly dented tin of Campbell's consommé, and a couple of enamel mugs. Slithering backwards and forwards along the plastic banquettes as the ship rolled from side to side, we spent the remainder of the night refilling our mugs and carefully cradling our precious bottle and tin.

From time to time Cameron and Paul came down in turn to join us for a drink. Cameron was beaming all over. 'I've never before been out in a storm like this,' he said. Paul did not even mention the weather but merely grunted, 'Those two other apes are useless. Green in the face and puking all over the deck.'

The storm gradually blew itself out and by the morning Xan and I had imbibed sufficient Dutch courage to clamber up into the wheelhouse. To our surprise, we found Tangier was still in sight. We had made hardly any headway and had simply tacked to and fro between the Straits all night.

'But the wind's veering,' Cameron assured us. 'We ought to be in Algeciras by noon. I'll have to put in there, as we've developed a leaking stern gland.' The alarm must have shown on my face, for he hastily added, 'Don't worry. It only means pumping out the bilges more often.'

It was a nasty phrase all the same.

Cameron's timing proved accurate. By midday we were entering the Bay of Algeciras. The wind had veered, just as he had predicted. It now dropped completely and we were becalmed, drifting slowly towards Gibraltar.

'Better start up the engine,' Paul suggested and disappeared below. His head reappeared at the engine-room hatch a moment or two later. 'The poxy thing *won't* start,' he announced. Meanwhile the Rock was looming closer and closer. 'Blimey!' he spluttered.

Before I could understand the reason for his haste, he had shipped the dinghy, made it fast to *Memory* and was rowing for all he was worth. 'Cor! Talk about a minnow towing a whale!' he shouted up to us. 'Am I making any headway?'

'None at all!' Cameron shouted back.

Luckily a faint breeze sprang up just then and *Memory* responded to it loyally. Paul climbed back on board.

'Phew!' he said, mopping his brow. 'After giving the C.I.D. the slip, I didn't fancy being arrested by bobbies from Gibraltar. . . .'

Safe in Algeciras, Paul dismantled the engine and found there was an essential part broken which he would not be able to repair himself. For some reason or other, which I have never been able to understand, this hunk of metal could not be taken openly to a mechanic in the town but had to be smuggled through the customs. It was therefore camouflaged in a large basket under a layer of fresh sardines and Paul loped off, swinging it lightly in one hand with all the nonchalance he could muster in order to disguise its weight.

Meanwhile Cameron attended to the leaking stern gland. By a natural association of ideas this reminded me of our blocked lavatory, which I now mentioned to him. 'Those damned maids must have stuffed their cleaning rags down it,' he said. 'I have to go ashore to replenish our stores, but I'll tell the apes to see to it. . . . Oh, by the way, you don't mind cooking lunch for them, do you? They've recovered from their sea-sickness and look famished.'

Down in the galley I saw from a calendar that the date was July 11. 'What a way to be spending my birthday,' I said, fearfully holding a match to the ancient stove. (Someone had told me that leaking gas in a ship collects under the floorboards, then rises like an invisible tide which the slightest spark is liable to ignite.)

'And our wedding anniversary,' said Xan, as he slipped on the greasy linoleum underfoot.

Soon we were both having difficulty in standing upright.

The floor seemed to have developed a pronounced list. We were too surprised to investigate this phenomenon, until the sound of gurgling water spurred us into action. We rushed back into the saloon.

Through the open door leading to our lavatory we could see lengths of piping all over the deck and, where the lavatory pan had been, a gaping hole through which the sea was pouring and at which the three Arabs were staring in bewilderment. No doubt they would have gone on staring till the ship had sunk to the bottom of the harbour, had we not exhorted them to block the hole.

'Don't worry,' said Cameron, inspecting the damage when he got back. 'It merely means pumping out the bilges again. But I'm afraid that lavatory will be out of use for the rest of the trip.'

Paul returned later in the evening, dropping his fish-basket on the deck with a metallic clang. 'Cor!' he said, taking off his peaked cap and shaking the sweat from it. 'I'll be needing a truss after this! Anyway, the flipping thing's fixed. . . . Now for a good strong handy Andy and a drop of the colonel's daughter . . .' And he poured himself out a nut-brown brandy-and-soda.

The two days we spent at sea after leaving Algeciras must have seemed disappointingly uneventful to Cameron. The stern gland was no longer leaking. The engine started when required. The weather was perfect. The wind was blowing in the right direction. The three Arabs had found their sea legs and were now more or less effective. No sharks appeared when we stopped to bathe. Paul, Xan and I basked on deck, lazing away the daylight hours, while Cameron, to console himself for the lack of excitement, spent most of his time in the galley preparing delicious meals over which we lingered until afternoon torpor and midnight sleepiness sent us reeling twice daily to our bunks.

It was not until our next port of call – Palma de Mallorca, which we reached late at night, in the dark – that this pleasant routine was disrupted. And it was not until we had entered the harbour – somewhat too fast, it seemed to me – that Cameron found he was unable to control the engine from the wheelhouse. This was a challenge which even he had not bargained for. 'My God, I wonder how much this is going to cost me!' I heard him mutter, as we headed at an alarming speed straight for a wharf, scraping through two serried ranks of expensive yachts.

Paul, however, had already seized a crowbar and dived into the engine-room. A sound of grinding metal and a stream of invective issued from the hatch, then the whole deck gave a shudder which set the soles of my feet tingling. But Paul had done the trick. Our propellers churned in reverse, our speed decreased, and we stopped within inches of the wharf.

But soon we were going backwards almost as fast as we had entered, once again scraping past the vessels we had just barely managed to avoid.

'Put her into forward gear!' Cameron yelled.

Paul's head appeared at the engine-room hatch. 'What did you say?' he asked. 'I can't hear you from down here.'

'Forward, I said!' Cameron shouted.

'He means Full Ahead,' Xan translated, stationing himself half-way between the engine-room and the wheelhouse.

'Reverse!' Cameron bellowed a moment later.

'Astern!' Xan echoed.

This was hardly the ideal way to berth a ship, but by means of these relayed instructions Cameron eventually brought *Memory* alongside the quay, right in front of the Yacht Club.

Dance music drifted out of the open club-house windows, through which we could see elegantly dressed couples waltzing sedately to a naval band in the background.

'Blimey!' said Paul, eyeing the ladies' bare backs and automatically assuming what we called his Robert Mitchum expression: a concupiscent leer. 'I've a good mind to go in there and give some of those birds the old cannibal-crutch signal!'

Before he could carry out this threat, however, an official immaculate in white uniform sauntered over, carefully keeping his distance as though he feared contagion from our scruffy vessel. Politely but firmly he informed us that this berth was reserved for the Admiral's launch which was expected at any moment. So we had to repeat our clumsy manoeuvres all over again and anchor in the outer harbour for the night.

After having the engine repaired once again, we headed for Corsica. The weather continued fair. 'It looks as though it's going to be plain sailing all the way to Ajaccio,' Cameron told us, scarcely able to conceal his disappointment.

It was so warm, even at night, that I took to sleeping in the wheelhouse in preference to the stuffy cabin. On the third night out from Palma, as I lay curled up on a narrow shelf between the chart locker and a bulkhead, I was woken by a dazzling glare, as though someone was shining a torch in my face. For a moment I thought that dawn had broken and a sunbeam had settled on my eyelids, but it was only the moonlight shimmering on the barely rippling sea.

I lay there for some time, gazing half-hypnotised at the phosphorescent streak of our wake disappearing into the darkness behind us, then turned my head to follow the antics of a couple of porpoises cavorting in the spray thrown up by our bows. Some distance ahead, and stretching right across our course, I noticed a second line of phosphorescence. The wake of another ship, I said to myself. But there was no other ship in sight. A mirage, then, an optical illusion? I rubbed my eyes and peered more intently. No, it was unmistakable: there seemed to be waves breaking in the middle of the flat-calm sea.

There was no one else on deck except one of the Arabs on duty at the wheel. I drew his attention to the phenomenon. He too peered straight ahead, then shrugged his shoulders, but made no attempt to alter course. So I concluded that my eyes were still playing tricks on me. Yet I was not completely reassured, for the vision seemed as clear as ever . . . and considerably closer. I decided to go below.

Cameron was sitting alone in the saloon, reading a paper-back thriller. He was so immersed in his book that he scarcely noticed my entrance. I felt all the more disinclined to disturb him by mentioning what I thought I had seen, I could imagine his reaction to my groundless fears. Yet supposing they were not groundless . . . I had almost made up my mind to speak, when the Arab at the wheel gave a shriek.

'What the hell's the matter with him?' said Cameron, reluctantly putting down his thriller. 'Oh, well, I'd better go up and see . . .'

He disappeared, leaving me alone with my guilt. A moment later the ship gave a violent lurch, which brought Xan and Paul stumbling sleepily out of their cabins.

'What the devil's going on?' Paul complained. 'That ape's handling the wheel as though he was driving a dodgem!'

'Don't worry,' said Cameron, reappearing from above. 'We missed it. . . . Only by inches, though,' he added cheerfully.

'Missed what?' Xan and Paul asked in unison.

'A line of rocks. We were heading straight for them. Didn't you notice them when you were up there, Daphne?'

'No,' I replied.

It was some time before I could bring myself to confess the truth, and then only to Xan.

He looked puzzled. 'But those rocks must be charted,' he said, 'and even Cameron wouldn't have plotted a collision course deliberately. His navigation must be faulty.'

Nevertheless we reached Ajaccio without further mishap.

On the final lap from Corsica to France, however, Xan secretly kept checking our course on the chart. Though he knew nothing about navigation, from his army days he remembered something about map-reading. 'The principle must be the same,' he told me, 'and, as far as I can see, no allowance is being made for magnetic variation.'

This was double-Dutch to me, but I felt there must have been something in what he said when we eventually approached the Riviera. This was the first landfall we had made in daylight, so that Cameron was unable to take his bearings from the lighthouses along the coast. 'Never mind,' he said to Xan. 'You were brought up in Nice, weren't you? You'll be able to pick out a landmark or two as soon as we're closer inshore. We ought to be heading straight for Villefranche.'

But even within hailing distance of the coast Xan failed to spot a single familiar feature. It was only after sailing parallel to the shore for some time that he recognised, in the far distance, the Rock of Monaco.

'As far as I can judge,' he told Cameron, 'we must be somewhere off San Remo right now.'

'San Remo!' Paul pricked up his ears. 'That's Italy, isn't it? Let's get away from here! The Eyeties only let me out of clink on condition I never came back.'

'Don't worry,' said Cameron, not in the least abashed. 'I can find my own way now. Let's have a drink to celebrate our safe arrival.'

Even at this stage I felt the suggestion was premature. There might still be hazards I had not even imagined. But nothing occurred to disturb our tranquillity for the rest of the voyage. We sat out on deck, sipping whisky-and-soda, revelling in the beauty of the evening. We berthed without mishap in Villefranche harbour. We went ashore and had a sumptuous dinner. We rang up Dirk and Tony at the Colombe d'Or in Saint-Paul-de-Vence and arranged to stay with them for a couple of days. Yet in spite of the pleasure of the moment and the prospect of the forty-eight hours to follow, I was already beginning to dread the return journey.

I confided my dread to Xan in the morning and even tentatively suggested inventing some excuse and flying back to Tangier from Nice. To my surprise, he agreed. 'I've never understood,' he said, 'why rats are disparaged for leaving a sinking ship. Surely it's the obvious thing to do.'

After two days on dry land, however, the rash I had developed on my thighs (from the plastic banquettes or merely from nerves?) began to fade, and so did my apprehensions. Xan, too, had second thoughts about abandoning Cameron and Paul. 'After all, *Memory* isn't actually sinking,' he said.

'And we did avoid those rocks, didn't we?'

'And the engine's working properly now . . .'

'And you can always check our course . . .'

So we decided to sail back.

The shining weather made us glad we had taken this decision. Basking on deck, stopping every now and then for a bathe in deliciously deep water, we congratulated ourselves. 'Think of missing all this,' we kept saying. But we had spoken too soon, failed to touch wood, defied the fates, pushed our luck too far. On the third night out the storm broke.

I was asleep on my makeshift bunk in the wheelhouse and was awakened by the motion of the ship which for so long had been almost imperceptible. Rubio, the cat, which had been happily purring on my stomach, now started mewing. Soon I was having to press my feet against the bulkhead and my shoulders against the chart locker to prevent myself from rolling off the ledge. Strangely I found Rubio's weight and warmth an antidote to fear and sea-sickness, as comforting and reassuring as a hot water-bottle. I was conscious of discomfort but not alive to any sense of danger.

All of a sudden, however, the boom which had so far been swaying gently from side to side in a narrow arc swung right over like a heavy pendulum. There was a noise like a whip being cracked and the ship gave a heavy lurch. The Arab who was steering was flung off his feet and I had a momentary glimpse of the wheel spinning round unchecked, then Rubio and I were likewise dislodged in a shower of pencils, protractors, compasses and notebooks. As I collected my wits and my belongings Cameron appeared, followed by Paul who at once seized the wheel.

'Better go below,' they advised me. 'We're in for a spot of fun.'

In the saloon I found Xan stretched out on one of the banquettes, shrouded in a tarpaulin to protect him from the water dripping from above. 'We can't get into our cabin,' he announced. 'The lockers must have come adrift and jammed the door from the inside. I can't open it more than a few inches.'

There was nothing I could do but follow his example. I picked up another tarpaulin and lay down on the opposite banquette. Conversation was impossible on account of the noise of the wind and the surging sea. We lay there without speaking. I tried to breathe in rhythm with the motion of the ship, inhaling as she rose, exhaling as she descended into a trough; but every breath became a groan, increasing in volume each time the water seeped in and pattered down upon me.

After one particularly big wave had swept over us, I was conscious of some new movement, some additional activity, inside the saloon itself. I raised a corner of my tarpaulin and saw Xan struggling with the door of the cabin. He had opened it sufficiently to get one arm inside and, when he withdrew it, I noticed he was clutching our passports and travellers' cheques, which he stuffed into the pocket of his jeans.

'What on earth are you doing?' I asked him, shouting to make myself heard.

'Oh, just to be on the safe side . . .' he stammered sheepishly. 'I thought we'd better have them on us . . . in case something happens.'

A few minutes later Cameron came in. 'Mustapha was almost swept overboard by that last wave,' he informed us. 'Paul managed to grab him just in time.' He rummaged about in a locker and produced half a dozen objects, two of which he tossed over to us. 'You'd better hang on to these,' he said. 'They're self-inflatable. Just pull the ring in case of . . .' he hesitated over the word . . . 'in case of emergency.'

We found ourselves holding a couple of patent life-belts.

Shortly afterwards Paul came down and joined us. For some reason he had discarded his trousers and was dressed in nothing but underpants and a short oilskin jacket. His fair hair dripped under his peaked cap. 'Cor!' he said, gazing at himself in the looking-glass. 'I look like a flipping elf in this gear!'

'What's it like on deck?' we asked.

'Pretty rough,' he admitted. 'The sails are tearing apart and the main block is cracked. If that doesn't hold . . .'

His voice was drowned by a series of rhythmic crashes overhead, as though a peg-legged giant was thudding across the deck.

'That does it,' he said. 'It hasn't held. Now I'll have to start the frigging engine.'

Simultaneously I heard Cameron's voice from above shouting, 'All hands on deck!'

To my shame, I pleaded with Xan. 'Don't you go up there,' I said. 'The waves are so big and you're so light, you'll be swept overboard and . . .'

But before I could finish the sentence he had followed Paul outside.

He came back a quarter of an hour later, accompanied by Cameron. Both of them were soaked to the skin and shivering with cold. 'Don't worry,' said Cameron. 'The sails have ripped but we've got a storm anchor out. Now that the engine's going, all we need do is sit tight and ride out the gale. Let's all have a night-cap.'

Paul joined us for a final drink, then he and Cameron went to bed. Xan too settled down on his banquette and, as he had been able to do even in the death cell in Digne, fell fast asleep. I envied him this ability to dissociate himself from his surroundings, and at the same time resented it; an unconscious companion is not much comfort in danger or adversity.

The wind seemed to have dropped – at least it was making less noise now that the sails had been lowered – but the seas were as mountainous as ever and sweeping over us at regular intervals. The sound of the engine, which at first I found reassuring, racked my nerves each time our stern rose and the propeller was lifted out of the water, biting on air and sending a shudder right through the ship. We seemed to be completely at the mercy of the elements.

Supposing the engine failed, supposing the Arab at the wheel was unable to keep us headed into the wind, supposing one of these waves caught us broadside-on . . . I could already envisage a sea-green anonymity of death by drowning. *Memory* . . . I kept repeating the name to myself. *In Memoriam* . . . 'In Memory of Daphne Fielding lost at Sea.' In my mind's eye I saw these words carved on a small grey granite stone set like a cairn on the Bodmin Moors . . .

By dawn we were all up on deck. The gale had blown itself out, but the sky was still overcast and the sea only slightly less rough than before. In the early-morning light I noticed something flapping in the rigging. It was a hoopoe, so exhausted that it made no attempt to fly away when I reached up and caught it. 'That means we must be somewhere near land,' said Cameron.

And so we were. Shortly afterwards we sighted a dark shape on the horizon, which Xan identified as Ibiza.

As we approached the island I prepared to release the bird, which I had been keeping safe in the front of my wind-jammer, but Mustapha asked if he could first handle it. Taking it gently in both palms, he rubbed its head across his eyes before launching it into the air. (The Arabs apparently believe the hoopoe is capable of curing eye diseases and averting blindness – no doubt by some sort of sympathetic magic, on account of the size of its own eyes which are as large and round as a woodcock's.) We watched it winging its way like Noah's dove towards Ibiza harbour, into which we wearily chugged some hours later.

After having our sails patched we set off on the homeward lap, still using the engine since the wind had now dropped again. My spirits soared, not only on account of the fair weather but because I felt that nothing worse than what we had just been through could occur during the two remaining days of the voyage. I was therefore only mildly disturbed when the engine caught fire and conked out in the middle of our last night at sea. Paul simply poured several buckets of water down the hatch until the flames were extinguished.

And I was amused rather than frightened when, almost within reach of our destination, a thick fog descended over the Straits, blocking out the familiar outline of Jebel Mousa which we could already see ahead of us. Visibility was reduced to a few feet and we were in the middle of a busy shipping lane, as we could hear from the fog-horns bleating all round us, but my fear of collision was as nothing compared with my horror in the recent storm.

Memory was not equipped with a fog-horn, but Cameron happened to have a toy trumpet and a wooden rattle on board: relics of a carnival party. With these instruments, supplemented at my suggestion (for I remembered Banjo Pier at Looe) by a number of pots and pans, we managed to kick up enough din to warn any other vessel of our presence.

The fog lifted as we rounded Cape Malabata, but I continued to whirl my rattle for the sheer joy of being within sight of home. Never before had I been so glad to get back to Tangier.

9

The Valley of the Wolves

In our absence the Moroccan government had instituted a fresh set of restrictive laws and passport regulations. For some time entrance visas had been necessary for visitors from abroad. We now discovered that *exit* visas were required, even for foreign residents. This was the last straw.

'It's getting worse than Russia,' Xan complained. 'Can you imagine being cooped up here, trapped, at the whim of some half-baked Arab policeman or customs officer! No, it won't do. We've got to get out of here. The next time we leave – if they let us – it'll be for good.' Even though the authorities recognised their folly and repealed the law a few days later, he remained adamant. 'They could easily change their minds again, or think up some new absurdity. No, we've got to go.'

'Where do you suggest?' I asked.

'Do you remember Uzès?'

Certainly I did: a delightful little market town in Languedoc, where we had once stopped – how many years ago? – for a drink. 'But we can't possibly afford to live in France,' I said.

'I know. But it was a nice idea. . . . Oh well, we'd better choose between Spain and Portugal.'

But the part of Spain we liked best, Andalusia, was rapidly being ruined. On each of our visits to the Davises we had noticed not only several new skyscraper hotels but entire new holiday towns disfiguring the coast. So we plumped for Portugal which, with its misty melancholy and rather old-fashioned atmosphere, had always reminded me of Cornwall.

Surprisingly – for by this time many other foreigners had left and their empty houses and flats were going for a song – we had no difficulty in selling our eagle's eyrie for a reasonable sum and, having stored our furniture, were soon ready to leave.

Apart from our luggage, we now had four dogs to transport, for we had kept one of the litter incestuously engendered by Salote and Trubshawe—a fluffy blond puppy with an engaging lop-sided face (which might have warned me, had I given it a thought, that he was eventually to become the canine equivalent of a village idiot). Since my second son, Christopher, also joined us for the journey at the last moment, it was a tight squeeze in our little Dauphine which had recently succeeded the Land Rover.

We arranged to travel via Algeciras rather than Gibraltar, where the dogs would have had to spend the night in quarantine – a wretched experience which Sunflower and Salote had already undergone on a previous visit when, failing to find rooms at the Rock Hotel which has its own accommodation for animals, we had had to leave them in the official kennels down by the docks: a row of ice-cold cells which were locked by a policeman and appeared not to have been cleaned since the last prisoner's release.

On our way through Seville, Christopher bought himself a guitar which added to the crush in the back of the car and gave an irritating twang each time he shifted his long legs or whenever one of the dogs moved. But we all managed to keep our tempers throughout the two-day drive.

Previously, when motoring through France with Sunflower

and Salote, we had always had to plan in advance, carefully consulting the *Michelin* to make sure that the hotel in which we hoped to stay did not have a 'No Dogs Allowed' sign after its name. How many times had we looked forward to a '*belle demeure dans un parc*' or dribbled in anticipation of '*paillardine à la sauge*' only to find these inviting words accompanied by that nasty little line-drawing of a dog's head barred by a diagonal line! This time, however, we had made no plans, for we knew the Spanish and Portuguese are less fussy in these matters than the French. We merely stopped for the night at the most convenient place – a simple but comfortable, spotlessly clean and ridiculously cheap *pousada*, where the dogs were admitted without a word – before driving on to Sintra, where we felt confident of finding somewhere suitable to live while we searched for a house to buy in the neighbourhood.

We did not have far to look. On the edge of the village we were at once attracted to an old stone building which, judging by the ornate iron-work sign above the massive front door, must once have been a coaching-inn. It looked as if it had been closed for years; all the windows were shuttered and no sound came from within. Yet something impelled us to persist in our knocking.

Presently the door was opened by a frail female figure clad in a shabby dressing-gown and bedroom slippers. Her fair hair was pinned on top of her head in an untidy knot and her prominent blue eyes were rimmed with red, as though she had recently been weeping. To our enquiries she replied in fluent cultured French with a pronounced central-European accent. Yes, the place was closed, but . . . she hesitated for a moment . . . but since we planned to stay for some time, she would let us have rooms, though no meals could be provided apart from breakfast.

She led the way upstairs and ushered us through a door on the first floor. We gasped. The bleak, rather dingy hall had not prepared us for what we now saw: a fairly small but perfectly proportioned sitting-room furnished in the height of eighteenth-century elegance. Each piece was so well preserved and tended that light was reflected from the beeswaxed surfaces of wood as intensely as from the gilt-framed looking-glass above the grey marble chimney-piece. The bedroom next door, and the dressing-room and bathroom leading from it, were all arranged in the same impeccable taste.

When we complimented the melancholy lady on her possessions she merely gave a shrug and murmured, 'These were Lord Byron's rooms.' At first we thought she must be raving, but we subsequently learnt that this inn was indeed the erstwhile Hotel Lawrence where Byron had stayed with Hobhouse in 1810 and from which he had written to his mother, 'The village of Cintra is perhaps in every respect the most delightful in Europe.' And remembering the poet's predilection for carving his name or initials – on his desk at Harrow, for instance, and on a column of the Temple of Poseidon at Sunium – I liked to think that the hieroglyphs I later discovered on one of the window-panes had been personally incised with his diamond ring.

Breakfast was brought up by an elderly grey-haired maid shaped like a cottage loaf and with the jovial temperament which is generally associated with this physique. At our attempts to thank her in our rudimentary Portuguese, she cackled with laughter, slapping her elephantine thighs and sobbing, '*O Jesu*', as the tears coursed down her appleskin cheeks. From Maria – for this was her name – we eventually learnt, by a process of dumb crambo and sign language which unfailingly produced fresh guffaws and tears of mirth, that her employer was a

Hungarian countess who suffered from chronic depression. This accounted for her accent and her red-rimmed eyes, but left many other questions unanswered. Why, for instance, with a large house full of exquisite furniture (the suites on the floor above were as well appointed as ours, we discovered) did she prefer to live in an almost bare servant's room in the basement with a mangy Pomeranian dog and a moulting parrot as her sole companions? This was a mystery we never solved.

For luncheon and dinner we had a choice between two restaurants, both within easy walking distance. The nearest was equipped with a marble font to which a piece of soap was attached by a chain. Before sitting down to his meal, each customer would make use of these amenities with an almost ritualistic zeal, soaping his hands and arms up to the elbow like a surgeon preparing for an operation. This public ablution was the only feature which distinguished what we called 'The Clean' restaurant from 'The Other.' In every other respect they were identical, with the same menu of soup, fried fish, steak and chips, and caramel custard, which never varied from day to day or between the midday and the evening meal.

For a change we would sometimes drive down to Cascais or into Lisbon but, for all the gastronomic shortcomings of Sintra, we preferred to remain in the immediate neighbourhood before sight-seeing or house-hunting further afield. The village itself provided us with enough diversion for the time being and, after so much motoring recently, it was delightful not to use the car for days on end but simply wander at will, on foot, down cobbled lanes lined with camellias where the silence was disturbed only by the clip-clop of an occasional horse-drawn cab or the wheezing trundle of a bullock cart. To exercise the dogs, we merely had to walk a little further into the surrounding woods where gigantic trees, lovingly tended by cohorts of state foresters – gnome-like figures in green uniforms – formed an unbroken canopy for miles, stretching upwards towards jagged outcrops of granite peaks tufted with cystus, heather and myrtle in aromatic profusion.

An invitation to luncheon, accompanied by a large bunch of garden violets, announced the presence in our neighbourhood of an old friend of mine, Bertie Landsberg. I had last seen him, several years before, at Malcontenta, the lovely Palladian villa he had restored outside Venice. I had heard that he had since married but had no idea until now that he had acquired a second house and settled in Portugal. His present home was only a mile or two from Sintra.

Even had I not been given the address, I would have identified the imposing mansion as his from a mere glance at the outside paintwork; no one but he had ever used this unique deep olive colour with bluish, almost black undertones. 'Bertie green', as I had always heard it called, was in fact his own invention and he kept its composition a secret. The interior of the house likewise bore the unmistakable stamp of his genius and, as he showed us round the sumptuous rooms, our pleasure was enhanced by his knowledgable comments on the decorative and architectural problems each of them had presented and which he had successfully solved.

When he heard that we too were looking for somewhere to settle in this area, he at once offered to act as our guide and suggested going off on a preliminary reconnaissance that very afternoon. This was to be the first of many such expeditions.

Since he had recently had a heart attack, his wife Dorothea naturally fussed over him. 'See that he keeps his hat on in the sun,' she would admonish us each time we set off. 'Don't let him walk too fast and get out of breath. . . .' But there was no holding him once he had sighted an old convent, a ruined abbey or dilapidated castle which he thought had possibilities; he would run towards it with arms outstretched, looking like an overgrown schoolboy in his blue blazer, grey flannel trousers and panama hat.

As we presently saw, he also had a schoolboy's sweet tooth. The Landsbergs employed a first-rate pastry-cook and any meal with them was bound to culminate in some delicious concoction which Bertie relished but which he was forbidden by the strict diet prescribed by his doctor and sensibly enforced by his wife. I could not help admiring the subterfuge and dexterity with which he would urge his neighbour at table to take a double helping of the pudding, half of which he would then transfer to his own plate and devour while Dorothea was still engaged in conversation with another guest. And one afternoon, while showing us round the little cottage nearby which he had equipped as an independent guest house, he opened the refrigerator, his forefinger raised to his lips in a mum's-the-word gesture, to disclose a large slice of the *vacherin* we had just had at luncheon but which he himself had been unable to taste by his usual ruse since Dorothea had happened to have her eyes on him while it was being handed round.

Alas, Bertie's idea of a suitable house for us did not coincide with ours. Everything he showed us was in proportion to his own grandiose schemes, far too big for us and well beyond our means. We were still homeless, and without any prospect of a home, when Christopher's holiday came to an end and I flew back to London with him.

On my return a fortnight later, however, I was greeted at the airport by Xan with the news that he had found something within our price range and which I might possibly like. 'I've only seen it from the outside so far,' he explained, 'but I've just

5 *right* Phyllis Della Faille

6 *below* Jorge Jantus with Xan in the wimming pool at the Cerrado, with *trompe oeil* decoration by Jorge

7 *bottom* Listening to *fado* at Coimbra, Xan nd Daphne with David Ponsonby

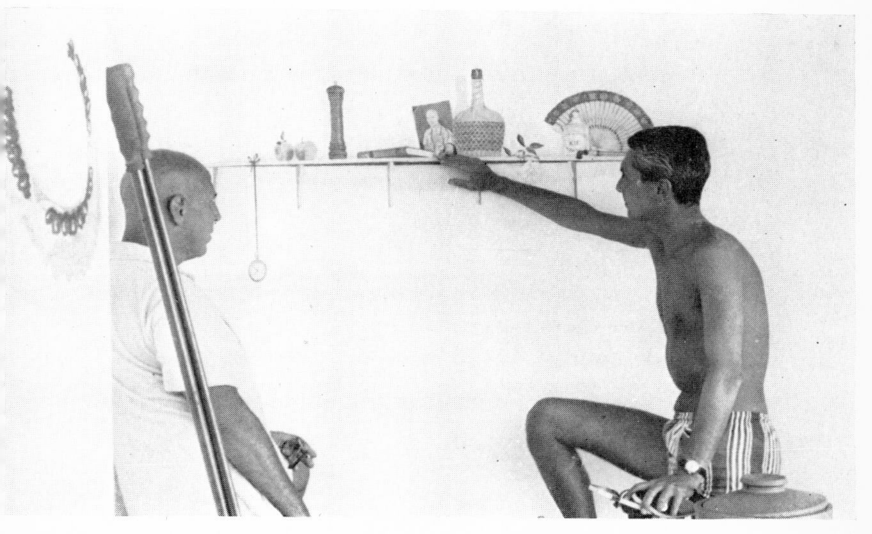

18 *above* Evelyn Waugh

19 *below* Emlyn Williams correcting proofs at the Cerrado

20 *right* Diana Cooper at the Cerrado

collected the keys from the owner, so we can drive out there at once and look it over.'

It was not far, only twenty-five minutes from Lisbon. Half-way to Sintra we turned off the main highway on to a minor road, then turned off again on to a still more neglected thoroughfare winding through a broad wooded valley. Soon, after passing a little hamlet, the slope on either side closed in and we were bumping along a rough track running parallel to a little stream. Here, for a moment, the landscape in the foreground seemed to turn all of a sudden snow-white, for, over a distance of several hundred yards, the low bushes on both banks of the stream were festooned with freshly laundered bedsheets drying in the sun – a surprising spectacle for which I was unable to account until I saw several groups of washerwomen at work in the series of pools formed by the meandering water. The valley, as it gently ascended, broadened once more into a shallow, irregularly shaped basin from which three paths radiated further up hill. We veered to the left, drove through a breach in a low stone wall – 'this is where the property begins,' Xan indicated – then up a short curving drive which led to the house itself.

At first I was too intent on the surroundings to pay much attention to the building, which in any case was half concealed on this side by a group of giant mimosa trees. I had eyes only for the beautifully terraced orchard in front of it, the small cork copse beyond, the pine-studded hillock rising in protection behind us and – to me, the most welcome feature of all – the crystal-clear rivulet at its feet, culminating in a reed-lined pool. From the platform of lawn above the orchard, on to which I advanced to get a better view, the cottage – for it appeared to be little more than that – looked like an illustration in a Grimm's fairy-story: the gingerbread house where the witch imprisoned

Hansel and Gretel. 'It's pure Humperdinck!' was my immediate thought.

To my surprise and delight, the interior was far larger than the outside suggested and as we wandered from room to room, throwing open the shutters, I could already see how we would arrange it. The first floor, which occupied only half the area of the building, lent itself automatically to our future personal quarters: a fair-sized bedroom, a slightly smaller work-room for me, a dressing-room for Xan, and a bathroom (so far the only one in the house). Downstairs, apart from the sitting-room, dining-room and three further rooms (which I earmarked in my mind's eye as two double guest rooms and a study for Xan) there would be space for two more bathrooms in addition to the existing servants' quarters and kitchen.

'It's perfect,' I said to Xan. 'How on earth did you find it?'

'Someone in Sintra told me it was for sale, and I was intrigued by the name.'

'Why, what's it called?'

'This is the address,' he replied, producing a slip of paper from his pocket. '*Cerrado das Fontainhas, Sitio da Tapada, Vale de Lobos, Sabugo* . . . which means: The Close of the Little Springs on the Site of the Parkland in the Valley of the Wolves. Sabugo is the hamlet we passed on the way.'

'Wonderful!' I said.

But when, a few days later, we proudly showed our find to Bertie, he remarked, 'Only a couple of mad children or a pair of besotted lovers would think of living in a place like this!'

10

Saudade

The title deeds of the house were drawn up in a notary's office in Lisbon. The documents were actually typewritten, but this was the only concession to modernity. The environment – a dark cell panelled in cork – was positively Dickensian and the procedure itself was designed for the days when literacy was less common. Every paragraph was first read out loud in Portuguese and then translated for our benefit by a clerk whose accent in English was so eccentric that the words he uttered were almost as incomprehensible to us as the original. After which, in addition to our signatures, we were required to append our thumb-prints. This simple operation assumed the qualities of an arcane ritual, as the clerk politely took Xan's thumb, guided it to an ink-pad, pressed it down, guided it back to the paper, pressed it down again, then repeated the process with me, making elaborate and genuinely embarrassed apologies for having to indulge in such apparent familiarity.

Not only our thumb-prints but the prints of every finger on both hands were registered a few days later, when we went to the police to apply for our residence permits. This time the atmosphere was less congenial. The office, with its white-tiled walls, felt as cold and antiseptic as a freshly scrubbed public lavatory, which it closely resembled. The procedure, too, was less genteel. I received no apologies for having my hand fondled by a strange man since, for the sake of decorum, there was a female official detailed to deal with me. The ridiculous charade reminded me of puppies having their noses rubbed in a mess and I could not help laughing at the grave expression of the people performing it – an expression which did not alter even when Xan ingenuously enquired if they would not like to have his toe-prints as well.

Since the house was already habitable we decided to move in as soon as our furniture arrived and thus be able to supervise on the spot the few structural alterations we had planned.

On learning that we were going to settle in Vale de Lobos, Maria begged to be taken on as our cook. She would be out of work as soon as we left the inn, since she was employed on a temporary basis only. Besides, her little daughter, a delicate girl, would be all the better for a change from the mists and damp of Sintra. (Maria-Elena was her only child, a lovely little creature in spite of her pasty complexion, and clearly the apple of her mother's eye for she was daintily and even expensively dressed. She was only five years old but looked even younger on account of her diminutive size, and I realised with a shock that Maria could be no older than myself.)

And so, on the day of our departure from the inn, they both came with us, two incongruous figures in the back of the car: a silent, elegant, pert and pallid little girl, and a voluble, globular, florid-faced woman, as ungainly in appearance as the wooden figure of Mrs Noah out of a toy ark.

As we approached the house, Maria started laughing. I looked round and saw that she was wobbling all over, shaken by the vibrations from the bumpy road which her own mirth kept intensifying. Her cackles were contagious and by the time we reached the front door all four of us were so convulsed that for a moment we were unable to climb out of the car. A fresh outburst of laughter was provoked, once we were indoors, by the discovery that she could barely squeeze through the narrow archway between the kitchen and dining-room. Clearly, this would have to be attended to at once.

From the previous owner we had inherited a gardener, Henrique, born and brought up within sight of the house. Though thirty years old, he had never been even as far afield as Lisbon and seemed perfectly content to spend the rest of his life in this valley, in the tumbledown shack nearby where he lived with a handsome gypsy-looking wife and two little sons, identical twins, who scampered about clothed in ragged vests, stark naked from the navel down. He had endeared himself to us at once by picking up a handful of our soil, burying his nose in it, holding it out to us as though he was offering us a pinch of snuff, then letting it trickle through his fingers, as he tweaked the lobe of his ear with his other hand and, for fear that we might not understand this sign of appreciation, murmured, '*Muito bom!*'

Within a few days we realised that Maria was an extremely good cook but could not be expected to do other chores as well. We therefore engaged two village girls, Salome and Lourdes, to undertake the housework. For them I designed a uniform, inspired by the regional peasant costume, in the bright checked cloth favoured by the Nazaré fishermen. Worn with a lawn headkerchief and flounced apron to match, it looked more like romantic fancy dress than domestic livery. At any rate both girls seemed to find it becoming, for they asked if they might wear it even on their afternoon off.

Meanwhile the alterations were proceeding apace. The servants' quarters and additional bathroom were our main concern. The previous owner's maids appeared to have slept in doorless, airless cubicles, with no sanitation or facilities for washing. Maria and the two girls were delighted but seemed surprised at our wanting to make their rooms more comfortable. They were also surprised when we provided them with meat and eggs to supplement their staple diet of bread, bean soup and dried cod. 'You're spoiling them,' we were told by the local gentry. Untrue, of course. But this remark, intended quite seriously, was an indication of how servants were usually treated in Portugal. No wonder poor little Lourdes was so upset when she broke a plate – she expected to have the cost deducted from her wages! Even so we were not prepared, on coming home at three o'clock one morning after an evening out, to find Maria still waiting up for us as a matter of course. 'You never told me not to,' she explained, 'and I thought you might be wanting something when you got back.'

In a surprisingly short time the house assumed the aspect I had originally envisaged. The kitchen, which we had found encrusted with the grime of ages, was tiled in gleaming white. All the other rooms were repainted. Curtains had been hung, bookshelves made. The new bathrooms were in working order; to prove it the village blacksmith who had been responsible for the plumbing insisted on our watching him as he turned on the taps one after another and, unconscious clown that he was, gravely went through the motions of washing his hands and having a bath. He even lowered himself for a moment or two on to each lavatory seat before pulling the plug. The necessary doors had been put up and the carpenter, a thickset elderly man with an adorable smile, had coyly pressed upon me a parting present of a cherry-basket fastened with a bow of pink ribbon and containing a pair of live turtle-doves nestling on a bed of moss. Oil lamps – dozens and dozens of them, for there was no source of electricity within miles – had been strategically sited and installed. The outside dining-room, an arbour of rambling roses and pink bignonia, had been refloored with bricks. Even the pond was freshly stocked with goldfish. We were now ready to give our house-warming party, which we planned to coincide with my birthday and our wedding anniversary.

Maria did not even flinch at the prospect of cooking for some fifty guests (drawn, incidentally, from ten different nationalities). In fact, on hearing that we planned to have fireworks, she even welcomed the idea. 'Splendid!' she said. 'My Maria-Elena loves fireworks . . . and I'll get her a new frock for the party.' Salome and Lourdes seemed equally enthusiastic, in spite of the extra work entailed in setting out trestle-tables in the garden and festooning the trees with Japanese lanterns and chains of coloured lights; while Henrique trudged off at once to engage some musicians from a neighbouring village.

What we expected him to find was the sort of bucolic trio we had often seen at the local country fairs: an old man in a cloth cap playing a fiddle, accompanied perhaps by a concertina and a drum. We were not prepared for the five-piece orchestra that eventually turned up, resplendent in scarlet dinner-jackets and black bow-ties, having marched over the hills for several miles carrying their instruments which included an electric guitar. The current for this was supplied by a heavy accumulator which they had also humped all the way.

As the evening progressed, the entire population of the valley – the washerwomen and their menfolk and children – drifted into the garden but, for all our persuasion, were too bashful to join in the fun. Diffidently they kept in the background, meek shapes among the shadows, friendly but undemonstrative, content but devoid of expression, apparently unmoved by any sentiment other than plain curiosity, barely smiling even when one of our guests inadvertently measured his length in the goldfish pond.

By this time we had grown accustomed to that indefinable trait in the national character, *saudade*, a sort of indolent wistful melancholy which colours every action, every attitude. Like all good tourists, Xan and I had made a point of spending an evening in a *fado* tavern and listening to the singing. We had not enjoyed the experience. We were able to put up with the mournful ululations, which were no doubt appropriate to the words, but what we found even more depressing was their effect upon the audience. Every man and woman in the place appeared to be sunk in sepulchral gloom, which persisted even after the songs had ended. Never in my life had I seen people take their pleasures so sadly.

There was no *fado*, thank heavens, at the local fête which was held later in the summer; yet there might well have been, such was the atmosphere. The site was idyllic: a broad upland meadow within sight of our house. But the fun fair erected there belied its name. All the sideshows were packed, but there was no sound of laughter. Outside the eating booths, sardines spluttered on charcoal grills, sucking pigs gyrated on turnspits, and barrels of red wine cascaded their contents into waiting canisters and beakers – a glorious spectacle. Inside, laden platters steamed on trestle-tables, plates and glasses were replenished as soon as emptied. But here again there was not the slightest evidence of merriment. Teeth chewed, jaws crunched, throats swallowed, as though in duty bound more than on pleasure bent. Somnolence rather than conviviality was induced by the food and drink.

This *saudade* seemed to be a universal affliction and deprived all public entertainment of gaiety. Every bar, every restaurant to which we had been was infected by it. We were therefore intrigued by a certain establishment lying just off the main road which we passed every time we drove into Lisbon. It looked like a motel but its neon sign proclaimed it to be a *boîte* and indeed, after dark, it sounded at least like a night club. The dance music issuing from the rather grim façade suggested unaccustomed revelry within. One evening we decided to stop and investigate.

As we entered the building our senses reeled, the glare from the harsh lights assaulting our eyes, the resonance from the bare walls playing havoc with our ear-drums. Beyond a large expanse of empty dance-floor, on a platform at the far end of the barrack-like room, we caught a glimpse of the orchestra: a woman in evening dress at a grand-piano and half a dozen male figures in tail coats and white ties. It was not until we had found a table and taken a closer look that we realised these figures were not flesh-and-blood. The woman was a wax mannequin, sitting bolt upright and immobile, one hand poised above the keyboard in an attitude of over-emphasised virtuoso. The other figures were tailor's dummies, staring sightlessly straight ahead, their fingers clamped round their instruments in a state of *rigor mortis.* The music was provided by a record-player turned up to full volume.

Our fellow-customers seemed almost as lifeless. A party of a dozen or so sat at one of the larger tables, understandably mute since the din precluded all conversation, but in the same frozen postures and with the same glazed expression as the orchestra itself. There were also a number of men sitting alone at individual tables, distinguishable from one another only by the degree of apathy with which they took an occasional sip of wine. The only other movement of which they seemed capable was to cross and uncross their legs as they glanced now and then with frustrated concupiscence at the pianist's rather dusty *décolleté*. No one danced. And, in the short intervals between one record and the next, not a voice was raised to break the silence.

At Christmas we gave a tea-party for the village children, about twenty or thirty of them, ranging in age from three to thirteen. They arrived all together, the younger ones competently herded by the elders, clean and scrubbed in their Sunday best, demure and courteous as their parents. Silently they filed into the dining-room. Silently, without jostling, they squeezed on to the benches round the long table. Silently they eyed the feast that Maria had prepared: bowls of rice pudding mixed with strawberry jam, jellies of various flavours, pyramids of *ovos moles* – those sticky bilious-looking cakes made of egg-yolk and sugar, to which the Portuguese of all ages are so curiously partial – and, in the centre, a yard-long chocolate Yule log decorated like a crèche, with a manger of candy-floss populated by miniature marzipan effigies of the Holy Family and the Three Wise Men.

Feeling the children might be intimidated by our presence, Xan and I withdrew next door, leaving Salome and Lourdes to look after them. I was hoping that during the meal their tongues might loosen, but still no sound came from the dining-room apart from the clatter and scrape of spoons and plates. By the time we returned, the food had vanished and they were sitting, silent as ever, gazing anxiously at the toys hanging from the Christmas tree. I fancied I could read their thoughts: 'Will there *really* be a present for me? . . . Will there be enough to go all round?' Their careworn expressions reminded me of little Father Time in *Jude the Obscure* and I hastened to put an end to their doubts.

It was impossible to get them to play any games; they didn't know any. Silently, sedately, they took their leave, filing out into the gloaming like a procession of aldermen, each clutching a present and an unopened bag of sugared almonds in one hand, the string of a balloon in the other.

11

Beasts

Such was the atmosphere we found whenever we went out that we felt more cheerful by ourselves at home. For days, sometimes for weeks on end, we never ventured farther than our front gates except to take the dogs for a walk. This was no hardship. Thanks to Maria, and to the two girls who were soon permanently infected with her high spirits, the house was like an oasis of gaiety in the surrounding desert of despond.

It was an active pleasure to wake in the morning to the cooing of the turtle-doves, to fall asleep at night to the rapturous song of nightingales. How they did go it, those birds, almost drowning the shrill sound of the cicadas, the creaking chorus of the countless frogs rising from the washing pools and the closer throaty bark of the solitary bullfrog presiding over our pond!

Except when it rained it was never too cold, even in winter, to spend most of the day in the garden. Everything we planted grew with rewarding ease, without the slightest effort (or so it seemed to us; Henrique, who worked from dawn till dusk might have had a different opinion). A datura, which I had carried back from the market in a small pot, shot up within a couple of years to the height of our balcony, the pungent smell of its ghost-white, bell-like flowers drifting through our bedroom window at night. Yet I remained untroubled by the dark dreams which the scent of this plant is said to induce.

The only barren part of the property was a field behind the house, which Henrique suggested might be turned into an olive grove. Nothing else would grow there. The subsoil was so rocky that he had to use dynamite to make the holes required for each sapling; into these he then inserted what looked like broomsticks. Only three weeks later, leaves began to sprout from this apparently dead wood and in less than a year each individual growth was a recognisable young olive tree.

As a substitute for bluebells, for which I pined but which I was unable to find locally, I planted some agapanthus in the cork copse. Soon these too had developed into a river of azure-headed flowers, reminding me with a stab of nostalgia of Longleat at bluebell time.

Meanwhile each season produced its crop of melons, peaches, strawberries, raspberries, plums, pears, figs, oranges and lemons, in such abundance that even after bottling and making jam we had to give them away by the sack and basketful; and peas, beans, zucchini, Indian corn, artichokes and sunset-coloured pumpkins, all of such succulence that we were tempted to become vegetarians for life.

In midsummer every bush and shrub was a buzz and a glitter with iridescent insect life. By day dragon-flies skimmed and coupled on the pond, fireflies flashed and flickered in the dusk, and at night furry moths spiralled round the lamps in suicidal convolutions. One particular veronica bush provided a hunting ground for Beelzebub, my pet chameleon. I would watch in fascination as he 'froze', fixing the prey he had sighted with an unblinking eye, inflating the pouches under his jaw. Then, with a rapidity of movement which never failed to take me by surprise, came the coral-coloured flash as his tongue uncoiled like a spring and instantly retracted, drawing the victim into his maw. He would also spend hours on the brim of my Portuguese hat, camouflaged against the pale honey colour of the straw. At night I used to place him on a pelmet in the bedroom, where he soon disposed of any fly that came within range.

I had always been told that the Portuguese were kind to animals, and on the whole I had found this to be true. But their kindness apparently did not extend to poultry. The local livestock market was a barnyard Belsen. Here, at high noon on one of the hottest days of the year, Xan and I came across a crate full of white ducks left out in the scorching sun while the stall-holder had gone off somewhere, presumably to lunch. The poor creatures were tethered tightly together; I could see the cord biting into their skin. They were limp and exhausted, their yellow beaks agape, panting like dogs; and I noticed tears, clear as crystal, coursing down their feathered cheeks.

'We've got to save them,' I said.

We eventually unearthed the stall-holder in a nearby wine-shop and told him we wanted to buy his ducks. He explained that they were already sold and waiting to be carted off. We pointed out that they would not live much longer if they were left out in the sun. He agreed to move them into the shade and, seeing that four of them were by now almost moribund (and would therefore, presumably, be turned down by his other client) offered to sell them to us. We bought them at once – three ducks and a drake – and drove back as fast as possible to revive them in our pond.

What a reward it was to see them, within minutes of being liberated, standing on their heads in the water, wagging their tails, stretching up to flap their wings, splashing and quacking with joy! From then on, every time I saw or heard them, my own joy was intensified.

Soon there was an addition to their chorus: the strident

raucous voice of a female Amazon parrot. I called her Judy because at the time I happened to be rereading Kipling, 'The Colonel's lady and Judy O'Grady. . . .'

But this Judy was no lady. In the pet shop where I bought her I was told that she could utter almost every obscenity in the Brazilian language. 'Let's see if she can learn some English ones,' said Xan. 'Fuck off,' he murmured gently through the bars of her cage.

Anxious to show him how clever she was, I kept repeating this phrase to her while we drove home and continued to do so at regular intervals for several days. Believing this to be the recognised mode of addressing a parrot in English, Maria and the two girls also took to mouthing these words at her. I had not the heart to disillusion them. Besides, it was good training for the bird and she eventually responded to it by shrieking 'Fuck off!' at the top of her voice and imitating Maria's cackle. From then on there was no stopping her. The phrase occurred in her everyday speech as frequently as on the lips of the most foul-mouthed private soldier.

One day Rosita Forbes came to luncheon with two rather prim-looking friends of hers. Throughout the meal she regaled us with stories about her travels in the Sahara, so intent on her monologue that she was not aware of Judy's running commentary in Brazilian punctuated as usual by the only phrase she knew in English. But the two other ladies, I noticed, kept glancing at the parrot's cage as though unable or unwilling to believe their ears. Luncheon dragged on till tea-time. Rosita rambled on. So did Judy. But by now her speech was slurred, as though she was bored or half asleep, and for a moment she did drop off, relapsing into silence. The two other ladies heaved a sigh, but their relief was short-lived. Judy woke up, blinked her eyelids, cleared her throat, steadied her voice, drew breath, and gave tongue: 'Fuck off!' The shrill spondee rang out loud and clear, so that this time even Rosita heard it. 'Well, yes, I suppose we really ought to be going,' she said, drawing on her gloves.

One of Judy's daily treats was a ration of white port. She would drink this from a coffee spoon which she held with the utmost gentility in one claw while balancing on the other, supping the liquid with her thick grey-blue tongue, making chewing movements with her beak, throwing her head back and closing her eyes in rapture like a professional wine-taster. As the alcohol took effect she would perform a sort of war-dance on her perch, stomping to and fro and flapping her wings. One day she flapped them extra hard and soared into the air. This flight seemed to be as unexpected to her as to ourselves. She gave a shriek of alarm and pleasure, like a small child on a fairground roller-coaster, as she swooped on to the nearest cork tree where she remained until the evening, mumbling incoherently. We tried to entice her down with the usual inanities one utters on such occasions – 'Pretty Polly! Darling Judy!' and, finally, 'Bloody bird!' – but she turned a deaf ear to our pleas. When it grew dark, however, she flew back to her perch of her own accord and allowed herself to be caged for the night without the slightest objection.

Her cage hung in an alcove above some shelves on which I kept my collection of china pussy-cats. These ornaments provided an obstacle course for the field mice that occasionally invaded the house. Sometimes we would see as many as a dozen of these engaging little creatures scuttling about in an endless steeplechase or else grouping themselves into *tableaux vivants*, striking attitudes on top of the cats' heads and nestling between their paws. Every so often one of them would leap into the cage above and steal a sunflower seed; whereupon

above Iris Tree with Aguri

right Daphne snowed up at Wuthering
eights

below Wuthering Heights, Xan dealing
ith the burning question

24 First sight of La G
des Pâtres

25 La Galerie des Pâtr
before the work begar

26 La Galerie des Pâtr
courtyard

Judy would give a squawk of fury and make an ineffectual lunge with her beak. But she had not the speed of Mr Brown, the Beatrix Potter owl, and, unlike Squirrel Nutkin, no mouse ever lost so much as his tail.

In the morning Judy would relieve her feelings by bullying the two doves, trampling all over the top of their cage and insulting them with an imitation of their cooing. If they happened to be nesting she would tug at the twigs they had laboriously collected, fly back to her perch with their building material and deliberately chew it to pieces.

One morning we were wakened by hysterical shrieks coming from the garden. At first I thought it was Judy and wondered how on earth she had managed to escape from her cage. Then I recognised the voice of Maria-Elena, Maria's little daughter. The child sounded genuinely scared, so Xan and I rushed down to see what was the matter.

We found her standing on the edge of the lawn in a histrionic attitude, one hand raised to her throat, the other pointing down the drive. Only then did we hear the growls and yelps which had so far been drowned by her shrieks. In the bushes a few yards away, Trubshawe was fighting with his son. Since we had been in Portugal the white puppy with the lop-sided face had grown into a hydrocephalic monster and was now far bigger than his father but, either from cowardice or stupidity, was no match for him. He lay on his back, one large fluffy ear firmly gripped in Trubshawe's rake-like jaws.

Xan separated the two dogs and gave them a good shaking; I patted Maria-Elena on the head to console her; and we would have thought no more of the incident had it not been repeated on the very next day, heralded by the same shrieks from Marie-Elena whom we discovered in the same histrionic attitude. When it again occurred later in the week, and again in Maria-Elena's presence, I could not help thinking that the child was in some way responsible, for Trubshawe had never before shown any sign of belligerence. This time, moreover, as soon as his jaws were unclamped from his victim's ear (still swollen to twice its normal size from the previous fights) he at once renewed the attack and, despite a thrashing from Xan, went for his son yet again.

From then on we had to keep them permanently separated. Maria, who for some reason preferred the idiot to any of the other dogs, was delighted when we gave him to her on condition that she kept him in the kitchen. Here he would spend all day curled up on a sack of potatoes, even though there was a comfortable bed for him by the stove, undisturbed except on the rare occasions when Trubshawe managed to slip in (or was enticed in by Maria-Elena?) behind Maria's back. Warned by the usual shrieks, Xan and I would arrive to find Salome and Lourdes performing a sort of tug-of-war, with the two dogs' interlocked bodies as the rope, Maria filling a bucket of water to pour over them (over the dogs, not the girls, though the latter were sometimes also drenched) and, inevitably Maria-Elena attitudinising in the background.

Sunflower was the next to cause us anxiety. By this time she was fairly old but had never had a day's illness in her life. I was therefore all the more unprepared when, one afternoon, without any warning, she sat up in her basket, gave a strange wail unlike any other sound she had ever made, then keeled over on to her side. She was unconscious only for a moment and seemed perfectly happy as soon as she recovered. But that evening she had a second attack and, in the morning, a third.

We sent for the vet, who diagnosed heart trouble and prescribed a course of injections. She responded to these at once and never had another attack; her appetite was unaffected and she was as active as before. She now seemed clumsier, however, and I noticed that when she jumped on to my lap she occasionally misjudged the height and distance. On one occasion she even overturned her water bowl by stepping on the edge of it. But it was not until I saw her walk straight into a chair leg that I began to be seriously alarmed. I picked her up and my fears were confirmed when I waved my hand a few inches away from her eyes. There was no reaction from them, not a flutter. The massive injections which had cured her heart must also have sent her blind.

Since her eyesight, like that of most Pekinese, had never been particularly acute, she quickly adjusted herself to this disability. Soon she was able to find her way all over the house without stumbling into the furniture, and after one fall into the duck-pond, which taught her to steer clear of it in future, she was just as confident out in the garden. Even when we took her further afield, up or down the valley, we never had to put her on a lead. She would stride out gamely, sensing the protection of Salote and Trubshawe who stuck close by her, one on either side, as though conscious of her need.

On these walks we were usually joined by another dog from a nearby farm, a ginger-haired mongrel with strange yellow eyes, and our pack was eventually further increased with the acquisition of Bacchus, a *cão de serra*, or Portuguese mountain dog.

We had seen this breed for the first time on a recent trip up north, to the province of Trás-os-Montes, a wild 'never-never land' sparsely populated by witch-like shepherdesses in sepia-coloured woollen cloaks falling in heavy folds from pointed hoods and by shepherds wrapped in three-tiered cloaks made of thatch, sartorial brothers of the Straw Man in *The Wizard of Oz*. The dogs guarding the flocks looked equally singular: as large as Great Danes but infinitely more hirsute and savage, wearing thick leather collars studded with iron spikes to protect them from marauding wolves, their natural enemies. Maria, who wanted what she called a proper watchdog, had advised us to get one of these. So we did.

Bacchus was still a puppy and looked anything but fierce. His constant playfulness irritated Sunflower and Salote, who put him in his place either by ignoring him entirely or, if his demands for attention became too unbearable, snapping at his paws which already were the size of their own heads; whereupon he would shamelessly turn tail. But he made firm friends with Trubshawe and the ginger mongrel and, when he was old enough to be attracted by a bitch on heat, used to accompany them on their predatory excursions, like a young dandy of the *belle époque* setting out with a couple of older *roués* on a visit to a fashionable brothel.

His size must have eliminated him as a serious contender, for he was at least three times bigger than any bitch within a radius of several miles. There was no doubt about Trubshawe's activity, however, and in due course we saw at least two other dogs in the valley with shaggy pelts and jaws like rakes – the False Trubshawes, as we called them.

From one of these expeditions Trubshawe returned alone. We were not very worried at first by the absence of Bacchus, whom we assumed to be still on the prowl with his other companion. But when, later in the day, we saw the ginger dog loping home by himself, we began to feel uneasy. Darkness fell, and there was still no sign of Bacchus. We stayed up all night waiting for him, in vain, and spent the next two days searching for him, fruitlessly. As a last resort we advertised his loss in the local paper, giving a detailed description of him and offering a reward should he be found.

The response to this advertisement was immediate. Early in the morning on the day it appeared, so early that we were not yet out of bed, someone rang up from Sintra to say that he had found our dog. Delighted, we made a note of the caller's address and said we would drive over at once. We had not finished dressing when the telephone rang again. Someone else, it seemed, had also found our dog, this time in Cascais. Before we were ready to leave, a third and a fourth and a fifth call came through, each from a different part of the country but each announcing that Bacchus had been found.

We spent that morning darting about the district, from one caller to the next, though we knew in advance that our quest was hopeless. Since Bacchus could not possibly be at every address we had been given, we felt we were unlikely to find him at any. Our fears were justified. Not one of the five dogs presented to us bore the faintest resemblance to ours.

That afternoon we visited half a dozen other people who had meanwhile rung up to claim the reward we had offered – pointlessly, as they must have known themselves, since the dogs they alleged to be Bacchus were not even remotely related to the mountain breed. At one of the addresses, where we were shown a small yapping Pomeranian, we were actually asked, 'Won't this one do instead?'

For the next week we followed up each of the further telephone calls that punctuated every day, though we knew by now what to expect. We even dropped in, on the off-chance, at an encampment of gypsies who were said to be professional dog thieves. There were dogs here indeed, dogs by the dozen, dogs tethered in groups to wooden stakes, dogs panting for water, dogs weak from lack of food, dogs whining in misery or growling in anger. But no Bacchus.

After a fortnight, when the telephone calls had ceased and we had given up all hope, one of our neighbours came to tell us that he had found a large mountain dog dead in his well. As a mere formality – for we knew at once this must be Bacchus – we sent Henrique to identify the body. Meanwhile we tried to work out how the puppy had met his death. Alone, he would never have fallen into a well. He must have slipped while romping near the edge with the ginger mongrel who had enticed him there to play and whom, for this reason, we henceforth called Evil Genius.

Shortly afterwards Sunflower died, unexpectedly but peacefully, in her sleep. I had known for some time that her days were numbered, for she had lately become paralysed in her hindquarters. Realising this condition could never be cured, that the paralysis was even likely to spread, I had been dreading the day when she would have to be put down, and was therefore less sad than grateful to her for relieving me of this decision by lapsing into eternal unconsciousness of her own accord.

Salote, on the other hand, seemed deeply affected by her mother's death. She too had been off colour recently, suffering from an irritation of the skin which defied all the remedies we applied. So far this had not appeared to disturb her unduly, but now her condition took an abrupt turn for the worse. She went off her food, her coat came out in handfuls, her eyes grew lustreless, and her nose, which had always been as cool and moist as a dewy blackberry, felt and looked like a lump of pumice-stone left out in the sun.

'This can't be due to grief alone,' Xan said, and he was right. The vet, whom we eventually summoned, diagnosed the trouble at once; intestinal cancer. 'Incurable,' he added. 'She might be in great pain at any minute. You'd better bring her to me tomorrow and I'll put her to sleep.'

So once again we were relieved of the horrid decision. Fortunately Salote's loss of appetite was accompanied by a feverish thirst. In the morning she lapped up her bowl of water, without noticing the barbiturate we had mixed into it, and presently fell asleep. She was still sleeping when we carried her into the vet's and, after being injected, never woke again.

Thus in less than a year we lost three of our dogs and within that space of time my chameleon had also disappeared, camouflaged against some unsuspected background. I felt bereft and all the more solicitous of Trubshawe's welfare. He continued to go off on jaunts with Evil Genius and I did nothing to stop him. How could I spoil his pleasure? Besides, I was not really afraid of his being led astray, as Bacchus had been. He was old enough to look after himself. It was a consolation, however, to know that there was little risk of his being run over. Apart from visitors' cars and our own, there was no motor traffic in the valley; and even the little road a mile behind us, between the hamlet and the quarry, was hardly ever used except by an occasional truck.

Trubshawe's health was now my main concern and I took every precaution to keep him fit, supplementing his diet with cod-liver oil, germ of wheat and yeast, all of which he devoured with pleasure. But he could not bear the liquid which I used for worming him, and would refuse to eat if he detected even a drop of it in his food. To me this represented a challenge, for I prided myself on being able to make any dog take medicine either by mixing it in his dinner or dosing him with a spoon. Since Trubshawe rejected the first method, he would have to put up with the second.

He struggled hardly at all as I picked him up, pulled one side of his cheek out in the prescribed manner, inserted the spoon, poured the liquid into his mouth and rubbed his throat to encourage him to swallow. But as soon as I put him down again he gave a faint whine, keeled over on to his side and passed out. I was horrified, remembering how Sunflower had collapsed in exactly the same way. For a moment I thought I had killed him. But he struggled to his feet immediately afterwards, shaking his head like a ham-actor registering bewilderment, then wagged his tail and licked my hand as though to reassure me. From then on I took care to dilute any medicine I gave him.

This experience seemed to tighten the bond between us, however. I felt all the more fond of him and he too appeared to cling to me more closely, his ugly mug suffused with affection. This expression of his struck me more forcibly than usual one summer afternoon, as he sat at my feet watching me paint a portrait of Judy posed against the datura tree; though I did not yet know I was seeing it for the last time. Intent on my painting, I never noticed the moment he moved away and was not aware of his absence until the evening, when Xan and I were sitting over a drink in the patio.

I assumed he was playing somewhere with Evil Genius and indeed, just as this thought occurred to me, I saw the ginger mongrel come scampering round the corner of the house. But Trubshawe was not with him and Evil Genius seemed to be behaving strangely, tugging at Xan's trouser leg with a sense of urgency rather than in fun, and so persistently that Xan finally stood up. Thereupon the dog started off in the direction from which he had come, glancing round to see if Xan was following.

'What on earth is he up to?' I asked.

'I'd better go and see,' Xan said.

No sooner had he disappeared than Maria rushed out from the kitchen to say that the milkman had just told her there was a small black dog lying dead on the road from the quarry. With sickening certainty I knew it could only be Trubshawe, even though there were several other small black dogs in the valley – the two False Trubshawes, for instance. 'Oh, let it be one of them!' I inwardly prayed, but without conviction.

Xan came back half an hour later, having collected the body and arranged for Henrique to bury it. 'Evil Genius led me all the way there,' he told me.

12

Nursery Landscape

Charles and Phyllis Della Faille had also left Tangier and settled in Portugal about the same time as ourselves. They too had had difficulty in finding a suitable house, but for different reasons. Whereas our choice had been dictated by the cost, their problem was to accommodate all their animals. When the ruined castle they eventually bought had been restored, Charles chartered a small cargo ship to transport the whole menagerie to Lisbon; while Phyllis, unwilling to subject the older and more decrepit dogs to the high seas, went to fetch them in a large American station-wagon.

On her way back through Spain she fell asleep at the wheel from sheer exhaustion. The car left the road, went over the side and landed upside down in a ravine. For over two hours, until help came, she was trapped inside, fully conscious though her head had shattered the windscreen, unable to switch off the engine and fearful of the leaking petrol catching fire, listening powerless to the whining of the dogs that had been hurt, unaware that two of them were already dead, and feeling the blood trickle down her face from her own injuries.

In hospital, for her wounds to be dressed, all her hair had to be shaved off her head. When I next saw her it was just beginning to sprout again and, to encourage its growth, she daubed her scalp every day with henna paste. The result was a fuzzy, fiery-red crop which made her look like a Picasso clown. Undaunted as usual, however, she was soon in the saddle again, risking further hazards from her horses which were wilder than ever after days of well-fed inactivity at sea followed by several weeks of an increased ration of vitamins and pep-pills to restore them from the shock of the voyage.

Foolhardily perhaps, I sometimes went out riding with her. The only way to master any of her demented broncos was to break at once into a gallop before it had time to start bucking, and keep galloping round and round the field behind the stables until it was sufficiently tired out to respond like a more or less normal horse. This at least was Phyllis's procedure and I was glad I always followed it, after hearing what happened to another friend of hers who did not.

This friend, a gallant Englishwoman who prided herself on her horsemanship, insisted on reining back instead of galloping off straight away. Within a minute she was bucked off. Looking over her shoulder, Phyllis saw her lying prone on the cobbles of the stable-yard, shielding her head from her mount's plunging hoofs. She was on her feet again when Phyllis raced past after her first circuit of the field, but instead of remounting she appeared to be searching for an object on the ground.

'Have you lost something?' Phyllis shouted.

'Yes, my ear!'

Even to Phyllis, who took the most startling incidents for granted and accepted the most extravagant statement without a murmur, this reply sounded intriguing. After completing her second circuit of the field she managed to draw up beside her friend.

'Your ear?' she belatedly echoed.

'Yes, the horse trod on it and it came off!'

The missing feature was eventually found. Unconcernedly, its owner put it in her pocket and drove off to the hospital in Lisbon to have it sewn on again.

'But the graft didn't take,' Phyllis told me. 'Her ear had gone cold and it should have been kept at body heat. . . . So if the same thing ever happens to you, remember to tuck it into your arm-pit or pop it into your mouth like a thermometer.'

Phyllis also introduced me to Portuguese fox-hunting. The local hunt had its club headquarters in the wild bull-grazing country on the far side of the Tagus and when I arrived there for the first time, after a two-hour drive, I was surprised to find what might have been a pre-war meet in the Shires. All the men wore pink coats, buckskin breeches, top hats, and violets in their button-holes; no one was dressed in ratcatchers or jodhpurs. Even the huntsman was English, from the South Notts, and most of the hounds came from English packs. But the field was international, consisting mainly of members of the various embassies, and the Master was a German baron.

The going was the roughest I had ever known: stony moorland, steep wooded hills, marshes into which the horses sometimes sank up to their haunches. There were few obstacles to jump except for an occasional drain or ditch, but the pace was extremely fast on this good scenting ground. To my secret delight – for I had always hated the kill – the foxes usually managed to get away into the thick undergrowth, through which we plunged regardless of our clothes being torn to ribbons and our boots being slashed and scarred. It was an exhilarating experience and, on the rare occasions when hounds failed to find, the whole hunt would gallop hell-for-leather back to the club-house where a lavish spread awaited us, served by liveried minions with appropriate Edwardian grandeur.

The Della Faille stables were managed by a Belgian ex-steeplechase rider, an impressively horsey figure in impeccably cut breeches, well-built boots and raffish checked cap. But he was horsey only on foot, having lost his nerve in the saddle, and I never saw him ride anything livelier than a bicycle. He spent most of his time in the kitchen, impelled there by a combination of gluttony and lust, both of which he managed to satisfy through sheer persistence, successfully wooing each of the cooks who came and went in a sufficiently rapid succession to offer him variety in bed as well as at table.

But his amorous activities were not confined to the kitchen. Force of habit made him ogle any woman who caught his fancy, no matter where or when. Once in a busy Lisbon street, he noticed an attractive girl at an upstairs window and could not take his eyes off her. Gallantly he blew a kiss and waved his hand. Unfortunately he happened also to be driving a car and, unable to concentrate on two things at once, mounted the pavement, grazed a bus queue and crashed into a lamp-post. Prompt payment by the Della Failles of the heavy fine he was given saved him from going to jail, and the withdrawal of his driving licence forced him to spend more time than ever in the kitchen.

Domestic disasters occurred so frequently to Phyllis that I sometimes believed she consciously encouraged them. Her choice of employees was certainly erratic, or so it seemed to me until I realised it was dictated by compassion. She would rather engage a lame duck than a normal one and welcomed the most cracked and twisted specimen of humanity as generously as she provided a home for any lost dog, injured bird or abandoned kitten. Who but she, with so many placid and willing Portuguese girls to choose from as an extra maid, would have preferred to employ a rather slatternly and sulky Spaniard?

'She's genuinely mad, poor thing,' Phyllis told me. 'Her

previous employers said so. According to the doctor, she might even develop homicidal tendencies. All the other servants are scared of her. I can't think why. Just because she mutters to herself, and howls all of a sudden for no particular reason. The dogs don't like it either, they all howl back, but I don't mind. She's perfectly harmless.'

But she was not perfectly harmless. One day she went for Phyllis with a carving knife. Somehow, for she was so much the smaller of the two, Phyllis managed to wrest the weapon from her, then sent for the doctor to come and take her away. While waiting for him to arrive, she rang me up to say what had happened. She sounded less alarmed than I felt.

'Are you quite safe now?' I asked. 'Is everything under control?'

'Of course I'm safe,' she replied. 'Why ever not?'

'But where's the girl at this very moment? What is she doing?'

'She's outside. Howling in the geraniums!'

Each time I visited the Della Failles I instinctively braced myself for a surprise. And so, when they asked us to dinner one Christmas, my immediate reaction was to say to Xan, 'What's going to happen this time?' Phyllis had gone to the trouble of ordering the food direct from England but, since she had never lived there herself and knew nothing about English customs, we wondered how she was going to interpret the 'real English Christmas dinner' she had planned.

She had found all the necessary ingredients. The turkey was delicious, accompanied by chipolatas, Brussels sprouts and chestnuts. That it succeeded instead of preceding the mince pies, which were served as a first course, was a minor aberration which I attributed to her usual eccentricity, until I realised that she had taken the word 'mincemeat' to indicate some sort of pâté. The turkey was followed by a traditional plum-pudding, decorated with holly and presented on a silver salver by a maid already flinching from the blue flames of the brandy in which it was drenched. But this conflagration was not enough for Phyllis, who seized a bottle of Courvoisier from the sideboard and gave the dish a further copious libation before any of us was able to intervene. The result surprised even herself. Her own eyebrows were singed as well as those of the maid, who looked as though she would have welcomed a pair of asbestos gloves as she handed round the miniature bonfire, adroitly juggling the red-hot salver from one palm to the other.

Later in the evening, since all the servants had by then gone to bed, Xan offered to get some more ice from the kitchen for a final drink before we drove home. He came back to the sitting-room considerably shaken.

'Phyllis,' he said, 'did you know there's a dead chihuahua in your fridge?'

'Oh, yes,' she replied, 'I should have warned you. I'm keeping him on ice for the autopsy. I think the poor little fellow was poisoned, but I can't get the vet to look at him until after the holidays.'

The Della Failles' parrots, which in Tangier used to be kept in the dining-room, were now housed in a separate conservatory vast enough to accommodate all the other birds as well. This was a decided improvement, for here they could chatter and shriek to their hearts' content without disturbing the rest of the house. Yet, with so many other rooms at her disposal, it was in this aviary that Phyllis chose to give a large fancy-dress party. And instead of hiring a dance band, she engaged a *fado* group.

Little did the singers know what they were in for. Accustomed to being listened to in reverent silence by an audience sober in manner and in dress, they were confronted by a whisky-swilling crowd in motley. As soon as they opened their mouths to sing, the inevitable happened: the birds followed suit. In no time the traditional melancholy strains of the human voices were drowned by what sounded like noises from a Tarzan film. Wolf whistles and bursts of sardonic laughter issued from various cages as their occupants bobbed up and down on their perches, stretching their throats in frenzy and flapping their wings. An elderly macaw in one corner kept booming, '*Bonjour, Monsieur le Comte*,' over and over again, while another voice that I was unable to locate repeatedly proclaimed, 'I'm a mynah bird!'

The dogs were also even more luxuriously housed than they had been in Morocco. A whole room was reserved for the old-age pensioners alone, and Phyllis's own bedroom was used as a night nursery for her favourites. On the floor stood a row of curious objects made of transparent plastic, like the lids of sewing-machines, which on closer inspection turned out to be draught-proof beds for the chihuahuas. Mice were allowed to nest undisturbed in the draped taffeta curtains, and the old macaw was brought up every night to perch on the foot of the bed. The wild acclamations with which he greeted the first chink of dawn did not disturb Phyllis in the least. But Charles, the most patient of husbands, had to draw the line somewhere and confided in me that he kept a water-pistol secreted beneath his pillow with which to silence the bird.

Trubshawe's sister, a tiny white puppy when I had given her to Phyllis, was now full-grown: an engaging little bitch whose Pekinese ancestry was hardly discernible. Her thick short coat had developed an apricot-coloured sheen and grew round her neck in a ruff which gave her the appearance of a dog in a Punch-and-Judy show. Her snub nose reminded me of a freshly scrubbed Tuscany truffle. Her kennel companion was a greyhound, over whom she had established complete authority, and her dominating character was apparent in her attitude to all the other dogs. At feeding time, after gobbling her own dinner, she would dodge fearlessly between the legs and under the muzzles of the Boxers, Alsatians, Dalmatians and Great Danes, making marauding darts at their plates and snatching mouthfuls of their food which she then kept pouched in her cheeks for future consumption.

Phyllis realised I still loved her and, on hearing of Trubshawe's death, immediately offered to give her back to me.

Princess Precious Pearl, as she was still called, was at first rather bewildered and subdued by the silence and tranquillity of our house after the hurly-burly of the Della Faille kennels. 'What do you think of her?' I asked Xan.

'Rather a dull little dog,' he replied, no doubt out of loyalty to Trubshawe. 'And she looks more like a pig than a princess.'

'Let's call her Piggy, then,' I suggested. And so her inappropriately regal name was dropped.

That evening I held Piggy's mouth open and spat into it – a trick I had learnt from an old keeper at Longleat who believed in the magical power of saliva for winning a dog's affection. She looked rather surprised, curled her lip, wrinkled her nose and yawned with emotion. But from then on she became as attached to me as a limb.

13

A Common-or-Garden Chestnut

Our friend David Ponsonby had lived in Portugal for many years and his enthusiasm for the country and the people reminded me of David Herbert's attitude towards the Moors and Morocco. So when we told him that we did not care for *fado* and found *saudade* a national affliction, I expected him to rise up in uncritical defence of all things Portuguese. Being an intelligent and civilized man, however, he merely said, '*Fado* isn't everybody's cup of tea. But have you heard it sung at Coimbra, by the university students? It's a far cry from the Lisbon taverns.'

From someone who had been a professional concert-pianist before turning to painting as a career, this was sufficient recommendation for us.

'Come up to Coimbra with me,' he went on, 'and I'll get you invited to my favourite *republica.* I don't think you'll find the atmosphere there at all melancholy.'

'What is a *republica*?' Xan asked. 'In Greek it means a trilby hat!'

'Well, in Portuguese it means a . . . how can I describe it? Something between an American college fraternity and a dining club at Oxford or Cambridge. Anyway you'll see.'

During a recent state visit to Portugal, Queen Elizabeth II had spent an afternoon at Coimbra. It was raining and the students, not to be outdone by Sir Walter Raleigh, had spread their black capes on the cobblestones for her to walk upon. The memory of her smile was still fresh in their minds and, although Xan and I were not given quite such a royal welcome, we were warmly received by our hosts and ushered ceremoniously into their dining-hall.

In front of each plate at the long table lay a raw potato impaled with toothpicks bearing miniature paper reproductions of the Union Jack and the Portuguese national flag. Dinner, consisting of a succession of regional dishes, was preceded by several small glasses of *bagaceira*, a local spirit as fiery as schnapps, and accompanied by *vinho verde* ('green' wine in the sense of 'young' or 'immature' wine, as one refers in equestrian jargon to a 'green' horse) dispensed in abundance from five-litre demijohns. By the time the post-prandial brandy began to circulate, the atmosphere was anything but melancholy. I glanced across at David, who gave me a complacent smile, as though to say, 'What did I tell you?' Language no longer formed an inhibiting barrier and our hosts delivered speech after drunken speech in broken English, to which we were by now sufficiently emboldened to reply in our rudimentary Portuguese.

Before the *fado* performance began, all the windows were thrown open. Three students' gowns, slashed and torn at the hems according to tradition, were produced for David, Xan and myself – not, as I at first thought, to protect us from the cold but to enable us to enjoy the singing all the more by being suitably dressed for the occasion. Whether it was on account of this additional formality or because our mood was by now more receptive, our enjoyment was certainly enhanced. The music was sad, but pleasantly so, and had nothing in common with the lugubrious caterwauling I had previously heard in Lisbon. To me it evoked the troubadours and the Courts of Love. As one serenade came to an end, it was echoed through the open windows by another group of singers in the house opposite, and then by yet another, the little flames of song licking up into the air, reaching out for one another and joining together, until, in a final chorus, the whole street seemed to be a blaze of melody.

But that evening in Coimbra was exceptional and, outside our own house, we continued to find Portugal universally dull in spite of the beauty and variety of the landscape and the wealth of architectural treasures. 'Man cannot live by sight-seeing alone,' Xan would murmur, as we sat despondent in some dreary bar or café after visiting one of the splendid churches or palaces scattered in profusion throughout the country. Luckily, we did not have far to go if we ever felt in need of a change in our surroundings. We could always nip over the border into Spain, and frequently did so, usually in the company of John Marks.

We had known John by name long before meeting him, having read his brilliant translations of Céline. We had also known he was an authority on Spain and bull-fighting, for the Davises had told us what Ernest Hemingway himself said: 'There's only one non-Spaniard in the world who knows more about the bulls than I do, and that's John Marks.'

It was ironical therefore that he should be living in Portugal, which, as a Hispanophile, he instinctively despised, when the country he loved was so tantalizingly close. But working for an international press agency, an uncongenial job in any case, kept him chained to an office in Lisbon. 'And to think I was once *The Times* correspondent in Madrid!' he used to moan.

Neither Xan nor I had ever been very keen on bull-fighting but, with John as our mentor, we began to appreciate its finer points and used to drive him over to Badajos, our nearest Spanish town, whenever there was a fight worth seeing. What I liked most about these jaunts was to watch the change that came over him as soon as we approached the frontier. His blue eyes would sparkle as he caught his first glimpse of a Spanish uniform and his ears would be almost visibly pricked to recapture the sounds of his beloved Castilian – 'a proper language after all that Portuguese shloishing and poishing'.

As we drove into the seedy little town, he would be beaming and chuckling with emotion. We would spend an uncomfortable night in one of the two fly-blown hotels, eat execrable food at any of the indifferent restaurants, and he would be as content as if we were staying at the Ritz and dining at Maxim's. But gloom would envelop him again as soon as it was time to leave. 'Ah, well,' he would mutter morosely, as we re-entered Portugal, 'back to the land of shloish and poish'.

For Xan and myself, however, Spain could never provide a sufficient contrast and we made a point of spending a few weeks every year in France. One winter we spent even longer than usual – in unaccustomed style at the Hotel Hermitage in Monte Carlo, where a suite was put at our disposal by the management to enable Xan to collect material for a history of the Casino.

At first we revelled in these luxurious surroundings and even enjoyed the vulgar opulence of the gaming rooms. But within a few days claustrophobia set in and we found the atmosphere oppressive. In the pouring rain the little principality seemed to shrink and retract until there was nothing left of it but the hotel bar and the green baize tables. We used to make our way between the one and the other by a series of lifts and underground passages which intensified the unnerving sensation of living in a vacuum, in a state of isolation, of mental and moral weightlessness. We began to long for unconditioned air and less confined horizons.

What depressed me most of all was the ugliness that seemed to be engendered by this short subterranean journey. People still looking their normal selves on leaving the bar by the first lift would emerge in the casino hall from the last one with their features transformed into predatory or zombie-like masks, and I could not help wondering whether my own appearance had undergone a similar change, whether my hands likewise resembled talons as my fingers curled round the plastic counters.

Compared to Xan, I am an unadventurous and unenthusiastic gambler, quickly bored even when winning. This time I had several runs of luck but, instead of following them and increasing my stakes, preferred to scoop up my modest pile of chips, cash them in and retire to the bar, happily reflecting that at this rate I would soon have enough to buy the lovely three-volume illustrated edition of Colette's complete works which I had seen in the window of a book-shop and on which I had set my heart.

Xan was also holding his own against the tables and, at the end of a week of fluctuating fortune, the hundred francs which each of us had set aside at the start and promised never to exceed, was still intact. While I stuck to roulette, he preferred *trente-et-quarante*, so we gambled separately. From a mere glance at him across the room I could never tell how he was faring, for he too seemed to develop a different personality in these surroundings and would adopt what I called his 'casino stance' – exaggeratedly poker-faced, with one eyebrow raised, as he swayed gently backwards and forwards on his heels, smoking a cigarette in an amber holder.

It was in this attitude that I saw him one evening, as I passed behind him on my way to the bar, negligently toss on to the table a couple of thousand-franc plaques which, to my horror, he promptly lost. 'What on earth are you doing?' I asked. 'Have you gone off your head?'

'Not at all,' he replied rather stiffly, still under the influence of his assumed personality. Then his eyebrow descended to its normal level, as he removed the cigarette-holder from his clenched teeth and smiled. 'Don't worry,' he said and produced a circular counter out of his pocket. 'Look, here's my original hundred francs. I've been doubling up on a winning run. . . . And this is the result.' He delved into his pocket and brought out a handful of rectangular plaques, one of which was even bigger than the couple he had just staked. 'Come on, let's celebrate with a really good dinner.'

'Lovely! Where shall we go?'

'Well, the restaurant here is said to be very good. . . .'

And so it was. It was also handy for the tables. He could hardly finish his coffee in his impatience to get back to them. 'Let's see if my luck still holds,' he insisted.

It did not. But he managed to drag himself away in time, and when we left the Casino we were still fifty thousand francs up.

But this good fortune did not make us any better disposed towards Monte Carlo. Instead, we regarded it as a means of escape. For we could now afford to stay elsewhere, although not in such splendour, and I gladly exchanged our free suite at the grand hotel for a cheap room in a little village inn above the Var. The absence of such luxuries as a private bathroom was amply compensated by the sense of freedom provided by the view from our window, by the atmosphere of peace and tranquillity produced by the sight of the river trickling down the valley in separate runnels, like veins in an outstretched arm.

Here I was able to resume work on my biography of Rosa

Lewis, *The Duchess of Jermyn Street*, while Xan commuted daily to Monte Carlo and continued his research on the Casino.

To get to London from Lisbon we had a choice of four routes, by air, sea, road or rail, each of which had its advantages. Lisbon airport, half an hour's drive from us and only ten minutes by taxi from the centre of the town, still had a certain rustic charm; but as I am frightened in an aeroplane and Xan is bored by flying, we scarcely ever used it except when meeting or seeing off our friends. Driving all the way through Spain and France was delightful but, since we were always tempted to linger on the way, this method took too long and proved more expensive than any other. The four-day voyage by boat provided a rest cure but little else, the vessels on this particular run having nothing special to recommend them. Best of all, we eventually decided, was to go by rail.

Travelling on the Sud Express always gave me an illusion of old-fashioned grandeur and evoked a nostalgic vision of massive wardrobe-trunks and dainty hat-boxes, silk parasols and silver-topped malacca canes, private couriers, gold sovereigns and first-edition Baedekers. Modern luggage, streamlined and zip-fastened, looked out of place against the dark panelling and faded plush of our compartment.

After a leisurely dinner in the restaurant-car we would come back to find our seats transformed into bunks, mysterious in the narrow beams of blue moonlight cast by the little brass lamp above each bed-head, and with unfailing pleasure I would hang my wrist-watch by its strap on the velvet-backed brass hook provided for the gold half-hunters of a previous generation.

Having to change trains at the frontier in the early morning was a further pleasure, emphasising the physical sensation, so rarely felt nowadays, of moving from one country into another, and I always looked forward to the contrast between the carriage we had just left and the sleek modern Pullman, all burnished aluminium and contemporary upholstery, in which we embarked for the remainder of the journey.

Whenever possible we spent a day or two in Paris before moving on to London. Thus it was that we found ourselves one evening in the big bar of the Ritz, celebrating our arrival and planning how to make the most of the next forty-eight hours. While we were still discussing the possible choice of restaurants for dinner, a waiter came up to Xan and said, 'Mr Hemingway would like you to join him for a drink. He's in the smaller bar next door.'

'There must be some mistake,' Xan replied. 'I don't know any Mr Hemingway.'

'It's *the* Mr Hemingway' the waiter insisted. 'Mr Ernest Hemingway.'

'There must still be some mistake,' Xan told him. 'I don't know Mr Ernest Hemingway.'

The waiter gave a shrug and moved off. A moment later he was back again. 'You are Mr Fielding, aren't you? Mr Xan Fielding? Then there's no mistake. Please come this way.'

Bemused, we followed him into the smaller bar.

Immediately we recognised two figures sitting at a crowded table in the far corner: Bill and Annie Davis. Thus the mysterious summons was explained. We knew that Hemingway had been staying with them in Spain, while working on his *Dangerous Summer*, though we had no idea that he or they were in Paris. But there was no mistaking those features which I had recently seen reproduced in countless press photographs: the tufted grey-white beard, the grizzly hair worn in a boyish fringe. What I was not prepared for was the high complexion: his cheeks glowed like a ruby-coloured stained-glass window with the sun behind it. Otherwise he looked exactly as I had always pictured him.

His manner, too, was what I had expected: spontaneous and expansive. He adopted us at once as part of his *cuadrillo* and took for granted our acceptance of his invitation to dinner, merely instructing the barman to ring up the restaurant and say there would be two more guests at his table.

That evening he concentrated almost exclusively on Xan, questioning him closely about guerrilla warfare in Crete and conditions in the death-cell at Digne – typical Hemingway topics, I thought rather huffily, vexed at being neglected. But at lunch next day I sat beside him and found him perfectly enchanting, largely because he was one of the rare people who ever agreed with me that the correct number of oysters to order at one sitting is nine, six being too few and a dozen too many.

At the end of the meal he delved into his pocket, fished something out and pressed it into my hand. 'Keep this,' he said. 'It will bring you luck for the rest of your life.'

It was a common-or-garden chestnut!

Or so I thought. But, unlike any other conker, it did not shrink or shrivel. I kept it in my bag or in my pocket the whole time we were in London, occasionally rubbing it against my nose as pipe-smokers polish their briar bowls, and by the time we left it was still as plump and firm as ever inside its tawny skin.*

On our way back to Portugal we stopped for a few days at Bayonne, where I decided to have it mounted in gold and hung on a chain. The jeweller was puzzled that I should be going to so much trouble and expense over an ordinary chestnut.

'This isn't an ordinary chestnut,' I told him. 'It belonged to Ernest Hemingway.'

* It still is.

'Ernest Hemingway!' the jeweller exclaimed. '*Hombre!* I saw him once, yes, with my own eyes. . . . He loves the bulls, he loves our town. . . . So this chestnut belonged to him, you say? It will be my pleasure and honour to mount it, but I cannot accept payment for the work. I shall charge you only for the price of the gold.'

14

Visitors

When we got home we found that Henrique, single-handed, had excavated the hole for the swimming-pool we were planning. Once again he had had to use dynamite to blast into the solid rock. The masons now lined the watertight crater with cement, surrounded it with a border of bricks in the same herring-bone pattern as the patio and, to protect it from the north wind, erected a wall which incorporated a small semi-circular summerhouse designed by myself and bearing a disconcerting resemblance to a Japanese tea-house in a musical-comedy set.

In the sunlight this large area of whitewashed masonry was painful to the eyes until it was relieved by some *trompe l'œil* murals executed by Jorge Jantus, our bald Argentinian friend from Tangier, who came to stay with us for the summer. On the wall itself he painted two grey stone plaques, the first commemorating the Daphne legend, depicting myself as the nymph with one raised arm already turning into the branch of a tree, on which basked a large green lizard; the other portraying Xan in the guise of a light-fingered Hermes, the messenger of the gods, who is said to preside over the month in which I was born. The inside curve of the summerhouse was decorated with a shelf on which stood various objects and ornaments, so life-like that I once saw a friend of ours stretch out her hand to pick one of them up before realising it was only two-dimensional; and, by way of signature, Jorge painted a portrait of himself as a shiny-pated Peeping Tom peering out of a window, with one hand holding back the curtain.

The pool, so much more pleasant than the crowded beaches we had so far used for bathing, kept us at home all the more and was an additional enticement for friends to come and stay. My grandchildren in particular loved it, splashing in and out of it at all hours of the day and running about the garden naked as water-babies, their pink bodies soon turning golden in the sun.

Since the house was so hard to find, we made a point of meeting guests from abroad either at the airport or at Lisbon station, or, if they were coming by car, at Queluz Palace, an unmistakable landmark to which anyone could direct them and which they would probably want to visit in any case. From there we guided them back, otherwise they were bound to lose their way. To most Lisbon taxi-drivers, the Valley of the Wolves was as remote and unknown as the Tundras or the Steppes, and even Portuguese friends living quite close to us were apt to miss several turnings until they had memorised the route.

So we could hardly conceal our surprise when, early one morning, we found Emlyn Williams standing on our doorstep flanked by a small suitcase and a large typewriter. His appearance there smacked of the supernatural. We were almost tempted to pinch him, to see if he was real. 'How on earth did you get here?' we asked, not meaning to sound so abrupt and unwelcoming.

'With the greatest difficulty,' he replied. 'But weren't you expecting me?'

A few months before, in London, we had urged him to come and stay, and he had said he would. So of course we were expecting him, and looking forward to his visit. But we were also expecting a telegram or letter to announce his arrival in time for us to be able to meet him. The telegram reached us only three days later.

'So that explains it!' said Emlyn.

'Explains what?'

'Your attitude when you found me on the doorstep. For a moment I thought you were going to slam the door in my face! I've already written to Mrs Patrick Campbell and warned her what to expect when *she* arrives.'

By 'Mrs Patrick Campbell' he meant a celebrated English actress whose grand manner had earned her the name we had privately bestowed on her. She was an old friend of Emlyn's and a girlhood heroine of mine and, shortly after meeting her at his flat in London, I had impulsively asked her too to come and stay. Her response had been somewhat intimidating: 'Of course you'll have a car and chauffeur waiting for me, won't you? In the old days, when I travelled all over the world, I was always met wherever I went by a car and chauffeur.'

'She's a very difficult lady,' Emlyn had warned me afterwards. 'No house is ever comfortable enough for her.'

'Do you really think she'll come?' I now asked him.

'Of course she will,' he replied, knowing that I had since regretted my rash invitation.

'Oh dear! But she'll hate it here, won't she?'

'Absolutely! Her visit is bound to be a complete fiasco.'

'Yet I can't very well put her off, can I?'

'No, certainly not.'

'Then what am I to do?' I wailed.

He realised my concern was genuine and for a moment

stopped teasing me. Yet he could not abandon the joke altogether.

'Leave it to me,' he went on. 'I'll just describe the house to her . . . in my own way, of course. Buried in the depths of the country, I'll tell her, the perfect place in which to put your feet up and relax, *because there's absolutely no distraction whatsoever.* You're left entirely to your own devices. Some people would find it boring, but you won't, I know. Just think what a nice change it will be from all those bridge parties of yours. The Fieldings don't even have a pack of cards in the house. . . .'

It was impossible not to enter into the spirit of this game and, from then on, the smallest incident or chance remark served as a pretext for elaborating on it. A stroll down the valley, for instance, was sufficient to launch Emlyn on a fresh flight of fancy:

'You'll love the walks there, darling. The Fieldings believe in a good ten-mile constitutional every day. And that road of theirs! Full of pot-holes. But then jumping over them is splendid exercise. Driving over them in a motor-car is better still. If you have a slipped disc, it will be knocked right back into place. . . . Oh, by the way, I forgot to tell you about the room you'll be given . . .'

'No, that's unfair,' I objected.

And so it was. The better of the two guest rooms was being repainted at the time and I had had to put Emlyn into the smaller one, which contained two bunks one above the other. And since he had arrived so unexpectedly, I had not had time to arrange it properly. In fact the top bunk was still occupied by a couple of sacks full of dried beans which Xan had harvested and two large lamp-shades which I had been sent on approval. Emlyn had taken one look at these and asked, 'Who are the ladies lying up there in garden-party hats?'

'Well, I shan't tell her about the room, if you don't want me to. But I must say something about the meals. . . .' And he was off again: 'Plenty of good healthy peasant food, my dear. Beans and lentils and dried cod. But then you can afford to put on a bit of weight. . . .'

Emlyn was then working on his autobiography and Xan and I also had books to finish, so that the house became a miniature prose factory. Except at meals we saw little of one another until the evening, by which time all three of us were quite content to stay at home and have an hour or two's quiet conversation before going to bed. There was one night, however, when Xan and I had to go out, to a dinner party to which we had been invited several weeks before. Emlyn could easily have come with us – we merely had to ring up our hosts and tell them we were bringing him – but he demurred.

'Just think what I'll have to say about this to Mrs Pat,' he told us. 'The Fieldings hardly ever go out in the evenings. Not that they're unpopular, it's just that they're not very social. . . . But when they *do* go out they leave you behind! So thoughtful of them not to force you to meet their boring friends. . . . And it's such fun to be on your own with the servants who don't speak a word of English, a perfect opportunity for practising your Portuguese!'

Emlyn had to leave for England a few days later. I never heard from 'Mrs Patrick Campbell' again.

Another pleasant surprise for us was the appearance of Henry Miller in Portugal. Xan had not seen him for over twenty years and I had never met him at all. Neither of us even had any idea that he was in Europe until we found ourselves lunching with him one day at John Marks's. From his books alone, which I much admired, particularly *The Colossus of Maroussi*, I had been able to form a mental picture of him; and Xan had often described him to me as well. What I had never envisaged, however, was a certain psychic quality of which I was aware as soon as I met him in the flesh.

'It's uncanny,' Xan told me afterwards. 'In twenty years he hasn't changed at all. I mean this quite literally, it's not just a phrase.'

The first words he addressed to me were, 'You're a sculptress.' He said this with such conviction that I felt I ought to have been one and almost agreed that I was. When I told him the truth, that my nearest approach to sculpting was modelling in plasticine, he merely repeated, 'You're a sculptress.'

What he liked about Portugal, he told us, was the peace and tranquillity of the country, which tempted him to settle here for good. When we drove him home after lunch to show him the Valley of the Wolves, his enthusiasm increased minute by minute. 'Just look at this view!' he exclaimed, leaning against the wooden balustrade of our bedroom balcony. 'Wonderful, wonderful!' he repeated, leaning further over still, unaware of the risk he was running.

We had been meaning to have the top rail of that balustrade repaired, for the woodwork was rotten and liable to collapse even under such a modest weight as his. But I dared not tell him so, for fear of startling him into an abrupt gesture of retreat which might prove fatal. Instinctively Xan and I stepped backwards into the room, without interrupting our flow of talk, feeding him conversation as though laying a trail of corn to entice a bird, and to our relief the small leprechaun figure automatically followed us inside.

I felt that apart from the landscape he was also attracted to Portugal by the apparent political stability of the country. It seemed unnecessary to disillusion him on this score by mentioning the more unpleasant aspects of the Salazar regime, such as the secret police, for Portugal *was* politically stable in the sense that there was no outward signs of unrest. That very evening, however, a bomb exploded in a post office in Lisbon. It was a very small bomb, it did little damage and injured no one, but the rarity of such an act of violence was sufficient to make headline news for several days on end.

When we next heard from Henry he was safely over the border, and in France. 'Just couldn't find what I wanted in Portugal,' he wrote, 'and don't think my kids could take it, especially the food. But it's a beautiful country. . . .'

Yet another surprise was a cable from Evelyn Waugh announcing that the ship in which he was travelling home from British Guiana was due to call at Lisbon at lunch time on a certain day, but only for a couple of hours. It would have been too much of a rush to drive him out to the Valley of the Wolves and back, and on second thoughts I felt this was just as well. He was accustomed to seeing me against the background of a stately home and would have thought I had fallen on evil times to be living in a modest cottage. So we took him out instead to a sumptuous restaurant which I knew he would find more appropriate.

Remembering the many hilarious times we had enjoyed together in the past, I was saddened and mystified by his melancholy mood which I noticed straight away. It was as though he had been afflicted by *saudade* within minutes of setting foot on Portuguese soil. For a moment his spirits were restored by the prospect of a dish of lampreys cooked with cream and brandy and port, a local speciality. 'I'm sure I shall die of a surfeit,' he said, beaming with greed. But just then he caught sight of a fellow-passenger on his ship, to whom he must have taken one of his unreasonable but typically violent dislikes. 'It's no good,' he said, 'that ugly mug has put me off my grub.' He pushed his plate away and relapsed into gloom.

It was perhaps unfortunate that the Portuguese colony of Goa had been invaded by the Indians only a few days earlier, so that the incident was still fresh in our minds and inevitably cropped up in the conversation. It would have been wiser to avoid such a controversial topic, but Evelyn kept harking back to it with outraged vehemence and, when I did not agree whole-heartedly with his views on colonialism, he gave me a quizzical glance, as though to say, 'This raggle-taggle life of yours has turned you into a left-wing hot-head.'

I tried to take his mind off the subject by talking about the new book on which I was working. He had done me the honour of writing the introduction to my recent biography of Rosa Lewis, in spite of hating the title I had given it: *The Duchess of Jermyn Street.* When I told him I was planning a life of Lady Cunard, he promptly asked, 'What are you going to call it? *The Duchess of Covent Garden*, I suppose!'

This characteristically caustic remark immediately relieved our tension and, even though a double crème-de-menthe failed to dispel his gloom, it revived the deep affection we had always felt for each other.

'Don't forget,' I told him, 'you inscribed one of your own books which you gave me with the words, *Undying love, come what may.*'

'I meant it, too,' he said.

This was the last time I saw him.

I particularly used to enjoy meeting Diana Cooper at the station. Her arrival was an entertainment in itself and, over the years, had assumed an almost ritualistic quality. No matter how crowded the train or the platform, I could always spot her at once, as though my eyes were automatically beamed in her direction by some inbuilt radar system of their own. Thus I never failed to delight in the sight of her dressed in her usual pale protective colours and invariably crowned with a plain broad-brimmed felt hat adorned only with her personal emblem, a golden unicorn. Then the luggage that I knew so well would be handed down to her: two plump suitcases and a matching hat-box of artificial leopard-skin, so comically vulgar that no one but she could get away with owning them.

By this time I would have drawn close enough to hear her muttering in anguish as she rummaged through the large straw basket she always carried: 'Oh dear, the spectacles!' or 'I've done it again . . . left my clock behind!' Sometimes it would be one of her elegant suède gloves that had been mislaid, but the missing object would always come winging back to her through the carriage window, retrieved by some fellow-passenger who had come under her thrall in the course of the journey.

On one of her visits she told us that her old friend Iris Tree was due to join her at our house. 'If she ever gets here,' she added. 'She's coming by road all the way from Barcelona, she hasn't driven for over thirty years, and her car's a second-hand old rattletrap.'

We were expecting Iris to arrive in time for luncheon on a certain day. She failed to turn up. But at three o'clock in the afternoon a telephone call came through for Diana. Iris, it appeared, was stranded on the road just this side of the frontier.

'I might have known it,' said Diana. 'Not a penny on her, not a word of Portuguese, and her car has broken down completely. But, trust her, she's already found a knight errant. They've just had lunch together and he's going to bring her here in his own car straight away. And – can you beat it? – it seems he's a diamond merchant to boot!'

I could imagine Iris standing by the roadside, guarded by Aguri, her great black Belgian sheep-dog, with her baby-soft hair blowing about her face like canary-yellow candy-floss, her fine skin etched with a network of lines (a chart marking many years of laughter) and her blue eyes screwed up to scan the horizon for a possible rescuer. I pictured her in her usual uniform of blue jeans and leather Red-Indian coat fringed and trimmed with blue beads – 'squaw-chewed', as she used to describe it.

And this indeed was exactly how she was dressed when she turned up in triumph that evening in a large limousine, with her diamond merchant at the wheel, her guardian-wolf in the back and her luggage (mostly dog food) in the boot.

To have either Iris or Diana as a guest was a rewarding experience. To have them both staying together was a stimulant which within a few days I found so habit-forming that I had to make a deliberate effort not to mar my enjoyment of the moment by dwelling in advance on the withdrawal symptoms which were bound to occur with their departure. I knew I should feel deprived of a daily delight when I no longer heard Diana's early-morning cry of 'Are you awake, doll?' delivered in that characteristic flat tone of hers, Iris's initial grunt of annoyance at being woken, and the hours-long conversation between them that subsequently ensued, consisting of brilliant repartee and sounding all the more ribald and uninhibited for being carried on at the tops of their voices as they shouted to each other from their respective rooms.

This verbal duel would continue intermittently throughout the day, punctuated by a chortle from the one or the other as a thrust went home or a point was scored. From time to time

Xan or I would be called upon to arbitrate, give an opinion or pronounce a diagnosis, but the role we preferred to play was that of a silent and spellbound audience.

On their last night with us, we all went out to dinner at a little restaurant on the coast. Undeterred by a larger public, oblivious of it even, they continued their conversational display. Iris's puns became more and more outrageous and, with typical prodigality, she lavished them even on the uncomprehending waiter. 'Shall I Campari to a summer's day?' she murmured to him, as he set her apéritif before her.

She continued in this vein for the rest of the meal, highlighting her performance with actions to suit the words. 'What's that fish you're eating?' she enquired of Xan.

'I don't know what it's called in English,' he replied,' but in Portuguese it's *cherne* – spelled C H E R N E and pronounced "share'n".'

'Share'n and share alike, then,' said Iris, spearing a morsel off his plate and handing him a fresh sardine on the end of her fork.

15

Disenchantment

One morning we woke up to find half a dozen strange men trudging about our olive grove with theodolites, plane-tables and various other land-surveying instruments. 'What the devil's happening?' Xan muttered, and went out to investigate.

He was back a few minutes later. 'They say they're going to put up a pylon there,' he announced incredulously. 'There must be some mistake.'

But there was no mistake. The erection of the pylon, it seemed, had been planned long before we bought the house and there was nothing we could do about it. We appealed to the local authorities in Sintra, who referred us to the ministry concerned in Lisbon, who told us that the pylon in question was only one of many which were due to be erected along our valley to carry a new electric cable right across the country. The manner of the official who gave us this information suggested that we ought to feel proud to be subscribing in our own little way to such a grandiose and progressive scheme. 'Besides,' he added, 'we shall even pay you compensation for each of your trees that we might have to cut down.'

'This is the last straw.' I said. 'We can't live here any longer.'

As a matter of fact we had already been toying with the idea of leaving Portugal. We had never been affected personally by the Salazar regime, and were not likely to be, but the mere fact of living in a police state was somehow distasteful. It also inhibited general conversation, for Xan and I refused to comment on the joys of dictatorship which seemed to be the only topic, especially among the more well-to-do Portuguese. Rather than disagree with them (and thereby risk being labelled dangerous communists) or remain silent in their presence, we found it easier to avoid them altogether. We were thus automatically cut off from a substantial section of the population.

What went on in the minds of the peasants and poorer people, we were unable to fathom since we had no social contact with them. Centuries of feudalism had made them ever more class-conscious than their so-called betters, with whom it would never have crossed their minds to consort on terms of equality. Submission to the regime was ingrained in them, or at least appeared to be, and if, say, Maria or Henrique had any opinion on it, they certainly did not vouchsafe it to us. It was so long since Salazar had assumed his role of father-figure that they never questioned it and seemed to regard themselves quite literally as his children, who had nothing to fear providing they behaved, but from whom blind obedience was expected. This attitude, combined with *saudade*, contributed to the impression of universal goody-goody inertia, unrelieved by the slightest trace of high spirits or insubordination, and engendered an atmosphere reminiscent of a vast well-disciplined nursery.

With few exceptions, the foreign residents, especially the British, were tedious in their praise of the regime. 'Where else can you live so cheaply?' was the burden of their argument. 'And the natives seem to know their place,' was another recommendation – rarely voiced, admittedly, though I heard those very words pronounced on one occasion, and not entirely in jest. The worst offenders in this respect were the mercantile families who had been established in the country for several generations. Though Portuguese was as much their mother-tongue as English, they made a point of speaking it with a pronounced Anglo-Saxon accent and took every opportunity to display an old school tie or regimental blazer.

'British colony' in fact was not an idle phrase in Portugal and, though Xan and I did not consciously form part of it – never, for instance, had we set foot in the Royal British Club in Lisbon – we could not help feeling that we were tarred with the same brush in the eyes of the Portuguese. Thus we fell between two stools. We had not been assimilated by the country but were merely using it as a background. An essential dimension was lacking in our lives.

These considerations apart, there were also questions of a more material nature which we found ourselves obliged to face. First and foremost, the damp. It would have been churlish to complain of a climate in which plants flourished with such rewarding ease. But it had its drawbacks. The house was never dry, even at the height of summer. Though we could lunch out of doors almost throughout the year, we could never dine outside even in mid-August. We tried once, and by the end of the first course were so drenched by the heavy dew that we had to move back into the dining-room for the rest of the meal. Our laundry, fresh from Salome's iron, would lose its crispness in a matter of minutes. Our books had begun to buckle on their shelves. If unworn or untended for any length of time, our shoes would develop a thin layer of powdery fungus. Our clothes were never entirely free from a faint smell of mildew.

Worse still, the damp was getting into our bones. Xan's joints began to creak, mine to ache. I tried the remedy by which Diana swore – a cabbage leaf applied like a poultice to the afflicted limb – but this proved too uncomfortable and embarrassing. In a crowded Lisbon street I found myself having to thank a perfect stranger for retrieving the discoloured fragment of vegetable matter that had dislodged itself from my elbow, worked its way down my sleeve and fallen on to the pavement.

All these disadvantages – the damp, the dullness, the distaste – had so far been outweighed by the delights of the private universe we had created round our own house and household. This refuge was now threatened by the pylon which, as though adding ironical insult to aesthetic injury, would not even give us the benefit of the electric light we needed since the high-tension cable it was due to carry was for commercial purposes and not for domestic use.

'Maybe we could grow some morning-glory up it,' Xan suggested.

But this improbable hope was scotched a few days later when he saw the area that had been marked out for its base. 'My God, it's going to be as big as the Eiffel Tower,' he exclaimed.

It turned out to be less big than that – but only just, so it seemed to me. Xan did his best to console me. 'You'll get used to it in the end,' he said, 'and just think what a good lightning-conductor it makes!'

It was not only the size and ugliness that disturbed me, however, but the actual *personality* of the monster. There were times when it seemed to be a living entity instead of an inert edifice of steel and copper. The design of the struts and girders lent it a recognisably individual countenance, in which, if I gazed long enough, I fancied I could discern each separate and loathsome feature. The pointed ears, adorned with turd-like ear-rings, were particularly offensive. It even had a voice of its own. By day I was often alarmed by its hollow boom or high-pitched whine, and at night I would lie awake listening to its crackling breath.

'It's no good,' I said to Xan, 'I'll never get used to it.'

'Then let's sell the place at once,' he agreed.

'If anyone will buy it now. . . .'

But my pessimism was unjustified. Within three weeks of putting the house on the market we had found a purchaser and Xan, in great glee, was again reminding me of Uzès: 'Remember that delightful little market town in Languedoc? And we *shall* be able to afford to live in France now!'

Yes. For by a heaven-sent coincidence he had just learnt that the protracted lawsuit over the Fielding estates in Nice was at last drawing to a successful conclusion and he would shortly be inheriting his share of a fortune that had been denied him for over thirty years.

By a further stroke of luck we also heard of a furnished house to let just north of Uzès. From the owner's description it appeared to be just what we needed as a temporary base, so we signed a six-month lease at once.

Ten days later we were ready to leave. Our furniture had been packed and stored. We had sold our car and ordered a new one, to be collected in France. We had booked our tickets on the Sud Express. We had ordered a taxi to take us to the station. The moment I had been dreading had now arrived.

Though I had loved the house and was deeply grateful for the six happy years we had spent here, thanks to the pylon I felt less sad than I might have been at the prospect of living here no longer. Though we had made a number of close friends in Portugal and were sorry to leave them, I was consoled by the probability of meeting them again elsewhere. But the closest bonds we had formed were with our own little staff and these, I knew – and so did they – were about to be broken for ever. The pang of parting was bound to be severe and I had to steel myself to accept it.

Henrique, Maria, Salome, Lourdes, Maria-Elena – the single file which they had instinctively formed outside the front door lent an air of formality to this last farewell. The tears in Henrique's eyes reflected those in mine, as we gravely and silently shook hands. No words were spoken either, as I embraced the four others one after another, for they were speechless from sobbing and so was I. Even Judy, whom we were leaving as a parting gift for Salome, seemed conscious of the gravity of the occasion and uttered not a sound.

We climbed into the taxi and drove off. I deliberately refrained from looking round and waving, in order to control my tears. But, as we turned the corner outside our front gate, a shriek echoed down the valley – 'Fuck off!' – and I started crying all over again.

16

Wuthering Heights

We were looking forward to our usual agreeable night on the Sud Express, but we had reckoned without Piggy. As soon as the train pulled out of Lisbon, she began to get restless. The movement and the noise must have reminded her of the voyage in the Della Faille ark – a traumatic experience even for a less highly-strung dog – and affected her all the more after the silence and tranquillity of the Valley of the Wolves. Even after I had dosed her water-bowl with bromide and she appeared to settle down, a whistle from the engine or the swoosh of another train rattling past in the opposite direction would revive her panic and start a fresh fit of trembling and panting.

'This means no dinner for us this evening,' said Xan. 'We can't take her into the restaurant-car if she goes on like this, nor can we leave her here on her own. We'd better order some sandwiches and a bottle of wine.'

During the night she grew even worse. I held her close to me under the bedclothes, but she kept trying to claw her way out. 'Here, you take her,' I said, and handed her to Xan in the bunk above. In a moment she was struggling to get back to me. A moment later she was struggling to get away again. I put her down on the floor; she tried to climb back into bed.

In the end, to keep her company, Xan transferred his own

bed to the floor and, holding her in his arms, fell into a fitful sleep. '*Your* dog has ruined *my* journey,' he told me in the morning.

But the ruined journey, the rotten night were banished from our minds by the joy of being in France again – this time, we felt sure, for good. Piggy recovered her nerve and Xan his temper, as soon as we picked up the new car and headed east. By lunch time we were skirting the circumference of Cyril Connolly's 'Magic Circle', striking it at a tangent as we bowled along a little departmental road south of Toulouse. Our own 'Magic Circle', which we planned to reach that evening, was a hundred miles further on; Uzès its centre.

Our spirits soared as we approached the well-remembered towers aflame in the horizontal rays of the setting sun. Though it was well past French provincial dinner-time, we headed straight for the café at which we had stopped for a drink so many years before. Here we had a ritual *pastis* before booking into the old coaching-inn, heedless of the indifferent food and primitive accommodation in our excitement at having reached journey's end.

In the morning we drove out to the house we had rented, only fifteen miles away. But these fifteen miles stretched across a vast plateau of unpopulated garrigue and the little hamlet we eventually reached seemed completely cut off from civilization. Completely deserted too. Clamped against the side of a hill, most of the houses were in ruins and the few that looked habitable were barred and shuttered, as though against an impending siege. Ours we recognised at once from the description we had been given: the last building right at the top of the slope, connected to the hamlet only by a stony footpath. To approach it by car, we had to make a further détour along a rough track winding up to it from behind.

On this side the garrigue was even wilder and more dense. Our mudguards scraped past ramparts of wild box, its pungent scent mingling with that of the thyme, sage, lavender, cystus and mint crushed beneath our wheels. I felt like some insect or fieldmouse scuttling through a herb garden that had run riot. Gradually this jungle thinned out, as though to make room for the house which towered athwart the topmost ridge like an ancient battlement. Up here the wind, which we had not even noticed before, was a tangible, audible, even visible force, each gust furrowing the undergrowth like the trace of a finger on a green velvet cushion.

'Wuthering Heights!' Xan and I exclaimed simultaneously, and from then on never referred to the place by any other name.

The hamlet was not completely deserted, as we had at first thought. While we unpacked and settled in, we could hear an occasional sound of rural activity in the neighbourhood – a hen cackling, a dog barking, a tractor clanking and rattling in the distance – and as we sat over a pre-luncheon drink on the broad stone terrace in front of the house, two wisps of smoke rose from the gently shelving roofscape at our feet, presumably from fires being lit for the midday meal. But still no sight of a living soul.

It was not until the evening, while preparing dinner, that we saw our first inhabitant. A tinkling of bells, the bleating of sheep heralded a clotted stream of woolly pelts which flowed past the kitchen, so close that we could have stroked them through the open window. Two dogs loped down the lane in their wake and, finally, the shepherd himself, a short swarthy man of indeterminate age, who stopped to wish us '*Bon appétit!*' before trudging on.

Shortly afterwards we received a more official visit, from a huge roly-poly of a man with a round moon-face as pink and creased as a new-born babe's. He and his old mother lived alone in the big farmhouse from which we had seen the first wisp of smoke rising that morning. The second marked the house which the shepherd, one of two brothers, shared with a sister. This was the entire population of the hamlet.

'Yes, just the five of us,' the baby-faced farmer repeated, as though underlining the loneliness of this tiny community. 'And to think,' he added wistfully, 'that when I was a boy there were still enough of us here for a game of *pétanque* in the evening. We used to play outside the café; yes, we even had a café in those days. . . . It's different in the height of summer, of course. People come here for their holidays: Parisians, foreigners like yourselves. . . . But you two are the only ones to arrive so late in the year. . . . Here, I've brought you something. . . .' From a capacious pocket he produced a dozen eggs, each carefully enclosed in a cowl of newspaper. 'Plenty more where these came from. In exchange, I'd be grateful if you let me have your swill for my poultry.'

Delivering the swill at the farmhouse became a daily ritual. After a few days the poultry learnt to recognise the sound of our clanking pail from afar and by the time we reached the yard we would be deafened by their clamour, which rose to a pitch of fury as we emptied our scraps over the wired enclosure into the flurry of feathered wings and gaping beaks.

Apart from providing us with eggs, this ritual also enabled us to get rid of most of our garbage – a problem that had never confronted us before. In Portugal, Henrique had always dealt with it – either he or one of the girls; we did not know which since we had never given it a thought. Other household chores, of which for years we had remained oblivious, now obtruded themselves on us – bed-making, washing up, laying the table, cooking – and while Xan occupied himself with what he called 'the burning question' (heaping whatever refuse was unsuitable for our swill pail into a bonfire, which had to be carefully tended for fear of setting the whole garrigue alight) I would find myself chained to the kitchen sink. It was a far cry from our leisured life in the Valley of the Wolves, but we both felt like pioneers and revelled in the novelty.

Since we were not self-sufficient like the farmer and the shepherds, who grew their own food, made their own wine and baked their own bread, shopping even for the most basic requirements of life was another occupation which had to be carefully planned. The nearest butcher's was in a little village five miles away, the nearest grocer's in another village five miles in the opposite direction, where we also bought our bread – and what bread! Kneaded by hand into loaves the size of dart-boards and baked in a wood-fired oven, it had nothing in common with the electrically produced and chemically adulterated staves of crusty cotton-wool for which the modern French palate has developed such an unaccountable weakness.

Uzès provided us with the rest of our needs and we used to drive in on Saturday morning, market day, to stock up for the week. In so small a town it was astonishing to find such a number and variety of foodshops, ranging from the most modest *épicerie* to a glittering supermarket. But to me the main attraction was the market-place itself: a Breughel crowd-scene come to life.

One street corner was commandeered by a group of men in cloth caps, heavy boots and corduroy suits, all with the roguish features and high complexions of professional poachers. These were the truffle gatherers, aristocrats of the agora. They exuded an aura of affluence, the pungent aroma of their wares clinging to their clothes as tenaciously as expensive perfume. Since they dealt wholesale at prices averaging a thousand francs per kilo, Xan and I were never even potential customers of theirs. But we would stop in their vicinity and inhale the air like Bisto kids. They were more interested in Piggy than in us. 'With a nose like that, she'd make a first-rate truffle hound,' they declared each time they saw her, though we never knew if this was meant as a joke or not.

They also told us how to hunt for truffles without a dog. 'There's a special species of fly that noses them out just as well,' they said. 'All you need do is pin-point the spot on which it settles, plant a twig in the ground there, then follow the fly until it settles again, and so on.... Then you excavate each spot you have marked, *et voilà!*'

Another joke of theirs? It was impossible to tell, for we could never bring ourselves to put this process to the test.

In any case, for the time being at least, truffles were not an essential ingredient for us. It was so long since Xan or I had done any cooking that we were out of practice and neither of us felt like tackling anything but the simplest dish. Sometimes, in fact, we would let several days slip by without cooking anything at all, living lazily on pâté, saucisson and tinned food, until our greed prevailed over our sloth and prompted us to further effort.

Meanwhile we had started scouring the country in search of a house to buy. What we had in mind was something slightly larger than the cottage in the Valley of the Wolves, but there seemed to be no local equivalent. At least nothing remotely resembling it ever figured on the lists of the various notaries and one and only estate agent to whom we applied. All they had to offer were modern villas vilely situated on main roads or else huge old farmhouses, some of them tantalisingly lovely, but well beyond our purse since the price invariably included hundreds of acres of valuable agricultural land which we neither wanted nor were able to afford. We were therefore reduced to persevering on our own, keeping our eyes open as we drove about at random and making tentative enquiries at any village that took our fancy.

This haphazard quest at least enabled us to explore the whole of our 'Magic Circle' in depth. It also occasioned a number of amusing encounters which we might otherwise have missed. While investigating the possibilities of St Maximin, for instance, we were accosted by an old man in charge of a flock of turkeys. 'Do you want to see the house where Racine lived?' he asked us. 'Come with me, I'll show you.' Wielding a wand which was fitted at one end with a bunch of feathers, he drove the birds into a courtyard, beckoned us to follow and closed the gate behind us. 'Here it is,' he announced.

We were already surprised that a gaffer like this should ever have heard of Racine. We were more so when he proceeded to declaim the opening lines of the *Cantique sur les vaines occupations des gens du siècle*:

Quel charme vainqueur du monde
Vers Dieu m'élève aujourd'hui?
Malheureux l'homme qui fonde . . .

There we stood, in the hot sun, knee-deep in gobbling turkeys, while the old boy continued to recite, maintaining the same theatrical pose until he came to the last line:

. . . D'où l'eau fuit à tout moment.

Only then did he release us from the courtyard and, without further explanation, bid us farewell.

Another village we inspected closely was Belvezet, a shallow fertile basin floating in an ocean of garrigue. This miniature Shangri-La was irrigated by countless streams which over the centuries had drilled through the surrounding cliffs, forming sinuous valleys like the tentacles of an octopus. These cried out to be explored. One of them even had a cart-track winding through it: an invitation we were unable to resist. After driving for a mile or so, however, we were brought to a halt on the edge of a morass caused by a recent rainstorm. Yet the track beyond still beckoned. We left the car and continued on foot.

'This must lead somewhere,' Xan persisted, blazing a trail through the mud.

Our perseverance was eventually rewarded. As it rose, the valley widened again into an irregular plateau hemmed in by a row of low hills as wrinkled and grey as an elephant's flanks. In the centre stood a compact group of farm buildings, surrounded by vineyards and orchards, approached by a noble avenue of mulberry trees: evidently a substantial and prosperous estate. The harvest was over; the trees stood fruitless and the vines were now leafed in purple mourning, bereft of their grapes. Yet, though the land bore every mark of careful husbandry, the house itself looked deserted. Part of it in fact – the whole of one wing – was in ruins. The heavy wrought-iron gate leading into the courtyard hung lopsided from one of its massive stone pillars which had been dislodged from its base by the roots of a venerable cypress tree. But the main block was obviously sound and straight away we started viewing it with the prophetic eye we had recently developed at the sight of any potential home, picturing it as it might be once we had converted it to our liking. Yet we had no reason to believe that it was even for sale . . .

As we plodded back, we went on discussing it:

'The road's a serious drawback, of course . . .'

'And there's no electricity . . .'

'It's not really worth considering, is it?'

'Not really.'

'But let's keep it up our sleeve all the same.'

After this fortuitous discovery we made a point of following any pleasant-looking track, however overgrown and disused, in the hope of finding an even better reward at the end. None of these expeditions led to anything worthwhile. More often than not the track merely converged on a main road or else petered out altogether.

On one occasion, after foolishly attempting a short cut across country, we lost our way in the middle of the wildest garrigue. After struggling through the undergrowth for over an hour we came across the vestige of a footpath, which we gratefully followed though by now we had only a vague idea in which direction we were heading. Within a few minutes it led us to a small clearing, a perfect circle of bare earth shunned by all vegetation, from the exact centre of which rose a gigantic prehistoric monolith.

The presence of this towering mass of stone in these surroundings was so unexpected, its effect so overpowering, that my immediate reaction was to throw up one arm across my face and avert my head, as though flinching from a blow. Though conscious of the warmth of the sun, I found myself shivering. This spot was in fact quite lovely – it would have made a perfect picnic site – but I could not dissociate it in my mind from weird and sinister rites, human sacrifices. There was a solitary eagle circling overhead, which my imagination immediately transformed into a vulture. I forced myself to draw closer, however, and even ran my hand over the rough granite. Though it should have absorbed the heat of the day it felt icy-cold, and I was reminded of A. L. Rowse's haunting story, *The Stone That Liked To Be Visited*.

'This place gives me the willies!' I said to Xan.

Luckily the footpath we had taken developed further on into a proper track, but the garrigue that still hemmed us in now seemed as evil and impenetrable as an Amazonian jungle and I did not breathe freely until we were literally out of the wood and had found our way back to the car.

One evening in late autumn, in that twilight hour *entre chien et loup*, I was sitting reading in front of the empty grate – it was still too warm for a fire – when Piggy raised her hackles, jumped off my lap and rushed across to the french windows, barking and growling. I too gave a start, for there in the gloaming stood a witch and her familiar, the figure of a woman with a wolf-like shape beside her. A grinning face framed in tow-coloured hair materialised at one of the window-panes, a flattened nose was pressed against the glass. Then I heard a familiar peal of laughter, which transformed this eerie vision into the welcome spectacle of Iris Tree and Aguri.

Since we had last seen her in Portugal she had been leading her usual nomadic life, stopping here and there for a few days or weeks as the fancy took her or wherever her car broke down. She had lived for some time in what she called 'my glass bubble', a small roof-top flat above the Spanish Steps in Rome. Then she had been drawn to Cadaques, near Barcelona, once a simple little fishing village which had meanwhile developed into an Iberian St Tropez. Now, like ourselves, she had come to this part of France in search of somewhere permanent to settle – 'an abandoned mill, a ruined tower, even an empty cave, anything I can really call my own'.

For the time being her little car contained all her worldly

possessions, with which she managed to convert even the most temporary abode into some semblance of a home. Bit by bit, we helped her to carry them inside – a portrait of herself painted on glass by Dora Carrington (a youthful Iris resembling Joan of Arc advancing into battle on a white charger), a large illustrated volume on mushroom identification, other books, manuscripts of her own poems, a roll of uncured sheepskins, a casket containing a silver chalice and a pair of brass candlesticks, a large sack of dog food for Aguri, a smaller sack of a special kind of porridge for herself, a battered suitcase stuffed with a heterogeneous collection of clothes which might have been drawn from various dressing-up boxes – and presently our anonymous spare room bore the unmistakable marks of her personality.

There was also a Dick Whittington bundle, a bulging red-and-white spotted handkerchief, which she handled as gingerly as if it contained a valuable porcelain or some precious archaeological find.

'What have you got there?' we asked.

'Ah-ha! A surprise! Something rare and strange . . .'

'Animal, vegetable or mineral?'

'Vegetable. *Now* can you guess?'

Of course we could; we knew our Iris. 'Mushrooms!' Xan and I replied simultaneously.

'No, not mushrooms. This is *one* mushroom, a particular mushroom, a very special kind of mushroom, a *hallucinogenous* mushroom . . . producing beatific visions in glorious Technicolor. It was given to me by a Swiss professor,' she added inconsequentially, as though the nationality and occupation of the donor guaranteed the pedigree of the gift. 'Only he didn't tell me what to do with it . . . Cook it? Eat it raw? I don't know. Perhaps we should chop it up and chew it like a quid of tobacco? Or rub it on our eyelids? That might induce a Midsummer Night's Dream. What do you think? Here, have a look. . . .'

She undid the bundle to reveal the most venomous-looking fungoid growth I had ever seen, as garish in hue and maculated as the handkerchief itself. She gazed at it in awe and admiration. 'Shall we try it tonight?'

'I don't think so, Iris. Let's keep it for a rainy day. I'll put it in the fridge.'

Throughout the evening she kept glancing anxiously into the kitchen. 'I can't bear the thought of it freezing in there,' she said.

'It will be all right,' I assured her. 'Mushrooms don't mind the cold. There are some which grow in the garrigue, called *gelées*, and they don't even appear until there's a frost.'

'But frost is a natural cold,' she objected, 'quite different from electrically produced ice. . . . Oh well, I'll have to console myself with wine.'

So we broached another bottle. By the end of dinner, which was washed down with further consolation, she could contain herself no longer. 'It's now or never,' she said, producing the schoolboy knife which she always carried in her pocket.

'You're not really going to try it, are you?' I asked, watching in alarm as the blade sliced through the fibrous flesh with a crunch of amputation.

'Just a little sniff,' she said. 'I shan't eat it if you don't want me to, but just a little sniff . . .'

By now she had reduced the beastly thing to a coarse powder and, before either of us could stop her, she took a pinch of it between finger and thumb and raised it to her nostrils, inhaling deeply. 'Now we'll see,' she declared defiantly, pouring herself another glass of wine.

We waited a quarter of an hour, half an hour, watching her

closely, not knowing what to expect. Nothing happened, even after she had taken a second pinch followed by further glasses of wine.

'Still no effect?' I asked.

'None at all. I'm afraid it's not up to snuff!' She gave a sigh of disappointment. Then a happy thought occurred. 'But it might work in my sleep! I think I'll go to bed at once and see what happens.'

She almost ran up the stairs in her delight at the potential dreams in store. I took this opportunity to throw the remains of the powder into the dustbin, making sure none of it fell into the pail we used for the swill. I did not want the farmer's hens to start laying white-and-scarlet spotted eggs.

There was no sign of Iris at breakfast next morning. There was no sign of her even two hours later. I was worried, but still could not bring myself to disturb her. It wasn't as if she had *eaten* any of the mushroom, after all; it was just a sniff, as she said. All the same I was relieved when she eventually appeared looking radiant and refreshed.

'Any dreams?' we enquired.

'None,' she confessed. 'I slept tight . . . *very* tight.'

Iris's quest for a house seemed to be no more successful than ours. Every morning the three of us would drive off, Xan and I in one direction, she in another. Every evening we would come back and compare notes.

'Any luck?'

'No. What about you?'

'None.'

She never came back empty-handed, however. Sometimes she would arrive with a couple of our baker's dart-board loaves clutched to her breast. 'There's nothing like nursing warm bread,' she would say, dusting the flour from the front of her coat. 'It's almost as comforting as carrying a live goose.' At other times she would turn up with a basket, a hay-fork or a wooden tub which she had found in one of the local markets. And always she would produce a crop of mushrooms which she had picked at random that day. Occasionally there were even some edible ones among them.

Then, one evening, she returned earlier than usual and carrying nothing, not even a toadstool. In her excitement and haste to get back she had denied herself her usual harvest. 'I've found something at last!' she announced.

'Iris! How wonderful!'

'Yes, but wait till you hear what it is! Too romantic! It's the tower of a medieval leper colony!'

'No!' I said, trying to introduce into my tone a note of enthusiasm which I did not feel. For I knew the tower in question, a pencil-thin minaret which I had seen several times from every angle during our excursions. Certainly it was romantic to look at, and possibly also to live in – providing one was prepared to spend the rest of one's life standing upright, since there was not sufficient room inside to sit or lie down. Who but Iris could even have toyed with the idea? Not wishing to be a wet blanket, however, I refrained from pointing out this obvious disadvantage and merely asked, 'Are you sure it's for sale?'

'I haven't the faintest. I only know there's nothing else I want. . . . But that's not all. Hold on to your hats now! I've found something for *you* as well, something which *is* for sale. I know because I've just seen the owner. He's an enchanting little gnome of a man and I think . . .'

But Xan and I did not want to hear about the owner and interrupted her:

'What's it like? Where is it? Describe it!'

'It's called the Galerie des Pâtres – there's a fine pastoral-poetic name for you! – and it's quite near Uzès, within walking distance I should think. There's a loft full of pigeons, and a courtyard with a big tree in it, and a *bergerie* for the beasts, and an old wine press, and . . .'

'But the house itself, Iris? What about the house?'

'Well, it's difficult to describe. It has a roof, and four walls, a front door, windows. . . . But you'd better go and look for yourselves.'

We did go, first thing in the morning.

The house had no architectural pretensions. A roof, four walls, a door, windows . . . just as Iris had said. Inside, it was dark and dank. It was also tiny, 'but too big for an old couple like us,' said the owner, who was indeed the enchanting little gnome of a man that Iris had described. 'Now that all our children are grown up and have homes of their own, it's lonely here for my wife. She wants to move into the town. That's why we're selling.'

In contrast to the squat little cottage, the *bergerie* next door looked as vast and spacious as a zeppelin hangar or the transept of a cathedral: a tall narrow building with walls as blank as the face of a cliff except for a few small apertures to admit the pigeons into the loft. There was also a large lean-to, forming a lateral wing to the courtyard, and it was easy to visualise these three separate structures combined into one harmonious whole.

Water was provided by two wells – 'they never run dry,' the little gnome assured us, and I believed him since neither he nor his wife could have drawn on them to any great extent. There was not so much as a bath-tub or wash-basin on the premises, and the only sanitation was a noisome pit enclosed in a wooden shack erected against the back wall. As for the electricity supply, a single wire furnished barely enough current for a couple of naked bulbs to shed a faint yellow light.

When we left Portugal, we had vowed never again to live without electricity, central heating and modern plumbing. 'Let's not even consider a house that isn't properly equipped,' Xan had said, and I had agreed. But now I felt his resolution wavering; I knew mine was. We were both seriously considering the Galerie des Pâtres.

What had shaken our determination was the setting, the view. From the terraced courtyard the landscape unfolded before us like a stretch of billowing ocean viewed from the deck of a trans-Atlantic liner. On one side, the edge of a thick wood encroached on the far horizon like the promontory of a distant island. On the other, further still, a range of snow-capped mountains merged into the clouds which concealed the higher peaks of the Cévennes. In front of us, beyond a patchwork of brown, green and umber fields quilting the bed of a broad valley, a line of silver poplars and willows suggested the presence of a river. This background resembled an escutcheon, dotted with the gnarled fists of mulberry trees and hatched with the marks of tractors, supported on the dexter side by a classical farmhouse from which rose a muffled chittering of guineafowl, on the sinister by a larger and still older *mas* turreted and colonnaded like a monastery. The middle base was represented by a small vineyard ('That's where the property begins,' the gnome indicated) separated from the foot of the terrace on which we were standing by a wide expanse of fallow ground buried in tall grass and fringed by a narrow vegetable plot terraced like the courtyard itself.

As we stood admiring this prospect we heard a distant rumble, then the toot of a railway engine, and a train appeared out of the woods on our left, rattling through the field as it slowed down, and came to a stop straight in front of us. We gazed in wonder at the three little wagons loaded with a variety of agricultural machines as brightly painted as children's toys: a delightful sight, and almost as improbable as that of a racing-yacht sailing down Piccadilly. For there was no sign of a railway-line (it was invisible in the grass) though I now noticed what looked like a level-crossing keeper's cottage half concealed in a clump of bamboos on the edge of the wood.

'The goods train from the Pont du Gard,' the gnome explained. 'It passes once a day. The driver's an old friend of mine.'

'But what is he doing?' I asked, for I had seen a small figure climb down from the footplate and disappear into the vineyard.

'Picking some wild leeks for his supper.'

Presently the driver climbed back into his seat, waved at us out of the window and, with a couple of cheerful toots, the train set off again through the grass.

This decided us. A train of our own! Well, more or less. . . . Then and there, over a glass of the little gnome's home-made walnut-wine, we clinched the deal. The Galerie des Pâtres was ours.

'And all thanks to you,' we said to Iris, when we foregathered again at Wuthering Heights that evening.

Her own deal had fallen through. Or rather, there had never been the chance of a deal. The leper tower was not for sale. 'Just as well,' I told her. 'I'm sure you can find something better.'

'No, it's the only thing I wanted,' she replied. 'I shan't go on searching any more in this area.' She was despondent, but only for a moment. 'I think I'll try the Pyrenees next,' she went on, brightening at the prospect of further gypsy life. 'There's no point in wasting time. I'll pack tonight and start off early in the morning.'

'I wonder why she's chosen the Pyrenees,' I said to Xan, as we watched her drive away next day.

'Maybe it's good mushroom country,' he suggested.

17

The Quest

As soon as the title deeds were signed and the little gnome and his wife had moved out of the Galerie, Xan and I got down to work. We had decided to concentrate first of all on the cottage, which could be tackled separately. Once it was made habitable and we had settled in, we would be in a better position to deal with the *bergerie* and lean-to. Besides, this was all we could afford at the moment for, although we continued to be assured that Xan's long-awaited fortune was about to materialise any day, assurances were all that we had so far received.

As a further economy, and also for the fun of doing the job ourselves, we decided to dispense with the services of an architect. So for several weeks we spent every day and all day inspecting our new acquisition, burrowing into every corner, climbing on to the roof, sounding each beam, every wall, assessing the structural repairs that would be needed, discussing the disposition of the various rooms, catering for new windows and doors to be pierced, and taking endless measurements. In the evening, at Wuthering Heights, we would collate these facts and figures which served as a basis for the series of detailed plans which Xan eventually produced.

For encouragement and advice, we used to call from time to time on Paul Hanbury and Bob Schootemeijer, old friends of ours who had restored a number of châteaux in this part of France and thus knew the ropes. They were now living in their latest masterpiece, the thirteenth-century Bastide d'Engras, and were about to embark on an even more ambitious project: the restoration of the erstwhile summer palace of the Bishops of Uzès. The vast scale on which they worked and the lavish result they produced had little bearing on our own problems and plans; nevertheless we shamelessly picked their brains.

We were probably a nuisance too to all our other friends in the neighbourhood, for at this stage we could think and talk of nothing but the Galerie. Walter and Barbara Robinson, for instance, must have known what they were in for each time we visited them at Vic-le-Fesq. Their manor house on the edge of the village was large enough to accommodate a nursery and playroom for their two small sons, a studio and storeroom for Barbara's paintings, a study for Walter the orientalist (lined with Chinese and Japanese manuscripts) and a workroom for Walter the handyman (equipped with electric saws and various other intimidating machines). It was therefore not the sort of house we had in mind for ourselves, but it gave us an idea of what could be done one day with our *bergerie*, and Xan was able to draw on Walter's do-it-yourself expertise.

Larry and Claude Durrell were further purveyors of useful information, having lived in the district for a number of years. Before we moved to France, Xan had not seen Larry for almost a quarter of a century and neither of us had met Claude. We had since made up to a certain extent for all this time that had been lost. The Durrells were hosts by nature rather than guests – only rarely could we entice them up to Wuthering Heights – and scarcely a week would pass without a characteristic invitation reaching us in the form of a lewd postcard or an urgent telegram: 'Come and have a glass and a jabber,' or 'What about a stirrup lunch by the fire?' or 'Duck on spit waiting to be eaten this minute!'

No wonder the Durrells preferred to stay at home. Where else could they have fared so well? Each time we entered their little *mazet* – an agricultural labourer's cottage in an olive grove just outside Nîmes, which they had converted into the snuggest of snuggeries – mouth-watering exhalations issued from the kitchen. In the diminutive sitting-room we would join Larry over a long succession of drinks – 'just another touch of the stockwhip,' he would urge, as he filled and refilled our glasses – while Claude would nip in from time to time to recharge her own. A ping on the bell of the clockwork turnspit announced that the roast was ready and we would settle round the plain deal table, greedily sniffing the steam rising from the golden crispness of whatever animal had been sacrificed for us that day.

Since Claude knew and shared Xan's fondness of pulses, the meal often started with a thick soup of lentils or chickpeas. 'Have some butter with it,' Larry invariably suggested, setting the example by putting a lump the size of his fist into his own plate. The pleasure he took in eating was contagious and he seemed even capable of injecting his appetite into others. Never before had I seen Xan do such justice to his food and I myself would devour more than twice as much as usual. How Claude kept her trim figure was a mystery.

Yet the stupor that elsewhere would have followed such indulgence never overcame me in the *mazet*. Even when reclining in the cushioned comfort of what Claude called 'my Elizabeth Barrett,' it was impossible to feel torpid in Larry's presence. His conversation was always a spell-binding display of legerdemain. His gift for mimicry was something I had noticed in other writers and we would sit entranced with delight or convulsed with laughter as he sprang into the air, gesticulated extravagantly or bounced on the balls of his feet, as though shadow-boxing, to illustrate some anecdote or imitate some character.

Sometimes we would play the gramophone and Larry himself would fall silent as he listened to the earthy songs of Georges Brassens. 'The fellow's a real poet,' he declared sincerely. 'He ought to be elected to the Académie.' When Brassens's deep meridional accents and haunting guitar were succeeded by a record of Greek folk music, Larry would be on his feet again, breaking with surprising agility into the intricate steps of a *syrto* or a *sousta*, encouraging us to link hands and join him. Claude, Xan and I would try to follow his movements as we circled round the confined circumference in front of the fire, but he was so much nimbler than the rest of us that our efforts appeared all the more ungainly and we would presently collapse into paroxysms of laughter which could only be alleviated by further touches of the stockwhip.

Late one evening, or rather early one morning, after the stockwhip had been administered even more liberally than usual, I was possessed with an irrational but irresistible urge to lift Claude off her feet and carry her round the room. She was no weight at all and I raised her off the floor with drunken ease which brought a cheer of admiration from Larry. But as I stepped forward I stumbled, overbalanced and, with Claude still in my arms, careered into the glass-panelled door dividing the sitting-room from Larry's study. Claude's slender buttocks shivered one of the panes like a battering-ram, but her thick brocade trousers cushioned the shock and shielded her against the flying glass. I was less fortunate and received a number of splinters in the face.

'I'm afraid you have a few shaving nicks,' said Larry. 'I'd better deal with them with my styptic pencil.' He picked up the bottle of Arquebuse which we had been sampling heavily and poured a generous measure on to his handkerchief. 'It's a *vulnéraire* as well as a liqueur,' he explained, dabbing at my cuts, 'macerated by monks to ease their digestion, and used by crusaders to staunch their wounds . . .'

'I'm sorry about the door,' I said.

'You've no need to be,' he replied. 'We've always hated it, haven't we, Claude? Been meaning to take it down for ages.' He drew back his foot, took careful aim, and sent another glass panel flying. 'I'll finish the rest off in the morning. Now what about another touch of the stockwhip. . . .'

Winter had come with overwhelming abruptness. After weeks of Indian-summer weather, during which we had been able to picnic every day in the courtyard of the Galerie, the mistral started to blow. Up on Wuthering Heights its impact was alarming. Venturing outside meant being winded at once – literally so, for our breath seemed to be squeezed out of our bodies by an icy grip and we would find ourselves choking, unable to inhale, as though the air was moving too rapidly to be drawn into our lungs. And as if this general onslaught were not sufficient in itself, individual gusts would lurk like footpads round every corner, ready to clobber us all over again.

Even indoors we were not protected. Here the assault was on our ears. The doors, the shutters, the windows – sometimes, it seemed, the very walls – rattled and clattered and shook, providing a percussion accompaniment to the wailing voice of the gale. One door in particular – facing north and therefore more vulnerable than the rest – kept bending inwards at one corner, leaving a visible gap under the lintel. We wedged it more or less tight with a broken kitchen fork, whereupon the volume of noise was increased by the sound of an Aeolian harp.

The thermometer plummeted. There was frost at night, and in the morning the garrigue looked as though it had been sprayed with thin white enamel sparkling in the bright sun which we found to be a natural adjunct to the mistral and a welcome compensation for it. The temperature inside the house was scarcely higher than outdoors. We had laid in a stock of wood, but the open fire smoked so much that we stopped lighting it, preferring the lesser torment of the cold to that of gradual asphyxiation. Since there was no other means of heating we took to living permanently in skiing trousers, anoraks, heavy sweaters, fur-lined boots, and several layers of thick woollen underwear which we did not remove even when going to bed. Piggy too was dressed as though for winter sports, in a smart tartan coat bought long ago at a shop in Cannes called Le Chien Chic, and at night she would snuggle under the blankets with us, fulfilling the role of hot water-bottle for which her Mexican ancestors were bred.

And still the mistral blew. One morning we woke up to find that a window-pane had been shattered, presumably by a gale-driven pebble. No one could be induced to come all the way from Uzès for such a minor repair. This we knew from experience, after blocking the kitchen sink. Xan, totally ignorant of plumbing, had been faced with the task of unblocking it himself. More by luck than dexterity (though he himself claimed it was by logic and sweet reason) he had done so. But replacing a window-pane was more of a challenge. Fortunately he had the presence of mind to buy three spare panes and twice the amount of putty that would normally be needed.

At his first attempt, after an hour's meticulous scraping round the empty frame, the glass cracked as he inserted it into its socket. The second pane also splintered as he fitted it into place. (His agonised yell – 'Oh no, not again!' – brought me downstairs, where I found him stamping, almost weeping with rage.) But with the last pane he was successful and by the time he had finished applying the putty he was wreathed in smiles of self-satisfaction. 'There's nothing to it,' he said, wiping his hands on the seat of his trousers.

The mistral went on blowing, so violently that we could hardly open the garage doors. Against such pressure our personal muscular exertions were inadequate. We had to prise the heavy wooden leaves apart by nudging them with the bumpers of the car, then edge forward through the gradually increasing gap between them until we were clear and they had slammed shut again. One day, however, the gap widened abruptly as we were scraping through; instead of snapping back together like the jaws of a trap, both leaves swung further open with the force of a boom gybing. Simultaneously they were torn off their hinges, lifted into the air as though made of cardboard and deposited several yards further off. Unable to shift them on account of their weight, we had to leave them where they lay.

But our bedroom was directly above the garage, and the floor in between was cracked in several places. That night the wind whistled in glacial jets through these apertures, fanning our faces and lifting the sheets from our bed. In the morning I woke with a miniature icicle on the end of my nose and we were unable to clean our teeth until we had thawed out the toothpaste. It was fortunate that we had a spare room into which we could move.

As suddenly as it rose, the mistral fell and was succeeded by a heavy snowstorm. The white shroud that covered the garrigue seemed infinite and intensified the illusion of stretching in an unbroken expanse right up to the North Pole. A lovely sight, but it had its disadvantages. In the first place, we found ourselves marooned. There was a slope leading from the garage to the point where the road descended into the valley. It was a gentle slope and only a few yards long. But, under snow, it proved an insuperable obstacle for the car. Secondly, we found ourselves without water. The cistern had frozen over and a sliver of ice had been sucked into the electric pump, cracking a vital part. This at least was our rough-and-ready diagnosis; all we knew for sure was that the pump was out of action.

Strange to say, neither Xan nor I felt like complaining. We were amused and exhilarated by the novelty of the situation. We had enough food to last for several days, we could wash and wash up in the snow, and if the plug didn't pull, why, there was always an alternative solution. Meanwhile the landscape in its new guise was waiting to be rediscovered. Every day we went for long walks, during which Piggy would stop from time to time to roll with delight in this unfamiliar substance blanketing the ground or to look back in surprise at the marks her own small paws had left upon it. Against this universally white background many of the indigenous animals which we had been unable to spot before now revealed themselves. All of them seemed abnormally large; the half-wild cats were lion-cheeked monsters; the foxes looked like wolves; and once we came face to face with a scarcely recognisable hare, charcoal-coloured and the size of a kid, for which we had at first mistaken it. There were traces of wild boar too, though we saw none of the beasts themselves. Nor, alas, did we ever catch sight of the badgers which we heard larking about in the woodshed every night and whose visiting-cards we found on the doorstep every morning.

Mending the water pump was beyond even Xan's newly acquired capacities. As soon as the snow melted and we could use the car again, we sent for a plumber. He told us he would be unable to do the job on the spot or at once, that the whole thing would have to be dismantled, that new parts would have to be ordered, that it might be several days, even weeks, before these arrived, that. . . . He rambled on, but we were no longer listening. He had already made it clear that we would have to abandon Wuthering Heights for an indefinite length of time, unless we were willing to continue to live in discomfort without even the excuse of being snow-bound. So we moved down to the coaching-inn at Uzès.

To the bumpkins we had now become, the sleepy little town seemed as busy and noisy at night as Soho or Manhattan. To begin with, this was a pleasant change. Meals that we did not have to cook ourselves were a further treat, and we enjoyed them all the more for knowing that we would not have to wash up afterwards. Yet after three or four days we began to tire of the hotel food. Or was it that Wuthering Heights, with all its inconveniences, still cast its spell on us? Whichever the reason, we found ourselves driving out there every evening with a jerrycan of water and tucking into a midnight feast of the special porridge Iris had left behind, followed by bacon and eggs, then driving all the way back again. A strange thing to do, in retrospect, yet at the time neither of us thought it the least bit odd.

It was actually a relief when the pump was eventually mended and we were able to move back to the house, back to domestic chores, to the burning question, back to the lack of heating, to the cold. But to combat the cold, we had now bought ourselves a portable sauna: a Heath-Robinson contraption consisting of a plastic cocoon to hold the steam provided by a sort of electric kettle. I was longing to try it out, for I had been putting on weight – all that porridge perhaps – and wanted to lose a few pounds. With the same laudable end in view, I had also bought myself a steel exercising bar which could be fitted between the uprights of a door.

The sauna, for all its eccentric appearance, worked perfectly. One session in it was sufficient to keep us warm for the rest of the day, and I also began to shed my porridge fat. The exercising bar was a great success as well, until, one day, I grew too venturesome and swung on it more violently than usual, picturing myself as the Empress Elizabeth of Austria getting into training for a season with the Quorn. The fixture came adrift from its moorings and I flew through the air, though not with the greatest of ease. I landed with a thump, catching my hip on the corner of an open drawer.

I lay there, too breathless from the pain to shout for help. But Xan had heard the crash and came rushing upstairs. 'What on earth's going on?' he said. 'Have you broken the furniture?' In his alarm he looked like an irate eagle.

'No, only my hip!'

It felt broken anyway, and I wanted a little more sympathy. Xan surveyed the damage which, almost to my disappointment, amounted to no more than a flesh wound – a deep one, admittedly – surrounded by a contusion that was already developing the stained-glass colours of a Rouault painting. The drawer was not even splintered. And the bar was still intact. It merely needed to be fixed back into place. But Xan picked it up and flung it out of the window. 'We shan't be using *that* again,' he said.

By this time work had started on the Galerie. The builders we had engaged were a small family concern, consisting of father and two sons, supplemented by casual Spanish and Arab labour. Unfortunately their method was to work on several sites simultaneously, so that it was impossible to map out a proper programme. After several weeks all they had done was remove the roof from the cottage, after which we saw no sign of them again for several weeks more.

There was some excuse for them, perhaps. Until a new roof

was built, they could not start tampering with the walls. But until they had water for their concrete-mixer, they could not start building the roof. And until an electric pump was installed, the water could not be pumped up from the wells. And until there was an adequate electricity supply, the pump would not work.

They must have known this all the time, of course, so that the premature removal of the roof seemed slapdash and irresponsible, to say the least. The wretched cottage now looked as though it had been scalped, and the scaffolding surrounding it reminded me of crutches or splints. We were distressed each time we saw it. 'It's like visiting the victim of a car accident or someone who's been coshed in the street,' Xan observed morosely.

We were all the more concerned when an alarmist friend of ours told us that without the weight of the roof to hold them steady the walls were liable to 'play'. '*Ils risquent de jouer*' was the phrase he used, and which impressed itself all too vividly on my mind. I imagined them, four feet thick though they were, shimmying by moonlight to the whistling of the mistral, shaking like dervishes or holy rollers, until they fell to the ground in a trance and joined the rest of the dust and rubble already there. Xan and I spent a sleepless night wondering whether we should not have employed a qualified architect after all. As soon as day broke we drove straight to the Galerie to make sure it was still intact. It was, but we still took the precaution of consulting an engineering expert and our fears were not completely dispelled until we received his reassuring report.

Meanwhile we goaded the electricity company into action with a substantial sum of money, euphemistically called '*participation*', and in a surprisingly short time we were provided with all the current we needed and our water pump was installed. With equally surprising despatch the builders then set to work and, more surprising still, went on working for several weeks on end. The new roof went on, a new floor was put in, apertures were pierced for the new doors and windows, and the rubble went on pouring out like blood from multiple wounds. Such a quantity there was that as I gazed with pity at the venerable carcase of stones and mortar, now so horribly lacerated, I found myself wondering like Lady Macbeth, 'Who would have thought the old man to have had so much blood in him?'

But gradually the little house, from the outside at least, began to assume the aspect we had envisaged. Inevitably there had been some last-minute alterations to Xan's original plans, depending on structural demands or as and when improvements suggested themselves. It was pointless, for instance, to insist on having a window in a specific position if the whole building was thereby liable to collapse. On the other hand, when changes could be made for aesthetic considerations, the builders proved singularly adaptable and uncomplaining. They merely gave a shrug of incomprehension at our wanting each bedroom to have its own bathroom. But since we had the space, why not? And they were flummoxed by our insistence on insulating the outside walls by means of brick partitions with an air gap in between. 'Totally unnecessary,' they maintained. Maybe, but after the damp of Portugal we were taking no chances.

The dreadful din of the concrete-mixer and compressor which greeted us every morning on our arrival became music to our ears: audible proof to confirm the visible evidence of progress. We were therefore disconcerted when we turned up one day to find the courtyard silent and deserted. We soon discovered the reason. There was no more water, both wells had run dry.

So much for the little gnome's reassurances, we thought. But we were doing him an injustice. There had been no rain to speak of all winter and the wells had had an unusual demand made upon them. Besides, the drought was not limited to the Galerie. Other houses in the area, we heard, were also suffering from it and Wuthering Heights itself was not spared. One evening the electric pump there changed its note from the whirring whine we had come to recognise as normal; it began to wheeze asthmatically, then broke into a death rattle and finally fell silent. The cistern was empty.

So once again we were waterless. 'Summon the fire brigade,' the baby-faced farmer told us. At first we thought he must be joking, but he assured us this was the normal procedure in the circumstances. He was right. The local *pompiers*, to whom we diffidently applied, seemed to see nothing odd in our request. 'Water? Certainly. We'll send a tank-wagon over tomorrow.'

We almost cheered out loud when we saw the clumsy scarlet vehicle wending its way towards us through the garrigue next morning. Now we knew how a beleaguered garrison must feel at the sight of an approaching relief force. For two pins I would have embraced both stalwart firemen who, in their uniforms and glinting helmets, looked as dashing and romantic as Victorian guardees. But they had no time for such dalliance and went briskly into action, as though the house was ablaze. In a minute, with a deftness and efficiency born of long practice, they had uncoiled a length of heavy rubber piping, passed it through the sitting-room and lowered it into the aperture on the terrace. A minute later this sea-serpent was writhing and gurgling, ingesting the contents of the tank and spewing them out into the cistern. Within half an hour the tank was empty and the cistern was . . . no, not full, far from it. The water inside it was only a few inches deep, but this was hardly the moment to look a gift horse in the mouth. We thanked our benefactors and after a quick drink they drove off.

Of course we should have exercised economy and harboured our bounty. But we didn't. We trusted to luck, or rather pinned our faith on an impending storm. Not a drop of rain fell and in a few days the cistern was again bone-dry. We dared not re-apply to the *pompiers* so soon after their last visit and were therefore reduced to fetching water daily in half a dozen jerrycans from the nearest mains five miles away.

Meanwhile Diana had come to stay. We warned her on her arrival of the discomfort in store, which was further aggravated, we now discovered, by a swarm of bees on the window-sill of the spare room. Characteristically, she took this inconvenience in her stride. 'Bees don't bother me,' she said. 'Don't you remember the hives at Bognor?' As for water, she rationed herself as strictly as a wayfarer in the Sahara, never once complaining of the lack of bathing facilities. When I brought the subject up she was quite sharp with me: 'Of course I have a bath if there's a bath going. But if there isn't I don't mind at all. I never *wash* in it anyway, do you?'

Still no rain fell. Each time a cloud appeared it was instantly dissolved or swept away by the mistral, leaving a faint trail across an otherwise completely clear sky in which the sun shone with an intensity that increased day by day. The first wild flowers of the year appeared in the garrigue: irises, grape hyacinths and tall pink-bloomed hellebores like tree peonies. Regretfully we bade them all farewell. The storm for which we had been waiting seemed more distant than ever, and we could not face the prospect of living indefinitely on our present water supply. Though our lease of Wuthering Heights still had several weeks to run, we packed up and moved out.

18

A French Wild West

The little inn on the banks of the Gardon, where we settled for the summer, had been recommended to us by the Durrells. It reminded me at once of an Impressionist painting. The group in Renoir's *Déjeuner des canotiers* would not have looked out of place on the broad balcony running the entire length of the narrow elongated building. Except for a group of ugly modern villas opposite, this stretch of the river would still have been instantly recognisable to André Gide who knew it in his boyhood and later described it in *Si le grain ne meurt*. The inn itself would have delighted Colette and might have served as the background for one of her tales of bourgeois summer holidays at the turn of the century. Xan and I fell in love with it at first sight.

The season had not yet started, so we had the whole place to ourselves. Except for an occasional fisherman who dropped in for a drink, for several weeks the only visitor we saw was the shepherd who passed twice a day with his flock. On his way back in the evening he would always stop and present a bouquet of thyme or sage to the innkeeper's wife, a swarthy statuesque woman for whom he obviously had a soft spot. Delivering these gifts in front of us made him mute with embarrassment until he grew accustomed to our presence, but soon he had overcome his shyness sufficiently to include us in his daily greeting and farewell.

We always knew he was coming long before he arrived, since Piggy kept her ears pricked for the sound of the sheep bells which heralded the appearance of her personal enemy, the shepherd's mongrel dog. At the sight of him her hackles would rise like a ruff; she would adopt an arrogant stance on the balcony, poking her head through the widely spaced bars, and bark insultingly at the flock below, like an aristocratic landowner upbraiding the jacquerie. One evening she barked herself right off her feet, lost her balance and fell through the railings. I had a glimpse of her sailing through the air, her tail extended like a rudder, her ears outstretched like wings, then I heard her land with a belly-flopping thud on the dusty path twelve feet below.

Her frenzied barking resumed at once – or was it agonised whining? For some time I could not bring myself to look over the edge and make sure, for fear of what I might see. When I did eventually peer down, the shepherd was holding her in his arms and examining her paws – 'just in case she has split them', he explained, as I rushed down and he restored her to me. She was completely unhurt, but what surprised me even more was the way she had allowed herself to be handled by a stranger.

But this stranger was an exception. I had always thought he looked more like a scholar than a shepherd – a gypsy scholar or retired schoolmaster; a Languedoc Thoreau perhaps? – and I had noticed that his voice bore no trace of the local plebeian accent. Now that Piggy's fall had broken the ice, as it were, he began to talk to me freely and I soon realised he was an educated, even erudite man. From him I learnt that in the fifteenth century the Bishops of Uzès minted their own coins, and he showed me the exact spot on the river bank – not fifty yards from the hotel – where they used to gather their gold by drawing a sheepskin through the gravelly water. Less romantically, I tried with a bath-towel and after two days' idle paddling collected half a dozen tiny sequins. I showed them to the shepherd, who was delighted.

'This country is rich in geological specimens,' he said. 'See what I found today.' He fished in his pocket and produced what looked like a miniature model of the human brain.

'What is it?' I asked.

'A fossilized walnut. Keep it if you like.'

From then on scarcely an evening passed without his presenting me with some treasure or other which he had come upon during the day: fossils usually, for this region abounded in them, petrified sea-urchins and oyster shells embedded in rock, but also fragments of marble, chunks of quartz, slivers of mica and, best of all, a small thunderbolt burnished by lightning.

The food at the inn was usually delicious, the service sometimes eccentric. One evening my face swelled painfully as a result of an abscess in a tooth. Since I felt too ill and ugly for dinner downstairs, I asked Xan to have a couple of boiled eggs sent up to our room. Then I went to bed. Shortly afterwards there was a knock at the door and a falsetto voice announced, 'I'm the waitress.'

At first I thought it was Xan trying to be funny, but the figure that entered bearing my tray was shorter and more thickset and wore, under a transparent nightdress, the sort of woollen pants in which Xan would never have been seen dead. Sunglasses, running mascara and clumsily daubed lipstick made the face unrecognisable, but the feather hat perched above it failed to disguise the close-cropped strawberry-roan hair which I identified at once as our landlord's. 'I thought you might need cheering up,' he said, disappointed at the wan smile which was all I could muster to show my amusement.

When he came back to collect the tray an hour or so later, he was in his usual clothes again but seemed more determined than ever to make me laugh, unaware that the swelling in my jaw prevented me from doing so. '*Le coquetier,*' he whispered, indicating the set of pretty porcelain cups in which my eggs had been served. Then, with a broad wink, he produced some cracked plates and saucers from his pocket, flung them down on the tiled floor and bellowed through the open door, '*Ah! Mon dieu!*'

We both knew what would happen, for I had seen him play this trick before and it had never failed. There was a shriek from downstairs and presently his wife rushed up, panting with effort and anxiety: '*Oh, mon beau coquetier!*' Did she really believe every time that her most treasured possession had been broken? Unlikely. Yet her anguish always seemed genuine, and so did her subsequent relief. And the words she uttered were always identical: 'I'd rather break my leg than break my precious *coquetier*.' I felt she meant it too.

Now that we were free from household chores and no longer had to deal with the wilful antics of Wuthering Heights, we were able to get down to work again, Xan on yet another translation from the French, myself on the double biography of Emerald and Nancy Cunard which I had planned in Portugal. For no extra charge, a large downstairs room was put at our disposal and furnished as a makeshift office in which we could keep our typewriters, books and documents – a welcome refuge, for by this time we no longer had the inn to ourselves. Other clients had arrived to stay, two nieces of the innkeeper's wife had also come to help in the kitchen and, with this additional audience to encourage him, our frisky landlord indulged all the more in his noisy horseplay.

With this new lease of leisure, I even found time for riding again. Ever since we arrived here I had been longing to explore this countryside on a horse and had often envied the groups of riders who were to be seen almost every day clattering down the main street of Uzès or watering their mounts at one of the many fountains. There were times when the little town looked like a scene in a Wild West film, for these horsemen all favoured American cowboy saddles and their gear was modelled on that of Buffalo Bill. Their natural 'sheriff' was the local printer, a lean middle-aged man with iron-grey hair and finely drawn features, who was so enamoured of all things Western that he frequently turned up at his office dressed in a ten-gallon hat, leather chaps and spurs, either on horseback or driving a spanking cob harnessed to a 'surrey-with-a-fringe-on-top'.

He kept a number of horses at his house on the outskirts of the town and, on hearing I was keen on riding, generously offered me a mount any time I liked. 'Come and have a look at them,' he said. 'Then you can see my llamas as well.'

Llamas?' I could hardly believe it and thought I must have misheard.

'Yes. A male and a female, and now there's a baby too.'

I was still puzzling about his llamas when Xan and I called on him that afternoon and, on finding him dressed in English riding clothes with well-cut boots and a velvet hunting cap, I could not help wondering whether this too might not be some elaborate joke. But the change of garb was merely in my honour – 'I have an English saddle also,' he told me – and his wife, whose vivacious features reminded me of one of Toulouse Lautrec's attractive female clowns, endeared herself to us at once by greeting me with an apology for not being able to speak our language, adding, with no intention to flatter but simply as though it was an undeniable statement of fact: 'You're very lucky to be English.'

And the llamas did in fact exist. As we walked past the stables on our way from the front gate towards the house, I noticed an animal which was certainly not a horse standing by the white painted railings of a small paddock – a shaggy jet-black beast with a contemptuous expression, its jaw rotating rhythmically and its underlip protruding as it chewed a mouthful of hay. 'That's the father,' the sheriff's wife told me. 'Stay quite still and he'll come over and say *bonjour*.'

I tightened my stomach muscles and remained frozen to the spot while the slobbering black muzzle gingerly approached the back of my neck, the jaws still champing. I hardly knew what to expect. A nibble? A deluge of saliva? What I received was a blast of warm breath delivered with a gentle snort from both tunnel-like nostrils.

'Good!' the sheriff's wife exclaimed, clapping her hands. 'Now I'll introduce you to the rest of the family.'

She opened the door of a loosebox and out stepped the dam, fawn-coloured, the epitome of feminine elegance, with the gait of a professional model, long lashes fluttering over eyes the colour of yellow Chartreuse and the same disdainful expression as the sire. This splendid creature was closely followed by its offspring, still unsteady on its long legs, as fluffy and cuddly as a teddy-bear.

One of the horses – a big bay mare – was then turned loose to join them and in a moment the paddock was transformed into a circus ring as the sheriff's wife put the animals through their paces, encouraging them to gallop and buck with cries of '*Vas-y, ma cocotte!*' while she herself bounced up and down as though on a trampoline, dodging and swerving to avoid the flying hooves. Throughout this impromptu rodeo act the big black sire remained sublimely aloof, still chewing his cud, until he was released on his own from the paddock; whereupon he lolloped up to a pile of horse manure in the garden, crouched over it, and calmly added his own alien contribution.

'Now let's have a drink,' said our host, who in his present guise looked more like a squire than a sheriff. But he reverted at once to his original role as he led the way, not into his house but towards a log cabin with the words 'Crazy Horse Saloon' painted above the double swing-doors. He pushed his way through in approved Western style and we followed suit, to find ourselves in a Hollywood film set. The wooden walls were hung with scalps, arrows, spears, bead necklaces, old-fashioned pistols and rifles. An open iron stove stood in one corner. Above it was pinned a poster offering a reward for a notorious cattle-rustler (whose photograph, on closer inspection, proved to be that of a local café proprietor). A bookcase opposite contained a library of cowboy and Indian literature. Above the bar was a large-scale map of the region, on which the name of every feature had been altered to suit the décor (Uzès itself, I noticed, had been rechristened Oozeville, and the gentle little valley of the Alzon masqueraded as Dead Man's Gulch). 'Take your choice,' said the sheriff, indicating a formidable array of Scotch and bourbon bottles which included every brand I had ever known and several I had never even heard of. Xan and I played safe and selected Dimple Haig. Our host, like his wife, drank Vichy water. 'I'm afraid neither of us likes whisky,' he admitted rather sheepishly, as though aversion to hard liquor was out of character.

In the saddle, however, he was tough and tireless and whenever we went riding together I found myself emulating him, viewing the landscape through his eyes, imagining myself as Calamity Jane or some other Wild West character.

Apart from the sheriff's horses, there was also a stable just outside Uzès which was managed by a young married couple,

Hélène and Michel. The first time I saw them I was bowled over by their appearance. They were both mounted on white stallions and wore identical black capes which fell in folds from their shoulders right over their horses' rumps. Straight and slim as javelins, he with high Slavonic cheekbones and slanting eyes the colour of pale malachite, she with a mane of dark-brown hair and a fierce sultry expression enhancing the beauty of her features, they looked like an over-romanticised illustration of a prince and princess in some Nordic fairy-story.

Their stable consisted exclusively of stallions, which they tended all by themselves, even acting as their own veterinary surgeon, saddler and farrier. Hélène treated any sick or lame horse with her own hands, sewing up wounds and giving injections. Michel made his own bridles, plaited with blue beads to ward off the evil eye. And between them they shod the whole stud without any outside help – not always with success, as I realised when I started riding with Hélène. Galloping behind her was like taking part in a cavalry charge, 'stormed at by shot and shell', as stones and flying horseshoes came whizzing overhead.

Michel never came out with us. 'He's shy of strangers,' Hélène explained. 'He loves riding, but only by himself. Do you know what his secret ambition is?' She tittered at the very thought of it. 'To ride alone, all over France, dressed in a suit of armour! And his hobby – do you know what that is? Designing tombstones!'

Hélène had idiosyncrasies of her own. For all her dedication to riding, she preferred horseflesh to the best beef. 'How could you!' I exclaimed, when she told me this. 'And you such a splendid equestrienne too!'

'Equestrianism has nothing to do with gastronomy,' she merely replied.

As a matter of fact her horsemanship was dashing rather than elegant. In the saddle, she broke every established rule. To keep up with her, I was forced to do likewise and I often thought my father, a cavalry officer and my original riding master, must be turning in his grave as I followed her, galloping on hard going, thundering blindly across main roads and racing back to stables at full speed on a sweating horse. Fortunately the stallions seemed used to such treatment, even if I was not.

What Hélène enjoyed most of all was to blaze a trail straight across country regardless of the lie of the land, spurning the contours, heedless of signposts natural or otherwise. She kept a large-scale map of the area in her pocket but, since she was unable to read it with any degree of accuracy, this was more of a hindrance than a help. As my own sense of direction was no less faulty than hers, we often used to lose our way.

Thus, on the way to the Pont du Gard one morning, we found ourselves skirting the edge of a lofty garrigue encircled by cliffs from which there appeared to be no exit. And no landmark was visible from which to take our bearings. We might have ridden round in circles for ever had we not heard a distant tinkle of sheep bells and headed in the direction from which it came. Presently we reached the flock and caught sight of the shepherdess in charge of it – scarcely a pastoral figure, for she was mounted on a big black stallion, dressed like a gaucho, and looked like a warrior queen – Boadicea, I felt, must have had just such a cast of countenance – as she galloped towards us, cracking a stock whip at the two boar-hounds yelping and snarling beside her.

At the sight of our mounts, the big black stallion reared and plunged, lips drawn back over champing teeth, hooves raking the air. But the woman sat him well and, leaning forward, dealt two swift blows with the stock of her whip on either side of his foam-flecked shoulders, then reined back off the path. To our enquiries she replied by rising in her stirrups and pointing to a clump of trees some distance away: 'The track starts over there. But be careful, it's a steep descent. . . . And watch out for wild boar!' Then, with a jab of her spurs, she was off at a gallop, disappearing almost at once in the cloud of dust she had raised. Hélène and I both rubbed our eyes and burst out laughing with relief and astonishment.

The descent was indeed steep, so steep that even Hélène for once followed my example, dismounted and led her horse on foot. But with her steady pace she soon outdistanced me as I slithered down the shaly slope, on my behind as much as on my feet. For some time I could still see the top of her head and her horse's saddle increasingly further below me, then both disappeared out of sight. I whistled to keep up my courage, imagining a pair of tusks aimed at me from every bush. Or would Hélène be the first target, I wondered? By the time I caught up with her down in the gorge, my nerves were as frayed as the seat of my trousers.

The main equestrian event of the season was the Rallye Latin, a sort of gathering of the clans, with horsemen from all over Southern France and even from as far afield as Spain converging on Avignon. Many of the cavalcades had to spend several days on the road to reach their destination. The Uzès contingent had only thirty miles to ride – a twelve-hour excursion at the most – and since the meeting happened to coincide with my birthday, I decided to give myself a present by taking part in it.

It was still dark when I got to Hélène's stables, which were already buzzing with disorganised activity. A little pony, the stable's mascot, was being harnessed to an old trap which Michel had picked up cheap, then repaired and refurbished. With its coachwork freshly painted in black and yellow, it made a smart turn-out escorted by a young man mounted on a good-looking Arab barb. As usual, Hélène had left all the preparations till the last minute and was now fuming ineffectually, giving vent to her feelings in a torrent of expletives which reminded me of the language favoured by Captain Haddock, the character in *Tintin*. Her temper was not improved when one member of our group, a young girl, turned up in a scarlet blouse instead of the white shirt which, with a black tie, black cowboy hat and white jeans, had been decreed as our uniform for the day. '*Sacré diable! Ça va faire un bougrement drôle d'effet!*' she stormed. But there was no time for the malefactor to go home and change. We were late already.

Eventually the last girth was tightened. We all mounted and were about to set off when Michel came running after us, waving an embroidered pennant adorned with a fox's brush attached to a long pole. In her haste Hélène had forgotten the stable banner, which she had constructed herself but had clearly never practised carrying. As she made a grab at it, her mount whipped round and the cumbersome object scythed through the air a fraction of an inch above my head.

In spite of the darkness and the banner, which, in her hands, continued to constitute a hazard for anyone rash enough to ride within its range, she set an even brisker pace than usual. At full gallop we clattered into Uzès, straight through the sleeping town and out the other side, where the sheriff and another posse were waiting for us to join them. Here there was a further delay. At the sight of our stallions, the sheriff's mare, which was temporarily hitched to a tree, broke loose and in a moment was several fields away, saddlebags flapping and reins trailing on the ground. A quarter of an hour passed before the café proprietor (he of the 'wanted' poster in the Crazy Horse Saloon) and the local jeweller, likewise resembling a cattle-rustler, rounded her up and led her back.

At last we moved off, in single file, wending our way down a steep track, first through thick woods, then along a broad rocky valley transformed by the rising sun into a Technicolor canyon. We forded the river within sight of our little inn and I was almost tempted to pay the landlord back in his own coin by leading our cavalcade in a wild charge past his bedroom window, whooping like Indians attacking a stockade. The sheriff, I knew, would have enjoyed such a diversion, but Hélène's sultry expression – she was still swearing quietly to herself about the girl in the scarlet blouse – deterred me.

The grass was misted with dew as we started across the wooded plain beyond. Crystal drops glistened on every leaf and twig, and I found myself instinctively turning my horse to avoid breaking the shimmering beadwork of countless spider's webs, much to the amusement of the youngest member of the group, the thirteen-year-old son of the Uzès horse-butcher, who happened to be riding beside me. This lad, a fine horseman already, was also intrigued by my hunting-whip which for sentimental reasons, if not from sheer habit, I had brought out with me despite its incongruity with my present cowboy gear. 'Is it for beating your horse?' he kept asking. When I tried to explain its purpose and went through the motions of lifting the latch of a gate with the horn crook, he looked as though he thought I was teasing him or else that I must be mad.

Suddenly, for no apparent reason, my horse shied and in the early-morning light I vaguely discerned the outlines of a body lying on the ground straight ahead, then a number of other recumbent forms all round me. At the sound of our hooves they stirred to life and in a moment the whole area seemed to be sprouting giant mushrooms as helmeted heads started popping out of the grass. We had come upon a detachment of soldiers bivouacking after night manoeuvres. 'The army!' Hélène snorted disdainfully. 'Cowboys wouldn't have let themselves be caught napping like that,' the sheriff agreed. 'Supposing we'd been Indians creeping up on them. . . .'

Just before noon we halted outside a village and tethered our horses by a stream. 'Time for a snack,' said the sheriff, and he and his posse started unpacking their saddlebags. Characteristically, Hélène had made no arrangements for feeding herself or her group. Had we been told, we could have carried sandwiches or a hamper might have been brought out in the pony-trap which presently caught up with us here. Between us we scraped up more than enough money to buy some provisions from the village shop, but all we got to eat was a loaf of bread and a few slices of *jésus*, the cheapest local saucisson, the rest of our combined funds being spent on a white shirt for the girl in the scarlet blouse. None of us minded, however, for Hélène's change of mood at this unexpected find was ample compensation for our short commons.

By this time other cavalcades had halted by the stream to prepare for the last lap across country. I noticed in particular a smart contingent of army officers from Spain and a well-equipped group of Swiss horsemen. All of them had brought a change of clothes with them and, after attending to their mounts, proceeded to spruce up themselves for their entry into Avignon. The only clean garment in either of the Uzès posses – and in contrast to our creased and saddle-stained gear it stood out like an advertisement for a brand of whiter-than-white soapsuds – was the new shirt now being worn by the girl with the scarlet blouse.

Though we may have looked like the rearguard of Napoleon's army in retreat from Moscow, I myself felt a surge of victorious pride at our achievement as we reached the Rhone and saw the Palais des Papes glowing on the far bank in the afternoon sun. Helmeted police on motorbikes were waiting to escort us across the bridge and, as we trotted over, I found myself thinking of my ancestor, Sir Hussey Vivian, who had led the last charge at Waterloo. This incident in the family saga had always fired my imagination and one of my girlhood ambitions was to ride into a foreign town at the head of a company of horse, a day-dream in which I pictured myself as a dashing young cavalry officer, or to be more specific, a captain in the Pomeranian Hussars, though I was not even sure if such a regiment existed. Riding into Avignon, I now reflected, was the nearest I had ever approached to realising this dream.

At the town gates we were greeted by groups of girls dressed in regional costume who handed each of us a small basket of peaches, like conquered subjects offering tribute to their victors. I accepted mine in my best swashbuckling manner, only to find that the gift was in fact a booby trap. The only way of dealing with the fruit was to eat it all immediately (or else adopt the posture of a child taking part in the egg-and-spoon race in a Pony Club gymkhana) but the juice ran down my chin and dripped on to my coat, making rivulets in the dust. A Pomeranian Hussar, I felt, would have handled the problem more skilfully.

A final and unexpected ordeal awaited us when we were paraded on the main square, in front of a panel of experts seated at a long trestle-table to judge the various groups and award points on the turn-out of horse and rider. Hélène had given none of us any warning of this jury. In spite of the last-minute substitution of the new white shirt for the scarlet blouse, our posse received no prize. But the day, and Hélène's face, was saved by the presentation of a small silver cup for the gallant little pony which had pulled the trap all this way.

There were further equestrian festivities on the programme for that evening and the following day, but I had arranged to drive home with Xan who had motored over in time not only to witness our arrival but also to prepare a pleasant surprise. 'It's our wedding anniversary, after all,' he said, as he led me into the shady courtyard of the Hôtel d'Europe, one of my favourite hotels in France, where a bottle of champagne was nestling in its ice bucket at the table he had booked in advance.

19

La Galerie des Pâtres

By this time work had resumed on the Galerie des Pâtres. Lack of water was no longer an excuse for inactivity. There had been several spectacular thunderstorms and our wells were brimming over. Whatever the demand made upon them, they were not likely to run dry again before being replenished by further rain. Yet progress on the building was constantly interrupted by lack of co-ordination between the various branches of our labour force. The masons would be held up until the electricians and plumbers had laid various pipes and wires, and this task in turn would be delayed until the carpenters had produced the required number of window-frames and lintels.

Since all these craftsmen lived in different villages, we spent days on end travelling to and fro between them in a vain attempt to get them to co-operate. Promises were made but rarely kept. '*Demain sans faute*' was a constantly reiterated phrase, which we soon came to dread, for we knew it meant anything but that. Tomorrow would come, bringing with it only a fresh batch of excuses or, in the case of the carpenters, the same old excuse. Whenever we called on them we would find them hard at work on yet another coffin. 'Emergency job,' they would explain in a tone of such reverence as to stifle any protest from us. In the end, however, Xan lost his patience and told them, 'You must stop your fellow-villagers dying off like flies.'

Nevertheless by the early autumn the last pane of glass had been put in, the last stroke of paint had been applied, and we were able to send for our furniture. All that remained was to floor the upper storey with the cork tiles which Xan had ordered specially and planned to lay himself with the help of Walter Robinson, since the local builders were not accustomed to handling this material.

It was a gruelling task, especially for Walter who had to drive from Vic-le-Fesq and back every day but without whose help and guidance Xan would never have been able to manage. They would start work at six in the morning and, apart from a short lunch break, would not stop until seven in the evening, by which time they both looked wan, exhausted and slightly drunk; for the weather was still torrid and the fumes from the glue they used acted almost like an anaesthetic, desiccating their mouths, parching their throats and encouraging them to consume vast quantities of beer in order to keep going. But even Walter, a perfectionist if ever there was one, seemed pleased with the result.

The delightful and immediate prospect of living once more in a home of our own was marred only by the sadness of leaving the inn where we had been so happy for five whole months. As I gazed for the last time at the familiar river, with the kingfishers streaking over the water like blue arrows and the swallows skimming and dipping in pursuit of flies, I was unable to decide whether the tears that kept welling in my eyes were prompted by contentment or nostalgia. Later that evening I was again near to tears, and not mere tears of laughter, when for the last time I heard the smash of crockery, our landlord's cry of '*Oh, mon dieu!*' and his wife's inevitable echo, '*Oh, mon beau coquetier!* I'd rather break my leg than break my *coquetier*!' And when, in the morning, she pressed this most treasured possession of hers upon me as a parting gift, my tears were finally unrestrained.

The arrival of our furniture was a mixed blessing. We were overjoyed to see the familiar bits and pieces again, but long before they were all unpacked from the vans we realised the house was far too small to accommodate them comfortably. For the time being it was useless even to attempt arranging each room as I should have liked, there was simply not enough space. When we had somehow crammed everything in, we could barely move. The main room downstairs looked like an over-stocked antique shop. The little anteroom next door, where I intended to work, was reduced still further in size by books lining all four walls right up to the ceiling. The walls of all the other rooms, even the two bathrooms, were similarly concealed behind a stockade of literature. Xan's dressing-room became a sort of glory-hole, in which he managed only with the greatest ingenuity to devise a minute working corner for himself. Our bedroom was slightly more habitable, though even here we had to be careful not to stub our toes, graze our shins and bruise our hips against the countless alien obstacles it contained.

Of course there was no question of hanging any of our pictures, which were stacked in the kitchen where, in the temporary absence of shelves and cupboards, the floor was already littered with pots and pans and dishes and plates and cups and saucers and glasses and decanters and knives and forks and spoons, not to mention my collection of china and other objects which I had unwisely unpacked instead of leaving them in the cases in which they had arrived. Here, as we ate our first meal in the house, from trays balanced on our knees, sitting side by side with our faces to the wall like two children in disgrace (there was nowhere else we *could* sit at the time) we burst out laughing simultaneously.

'We can't go on living like this indefinitely, can we?' I said.

'Piggy can't anyway,' Xan replied. 'It's not up to her standards.'

We had known all along that we would have to convert the *bergerie* as well as this part of the house if we wanted to live in moderate comfort. We had also expected to have enough money by now for the builders to go ahead with the work at once. Meanwhile we had spent every penny from the sale of our Portuguese house and Xan's ship had still not come in, though it was reported on the horizon almost daily. In fact, on a recent visit to Nice, he had been categorically assured by his trustee that the financial question would be settled by the end of the year at the latest. This was good enough for us. We took the plunge, drew up our plans, presented them to the builders and told them to get busy. Within a week the courtyard was echoing once again to the sound of the concrete-mixer.

Thus we embarked on our second Languedoc winter, fending for ourselves once more since we still had no servants, but in conditions of luxury compared to what we had known at Wuthering Heights: central heating instead of a smoky fire, a proper incinerator in which to burn refuse, ample water (for by this time we had been connected to the mains and were no longer dependent on the wells), doors and windows that defied the mistral, and, above all, the glorious sense of ownership.

There were drawbacks too, admittedly. First and foremost, the lack of space. But this problem, I knew, would eventually be solved. What frightened me – to begin with anyway – was something far more serious: rats. The house must have once been infested by them, for even while the building was in progress they had continued to emerge out of every nook and cranny until the new roof and double walls were built. I had been thankful to see what I thought was the last of them. But they must have fled no further afield than the *bergerie* and, now that this refuge was denied them by the activity there, they had presumably chosen to return to their old haunts. Fortunately they confined themselves to the rafters, so I was spared the sight of them. But the sound of them was enough to disturb my sleep, or anyone's sleep for that matter. Even Xan was roused by their revels in the attic above our bed. 'My God, they must be wearing ammunition boots!' he would grumble, as the ceiling thudded and the rafters echoed with uninhibited squeals and furtive susurrations.

'Perhaps they'll stop if we ask them politely,' he suggested one evening, then bellowed at the top of his voice: 'Shut up!' Unbelievably, a dead silence ensued. But not for long. In a moment the rattles and rustles and squeaks and thumps had started again. 'We'll have to shout them down, that's all,' he decided. 'Sing something. Go on sing! Anything you like, but as loudly as you can.'

I broke into *Onward, Christian Soldiers* while he kept time by banging a broom handle against the ceiling. It was a restless way of spending the night, but better than lying awake and doing nothing. Besides, it seemed to be having an effect. Each time we paused for breath the period of silence overhead grew progressively longer, until, just before dawn, the noises stopped altogether.

We repeated this performance on the following night, and again on the night after that. On the fourth night there was no further need for it. The rats had left for good.

Scorpions were another hazard. They too had been routed from their nooks in the old masonry and now emerged, not in cohorts like the rats but individually, traversing a freshly painted door like a refugee in unfamiliar country or stealing over the new floor-tiles like a displaced person clandestinely crossing a frontier. I minded them far less and often stopped to admire their immaculately cuirassed torsos, their heraldic shape and posture . . . before giving them a good clout with the heel of a shoe. Though we had been told they were not lethal, we were not taking any chances and went on slaughtering them until they finally lay low.

Meanwhile there was other animal life to study and enjoy from my favourite vantage point, the bedroom window. On moonlit nights the huge Chinese mulberry tree stood etched against the steel-coloured sky, each of its branches providing a natural perch for the little owls which I would lure closer and closer with imitative cries. 'Qu-weck! Qu-weck!' they would reply. Every morning the low wall of the terrace, on which I had left out breadcrumbs, rice, nuts, raisins and bacon-fat, was transformed into a stage for a feathered comic opera. I came to know each separate performer: the solitary robin displaying his gaudy waistcoat, the wren (I felt sure it was a female) flirting her tip-tilted tail, the couple of slim pied wagtails, the supporting cast of blackbirds and thrushes, jackdaws and chaffinches, house-sparrows, and great tits with clownish white cheeks. Then the magpies would make their entrance, as clumsy and out of scale as papier-mâché carnival figures, and finally the pigeons would streak across the sky like a flight of aircraft in close formation, taking off from the loft above the *bergerie* which they still refused to abandon despite the removal and renewal of the roof. This daily delight ceased only with the arrival of the builders and the subsequent din of the cement-mixer which cleared the stage and drowned all song until the following morning.

Our nearest neighbours were a family of gypsies who lived in the little house at the level crossing. At least I presumed they were gypsies from their appearance. I had often noticed them in Uzès, the mother in particular. It was impossible not to notice such a flamboyant figure, short and stout, invariably wearing three layers of clothing – tunic, skirt and trousers, all of garishly contrasting colours – high-heeled boots, a turban of yet another colour clashing with lipstick applied as though with a palette knife to a mouth from which most of the teeth were missing, and heavy ear-rings dangling from lobes as thick and rubbery as motor-car tyres.

Never once had I seen her unaccompanied by all three of her children: two adolescent boys, both gig-lamped, and a lanky girl of school age. They would stand in the street together for hours on end, a compact gawping group, doing nothing, saying nothing, never shifting from their position, until they rode home in close column, the mother on a powerful motorbike painted in colours as glaring as her clothes, the two boys each on a scooter, and the girl on a push-bike, her spindleshanks working like pistons as she strove to keep pace.

The father of the family appeared only at rare intervals. We would sometimes come across him squatting in a hedgerow, invisible from the waist down so that he looked like a toby-jug. With a gesture of exaggerated courtesy he would doff his cap, revealing a growth like a vestigial or incipient unicorn's horn planted with perfect symmetry in the middle of his forehead above a pair of benign blue eyes glazed with drink. We found him rather endearing but he must have been a bit of a trial to his family, judging by the shouts and screams that rose from the little house whenever he tottered home.

One evening, after a particularly violent row which shattered the tranquillity of the whole valley for over half an hour, Xan and I felt we ought to intervene. It was not so much a sense of civic duty that prompted us. Our main concern, to be frank, was to spare our ear-drums further injury. I was also rather curious to see what the little house was like inside and how all of them managed to fit into it.

By the time we strolled down there, all was quiet. The old man had been bundled out and was squatting in a nearby ditch, from which he greeted us with his usual affability. The rest of the family, whom we found at supper, welcomed us warmly and invited us to sit down and share their meal: a cauldron of boiled potatoes. But there was nowhere to sit. Most of the space in the tiny front room was occupied by the motorbike, the two scooters and the push-bike. Not only space but even the most rudimentary comfort seemed to have been sacrificed to these gleaming household gods. I had not been prepared for such squalor, which surpassed that of the poorest Portuguese hovel. What light there was came from a single wick floating in a tin saucer of olive oil. Soot from the smoking stove clung to the bare rafters in the ceiling. The walls glistened with damp which had condensed into rivulets, turning the earth floor into a shallow quagmire. As the mother rose to her feet she had to disentangle herself from her chair, the bare frame of which encompassed her broad posterior like a tightly fitting girdle, its cane seat having long ago rotted away and never been replaced. The three other chairs were also seatless but their occupants, being slimmer, avoided being similarly trapped and merely ran the risk of falling through into the mud underfoot.

In the circumstances we felt it would have been unkind to complain of the noise they made, so, pretending ours was merely a social call, we wished them '*Bon appétit!*' and went back. But the visit had given me an idea. 'Do you think she'd be too proud to help us with the housework?' I asked Xan. 'They could obviously do with the money . . .'

'Yes, if only to spend on their bikes,' he agreed. 'Why not? There's no harm in asking her.'

So I did, two days later. She accepted at once.

For a week or two the arrangement worked perfectly. The daily presence of such a preposterous figure was an active pleasure. Her conversation was as colourful as her clothes and I was delighted to improve my vocabulary with the phrases I picked up from her. She too seemed to enjoy my company . . . or was it only the vacuum cleaner she liked? Did its noise remind her of her beloved motorbike? At all events an expression of deep content, almost of ecstasy, would come into her eyes whenever she used it.

One morning, however, she burst into tears on my shoulder. 'I can't go on like this,' she sobbed. 'It's not the work, that's nothing. And you're paying me handsomely too . . . But I can't stay indoors, I must be out and about.'

Then and there she strode back to her house, and a moment or two later I heard the sound of motorbike engines. I looked out of the window and saw her bouncing along astride her huge machine, followed by her familiar retinue. Each of them gave me a cheerful wave before vanishing over the brow of the hill.

It was not so easy to replace her. Though we lived quite close to the town and often walked in ourselves, no *bonne* could be expected to make the daily journey on foot and the road was so bad that even on a motorbike or scooter hardly anyone ventured down it apart from the gypsy family. Eventually we heard of someone – 'she's slightly dotty, mind you,' we were told – who agreed to come to us providing Xan drove her to and fro from work

She was a middle-aged widow, sound in wind and limb, but, as we had been warned, not in mind. In the first place, she was a compulsive chatterbox and, since she was incapable of working and talking at the same time, even such a simple chore as drying a plate would take several minutes. Fascinated, I would watch her drop it back into the sink as she thought of some remark to make, then retrieve it and start drying it again until a further remark occurred to her. Refusing to listen to her was no solution, she needed no audience and was perfectly happy to talk to herself. In any case she could not be left to her own devices and required constant guidance and supervision. When in doubt – and she appeared to be perpetually so – she had no hesitation in seeking advice.

'What do I do with these?' she once asked me, creeping up from behind as I sat at my desk and unclenching her fist to disclose a handful of dead flies. I was able to restrain myself from replying, 'Put them in your pocket,' and merely grunted to show I was busy. She, to show that she had understood, raised a finger to her lips and tip-toed out of the room. But a little later she was back again, entering as quietly as she had left. I sensed rather than heard her presence behind me, and went on working. Presently I was conscious of something tickling my forehead and looked up to find a piece of string dangling in front of my face. The widow was holding it over my shoulder, as though trying to catch a fish on a line. 'I didn't want to disturb you by asking,' she explained.

'Asking what?'

'Where do I put this piece of string?'

It was a relief when Xan went to fetch her one morning and she failed to turn up at the usual meeting-place. Later we heard that she was undergoing another of her 'cures' in the local loony-bin.

As the winter imperceptibly softened into spring, the rubble continued to pile up in the courtyard. But the house was gradually assuming its final shape. The *bergerie* and the cottage were now united, the intervening space already recognisable as an entrance hall. We had had to dig in our heels over the well which stood here and which the builders wanted to block. 'A well *inside* the house?' they demanded. 'A well inside the house,' we insisted.

We also had the greatest difficulty in persuading them to make the ceiling high enough for the double-cube drawing-room we had planned. 'But it will be as tall as it is broad!' they objected. 'So it will,' we said.

The arboured terrace outside the front door presented a further bone of contention. An old vine, which to my grief had been sacrificed in the course of the work, gallantly thrust a new shoot right through the fresh cement on which the flagstones were to be laid. The builders were intent on destroying it again, and Xan almost gave into them. 'It will never grow properly,' he insisted, turning a deaf ear to my pleas. Fortunately, the day before the execution was due to be carried out, Larry Durrell dropped in and supported my protest. 'You'll be destroying the spirit of the house,' he told Xan, who was immediately persuaded by this argument and relented. I felt that in gratitude to Larry I ought to commemorate the reprieve of the vine by erecting at its foot a stone plaque engraved with the words, *Saved by the Apostle of Love*.

By the early summer we had once more reached the stage of having to travel to and fro between the plumbers, electricians and carpenters in an attempt to co-ordinate their work. Once more we heard, again and again, the dreaded reassurance, '*Demain sans faute*'. Once more we found the carpenters occupied with coffins. But the death rate in their village appeared to be less high than before and our doors and windows were soon in position.

Meanwhile the stone staircase in the hall had been completed as if by magic, for it seemed to be supported by nothing. Xan and I had watched it go up step by step, as fascinated as though we were witnessing the Indian Rope Trick. 'How on earth does it stand up on its own?' we asked the expert working on it. 'It's a Saracenic arch,' was his reply, which merely mystified us all the more.

Our fireplace too had now been erected: a massive but graceful edifice based on a traditional design and stretching almost the whole width of the drawing-room. The young sculptor whom we had commissioned to carve it had personally selected the golden stone from the quarry used by the Romans when building the Pont du Gard. He had also put it up himself, single-handed: a feat almost as miraculous as the construction of the staircase, for the heavy blocks likewise seemed to float in mid-air without any visible support. This work of art was by far the most costly item in the house, but Xan and I both felt that no expense should be spared on something as symbolically and materially important as our hearth.

The final job was the conversion of the lean-to into separate servants' quarters, connected to the main building by a broad covered passage. While this was being completed, we were at last able to rearrange the furniture and make more space for ourselves. Down came the stacks of books lining every wall of the cottage, to be transferred to their ultimate destination: Xan's workroom and library at the far end of the *bergerie*. Piece by piece we cleared the room in which we had been living all winter, until it resembled the dining-room which we had originally intended. Meanwhile the double-cube assumed its role of drawing-room. By gradual stages we shifted our personal belongings from what were henceforth the guest rooms to our new sleeping quarters occupying the whole of the top floor under the pigeon loft. At last I had enough space for my clothes – thirty feet of hanging cupboards, no less – which Xan had cunningly contrived in the passage linking our bedroom to his dressing-room, each with its own adjoining bathroom. The vast Sheraton four-poster we had bought from a friend was finally set up and we were ready to move in.

To celebrate the event, Xan engineered a system of concealed rubber pipes which, at the turn of a tap, sent a flow of water cascading gently into the indoor well, transforming the niche above it into a trickling grotto. Although it was midsummer we ignited a five-foot Yule log in the fireplace, for practical as well as festive purposes, to see if the chimney drew properly. It did. Then we poured a libation at the foot of the vine. With a spirit to protect it, a hearth to warm it, and a captive waterfall pulsating through it like a vein, the Galerie des Pâtres had come alive.

20

The Reckoning

Now came the reckoning.

The bills began to pour in, but there was still no sign of Xan's legacy on which we had been relying. All we had so far received, apart from the usual assurances, were a few payments in advance constituting a minute fraction of the sum that was due and nowhere near sufficient to cover even our most immediate debts. Meanwhile we were again informed that the matter would be settled any day and there was therefore no need for us to take a mortgage on the house.

'But how else can we pay our creditors?' we asked.

'Keep them waiting,' was the unhelpful reply.

We did so for as long as we could, but their patience and understanding finally put us to shame. I raised what capital I had, and Xan borrowed a large sum from a friend, in order to meet the most pressing claims. But there were still further claims, which in their turn became pressing. We continued to receive the usual promises from Nice, but nothing else. This time, on pointing out the urgency, we were told, 'Then you'd better take a mortgage.'

So we did, even though the very word filled me with alarm, recalling my childhood at Glynn when I used to overhear my father and stepmother discussing 'rates of interest' and 'fore-closures' – terms which I barely understood but which I knew presented a menace. I had visions of our home being sold over our heads and pictured myself as Little Dorrit visiting a father in a debtors' prison.

The same anxiety assailed me now and I could see that Xan was also worried, even though the reports from Nice were as optimistic as ever. More than once we were even given a specific date for the final settlement, but each time there was a further delay. Meanwhile, though we were keeping our heads above water, our income had been so drastically reduced that we could not even consider engaging the staff which the house needed and deserved. Thus the comfortable servants' quarters we had built – a large living-room and kitchen, two bedrooms and a bathroom – remained unoccupied. This seemed a horrid waste.

Eventually we came to an arrangement with Jorge Jantus, our Argentinian friend who had painted the murals on the wall of our swimming-pool in Portugal. We heard that he had left Tangier and was now living in Paris, in a tiny attic in a cheap Montparnasse hotel where he was employed as the night porter. He was hating the job and longing for a change. 'I haven't seen daylight or touched a paintbrush for over a year,' he wrote. We suggested he might come and cook for us – in his spare time he would then be able to paint again – but explained that all we could offer was board and lodging and pocket money. The deal was in our favour, for we knew how well he cooked and the servants' quarters were going begging anyway, but he jumped at the suggestion – 'I'll even risk housemaid's knee,' he added – and within a week he had moved in.

From then on we fared extremely well. Xan's everlasting curries and my eternal omelettes, good though they were, made way for dishes that were far more varied, exotic and professional: *carbonada*, a subtle combination of beef, peaches and sweetcorn; *pasqualina* – traditionally an Easter dish but so tasty that we found ourselves celebrating the Resurrection at least once a week – a timbale of cinnamon-flavoured spinach dotted with hard-boiled eggs and enclosed in a crust of short pastry; an Argentinian version of shepherd's pie, made with maize instead of potatoes; and Jorge's speciality, requiring the dexterity of a surgeon combined with the skill of a seamstress – boned chicken. On the first of every month, humble lentils always figured on the menu – not for dietary or gastronomic reasons but because they were prescribed by Argentinian folklore to bring us luck, on the same principle as saying 'Rabbits'.

What a blessing to have such a chef! A double blessing, to have such a chef who was also a close friend! A treble blessing, to have such a chef who was also a close friend and, furthermore, unsalaried! We became the envy of the neighbourhood, and anyone we invited to luncheon or dinner accepted with greater alacrity than heretofore. Thanks to Jorge and the mortgage we had taken, we were able to give a party that Christmas for over thirty people – something we would never have attempted on our own – and, since our dining-room was too small for entertaining on this scale, we transformed his own living-room for the occasion into a *fin de siècle* bistro, incorporating the personal touches he had already introduced to create the setting he most enjoyed.

He took great pride in this little refuge of his, and lack of money did not deter him from embellishing it. He used ingenuity instead. Shells, pieces of cardboard, remnants of material, *objets trouvés* – anything served to achieve the decorative scheme he had in mind. If he wanted a lampshade of a certain design, he made it with his own hands. A cushion cover? He crocheted it himself. An indoor garden? Old whisky bottles filled with a mixture of earth and sand were transformed into miniature Wardonia boxes, the plants inside them keeping fresh through their own humidity. Even his pots and pans served a secondary, artistic purpose. Hanging on hooks from an old worm-eaten door attached to the wall above the stove, they formed a still life harmonising with his own *trompe l'œil* paintings.

To conform with this change in his surroundings, he decided to alter his appearance as well. 'I'm sick of my face,' he said. 'I'm going to grow a beard.' He also allowed his hair – what there was – to grow, and in due course a curly grey fringe sprouted from the back of his neck, uniting below his ears with the new growth on his cheeks and chin. 'You look like an El Greco,' we told him, truthfully, 'one of the figures in *The Burial of Count Orgaz*.'

But he was still unsatisfied. 'Grey!' he moaned. 'It makes me look too old.' So he experimented with various shades of hair-dye, which he applied in quick succession and no doubt over-lavishly; for his beard and neck-fringe first turned a bright Tyrrhenian purple, then a more subdued tone of navy-blue, and finally a delightful yellowish-green which reminded me of those pottery heads in which children grow – or used to grow (do they still exist, I wonder?) – mustard-and-cress.

Despite the pleasure he derived from having a home of his own (more or less), from cooking (as a duty, admittedly), and from painting (when he had the time), there were periods when he suffered from acute melancholia and lost all zest for life. This was understandable. Uzès offered him none of the diversions that could be found in Paris or Tangier. Xan and I were both hard at work and therefore went to bed early, leaving him to his own devices. It must have been a dull and lonely existence for someone so fond of night life.

These moods – his 'black monkeys' as he called them – assailed him less severely during the winter, but with the coming of spring he became positively feverish with depression. He stopped painting, his beard became shaggy and unkempt, even his cooking went off. 'I think I'll get a cat,' he announced. 'Maybe that will cheer me up.'

Xan and I were not fond enough of cats ever to have owned one. Besides, Piggy might have been jealous. But in the circumstances we could not very well deny Jorge his wish. 'So long as you keep it in your own house,' I told him. 'And do make sure you get a male, not a female. . . .'

It was a female he brought back, and not only a female but the ugliest cat I had ever seen: a tortoiseshell, though no self-respecting tortoise would have been seen dead under so ill-favoured a carapace. There were blurred pinkish markings over mouth and jaw, giving the impression of a hare-lip. The wretched animal seemed to be afflicted by a permanent leer, which reminded me of the Tenniel illustrations of the Cheshire cat. But Jorge appeared to be enchanted with Inez, as he christened her, and his depression lifted. And he did keep her to his own quarters, as he had promised. Whenever I passed his door I could hear him addressing her, at great length and with sentimental passion, in the Spanish equivalent of pussy language.

Meanwhile our nights were disturbed by the howling and yowling of prospective suitors, domestic cats from the neighbouring farms as well as those running wild in the garrigue. I warned Jorge, 'Do be careful of Inez, otherwise we're going to have kittens all over the place.'

'Never fear,' he assured me. 'She is always by my side. But to make sure, I'll have her operated. I'll go and see the vet tomorrow.'

He may have seen the vet, but he went no further. He never had Inez operated, nor – for this was impossible – did he keep her beside him every minute of the day and night. In due course she was pregnant.

'You're not to worry,' he told me, when her time came. 'I'll deal with the kittens myself.'

'Get some chloroform,' I advised him. 'It will be kinder to them, and easier for you.'

'I'll get some tomorrow,' he said.

He never did. The kittens were born, and he was faced with the grisly task of drowning them in a bucket.

'Don't forget to keep one back,' I told him, 'otherwise Inez will have milk fever. But this time do make sure it's a male.'

He did keep one back. It was a female.

One Saturday morning, in the market, I saw a small white pigeon for sale. It was hanging upside down on a hook by a piece of string tied round its pink legs and looked so pathetic – a crucified dove of peace, I thought – that I bought it at once. 'It will make a nice Sunday dinner for you,' said the stall-holder, as he handed me my change. I could not bring myself to tell him that my purpose was precisely to save the bird from this fate. Instead, I bought a cage for it and took it home.

It was a mere squab, its beak was still quite soft, and it had not yet learnt to coo like an adult; a mouse-like squeak was all it was able to utter. It seemed utterly defenceless and, with two cats on the premises, I dared not release it at once.

'Surely it can't enjoy being cooped up like that,' Xan objected.

'Better than being made into pigeon pie or done to death by Inez,' I replied. 'Anyway I plan to set it free, but not until it's older and can look after itself.'

When the time came, however, I was reluctant to let it go. Mr Coo, as I had christened it (for by now his voice had broken, as it were, and he was making proper pigeon noises) appeared to be equally attached to me, feeding from my hand, even from my lips, and allowing me to stroke him and ruffle his feathers. To begin with, I gave him the freedom of our bedroom only, after clipping his wings so as to be able to catch him more easily. I need not have taken this precaution, for rather than fly he preferred to perch on my shoulder or else return to his cage. Soon I felt sufficiently confident to let him out in the courtyard, keeping an eye open for the cats. Even here he made no attempt to escape, still apparently preferring the company of humans. At luncheon parties, with complete trust, he would flutter from one guest's head to another, reminding me with a pang of my beloved Bumpy, and I kept him well supplied with small olive twigs which he used to carry in his beak – a living model of the symbol of peace.

By an odd coincidence another pigeon fell into my hands that summer – a woodpigeon with an injured wing, which I caught while walking in the fields and brought home in the hope it might make a companion, maybe a mate, for Mr Coo. I kept it in a separate cage and nursed it carefully, but it did not respond to my attentions. There was nothing wrong with its diet, for it ate ravenously, but when not eating it would merely sit on its perch glaring malevolently. Its grumpy disposition and appearance reminded me so forcibly of a dyspeptic judge that I christened it Lord Merriman. It ignored Mr Coo's attempts to fraternise, and whenever I tried any blandishments it would make a jab at my hand with its horny beak or give an admonishing thump with its good wing. I was glad when it was sufficiently able-bodied again to be released and join the other pigeons in the loft.

When the shooting season opened, in the autumn, I continued to keep Mr Coo's wings clipped, not for fear of his deserting me but lest he be murdered by *chasseurs* (impossible to refer to them as 'guns' in English sporting parlance; 'gunmen' in the American sense would be more appropriate). As soon as these sinister and faintly ridiculous figures made their appearance, accoutred as though for jungle combat rather than sport, the experienced pigeons in the loft steered clear, knowing that anything moving in the air or on the ground, whether a legitimate target or not, was liable to be shot at. Anyone moving, for that matter, was open to the same risk. Not a season passed without a certain number of *chasseurs* (never enough, Xan complained) being shot by mistake (presumably) by their fellows. Even unarmed civilians (to distinguish them from the 'soldiers' in their silly camouflage uniforms) were sometimes peppered while going about their lawful business. Hélène, my equestrian companion, was one such victim. While out riding she had received a couple of pellets in her pretty face, being mistaken presumably for a female centaur. So whenever Xan and I went for a walk at this season, at the first sight of gunmen crouching in the hedgerows we would burst into loud song, not only in the hope of disturbing their aim but as a measure of self-protection.

In his innocence Mr Coo was unaware of these hazards, so I dared not let him out in the courtyard except in a cage, and even then under my constant supervision. (I had visions of him escaping and fluttering trustfully towards a *chasseur* – to him just another human being, after all – only to be blown to bits.) For proximity to a house was no guarantee of an animal's safety. Xan and I had already seen five grown men spend three quarters of an hour stalking and finally shooting a rabbit within five yards of our own kitchen door. And there was nothing we could do about it, apart from cheering when one of them tripped up and measured his length in the long grass while his companions ducked for safety as his gun went off. Legally they were entitled to trample over private property, providing they came no nearer to a house than fifty yards. But

, 28, 29 La Galerie des Pâtres after
storation

30 Daphne riding into Avignon

31 Jorge Jantus in fancy dress

32 Daphne with Claude Durrell outside the Durrell house

33 Larry Durrell outside his house

by the time we had measured the distance and taken the miscreants' names. . . . Anyway, in a court of law – if it ever came to that – it would merely be a case of our word against theirs.

To add insult to injury, after disturbing our peace with their fusillades they would call on us and ask for water – a request we could hardly refuse – or pester us with enquiries about dogs they had carelessly lost. One of them even managed to lose two dogs in one day and asked us to look out for them.

'What are they like?' we enquired.

'One of them is black, the other is brown, and they both answer to the name of White!'

English dog names seemed to be very popular with the shooting fraternity, and the countryside would echo with cries of 'Whisky!', 'Jack!' and 'Vicky!' I used to cry 'William!' myself when putting out food for the dog belonging to our gypsy neighbours, for that was how they addressed him, at least I thought so, until one day the skinny daughter shyly pointed out that I must have misheard. The dog had a perfectly good French name, Brillant, and was not called William at all. Which, after all this time, made me feel a bit of a Charley.

When his owners moved from their little house that winter, they asked us to look after Brillant since they could not take him with them. We were only too glad. We had been feeding him ever since our arrival at the Galerie, so he already knew us well and always joined us on our walks with Piggy for whom he represented a sort of beau ideal, being large, muscular, of indeterminate breeding, but singularly clever and affectionate.

For some time, though he knew his masters had left, he continued to sleep at the little railway house, curled up on the doorstep like an Indian bearer outside his sahib's bedroom. Eventually, during a particularly cold spell, he consented to use the bed we had made up for him in the garage, and from then on he spent every night there. In the daytime he kept moving to and fro between the Galerie and his previous post, as though unable to decide which house to guard. Finally, however, he settled down with us but, as though knowing his place, never once followed Piggy into the house or even into the courtyard.

As spring came round again, Mr Coo began to show unmistakable signs of adulthood. Whenever I set him free in my bedroom he would make straight for my hairbrush, then preen and strut round it as though it was a female pigeon. A china pheasant I kept in the dining-room proved even more irresistible to him; he would bob up and down before it, wings outspread, then mount its ice-smooth back off which, after a brief flutter of feathery ecstasy, he inevitably slipped.

When the shooting season came to an end, I released him out of doors. He at once made advances to the first live bird he saw, a sparrow, which responded with the indignation of an outraged spinster. Frustrated, he then raised his sights and ventured into the loft. But the other pigeons must have resented the intrusion of this cheeky young rival, for an angry altercation ensued. I saw a number of white feathers drift over the roof like snowflakes, and once again heard a series of mouse-like squeaks as Mr Coo in alarm reverted to the voice of his squabhood and flew back into the house, taking refuge in his cage.

For some time he led a solitary existence and continued to seek human company, sometimes waking us up early in the morning by flying into our bedroom through the open window and perching on the foot of the four-poster, his feathers gilded by the rising sun. Eventually, however, he found himself a mate, a little blue-grey Lolita from one of the neighbouring farms, with whom he took up residence. But he continued to use our bedroom window-sill as a restaurant, which he kept secret from his companions, arriving alone twice a day to eat the seed I left out for him. And even though he was now mated he did not reject me entirely. When he passed overhead with the flock which had adopted him, I would merely have to wave my arms and call his name for him to wheel away, like a fighter plane peeling off from its squadron, and land beside me on the balustrade of the courtyard.

Jorge was also affected by the coming of spring, which revived his melancholia. His two cats no longer provided sufficient consolation and were of no avail against his 'black monkeys'. The tranquil fields and woods, the distant mountains, simply aggravated his longing for city pavements and urban activity, for the noisy comradeship of bar and café. Once again he allowed his beard to go untended and began to put on weight. Gloomily he devoured increasingly greater quantities of food at every meal, driven daily more frantic with compensatory hunger. Even in the middle of the night the 'black monkeys' would continue to sharpen his appetite, urging him across the courtyard in his dressing-gown towards the kitchen, insidiously whispering in his ear, 'Something tasty for you in the fridge.'

'I'll have to go back to Paris,' he finally decided.

'But what about your cats?' I asked.

'I'll find a home for them both before I leave.'

And so he did, safely depositing the docile Inez with her future owners in Uzès. But her daughter, named Krikri and now fully grown, managed to escape from her basket just as he was delivering her. Panic-stricken by the noise, smell and sight of a town, she fled down the nearest lane and vanished into the open country. At first we thought she would make her way back to the Galerie, but she failed to turn up. We searched high and low and made exhaustive enquiries, to no avail. She was still missing when Jorge left.

21

The Kiss of Life

So once again we were back where we started, beset by household chores, and with no immediate prospect of a change in the situation. Though Xan's trustee had once again given us a firm date for the settlement of the legacy, that date had long since passed. Meanwhile even the interest we had to pay on the mortgage was a severe strain on our resources. Furthermore, the day was fast approaching when the full sum of the mortgage would have to be repaid and already I was haunted by the dread of foreclosure.

Out of the blue, Diana Cooper came to our rescue. She was looking for something in the country instead of her flat in Paris and, knowing our difficulties, suggested buying part of the Galerie. It was easy to divide the house, since it had been two separate buildings to begin with. The original cottage, now the guest wing, could be put in her name without any further alterations being made. This was done, but not before endless legal formalities had been settled which demanded her presence on the spot.

Thus the three of us – she, Xan and myself – spent several days with the local notary ('our beauty', as she called him, and indeed he might have been the model for a portrait by David – I could easily visualise him in Napoleonic uniform) who eventually drafted a lengthy document which we were all required to sign. After reading the text out loud to us, he asked if we had understood.

'Not a word,' said Diana, 'but it doesn't matter in the least.'

Nor had Xan and I understood; likewise we felt it did not matter. But the handsome notary, before allowing us to append our signatures, insisted on explaining the various clauses and in particular something called *droit d'échelle*, which stipulated that Diana's part of the house should include a strip of land round it broad enough for her to put a ladder up against the wall – 'otherwise, Madame, in the event of your quarrelling with your co-owners, you would find yourself immured and unable to escape.'

'*Droit d'échelle!*' she exclaimed. 'It's like something in a fairy-story.'

For us the whole arrangement was a fairy-story, and she the fairy godmother who had saved our bacon. With anyone but her it would have been hateful to divide our house, but if the present deal meant that from now on we should be seeing more of her, then we were doubly rewarded. Not only was our bacon saved, there would also be eggs to go with it.

Shortly after she left, we were paid another visit which was more unexpected and less pleasant. Krikri, Jorge's missing cat, turned up. She had been at large for over a month and heaven knows how or where she had survived. That she had suffered some traumatic experience was obvious straight away, for although she was starving – this too was obvious – she arched her back and spat at me when I approached her with a saucer of milk. Gradually, however, I managed to entice her into the kitchen where I intended to keep her, for I noticed that besides being famished and half wild she was also pregnant. I had never wanted a cat, even less a neurotic female cat, and least of all one that was about to have kittens, but what else could I do?

The kittens were eventually born in the cupboard under the sink. Neither Xan nor I could face the ordeal of drowning any of them, so we kept the whole kindle of five. Fortunately motherhood made Krikri far tamer, towards me at any rate, though she was still scared of Xan and Piggy, both of whom ignored her. But I found myself spending more and more time with her, observing how she brought up her young. Scarcely were their eyes open than she began to train them to hunt, bringing tiny little shrew mice in from the garden and depositing them in their midst. It was fascinating to see how they imitated her after the very first demonstration.

One evening I was interrupted in my work by a dreadful caterwauling in the kitchen. I rushed in to find the kittens cowering in a corner, tufts of fur still floating in the air, and Krikri arched like a bow and spitting at the open window through which I could see a strange cat which she must have just put to flight. The intruder returned several times during the next few weeks and each time the same hullabaloo ensued. But eventually, as soon as the kittens were weaned – and it was not long before they learnt to lap and I started feeding them on raw meat – I noticed that far from discouraging her suitor, Krikri went out in search of him. But she never stayed away for more than an hour.

Then one night, by the ice-blue light of a full moon, I saw her sitting patiently on the branch of the big mulberry tree. It was only too clear that she was keeping an assignation. As I expected, the strange cat presently appeared on the wall of the terrace, then sprang on to the same branch. For several minutes the two of them sat watching each other in silence. Simultaneously, still in silence, they crept closer together. They were almost nose to nose when they started ululating like a pair of flamenco singers. Then, with a dual gymnastic leap and an ear-splitting howl, they met in mid-air before disappearing over the wall in a tangle of fur and claws and teeth.

I heard them again several times during the night, in the distance. But neither of them reappeared. Krikri had taken to the wilds again, for good.

I would have had no difficulty in getting rid of all five kittens, but by this time I had become converted to cats and was resolved to keep at least one. My choice was a male, the smallest but the most advanced of the kindle, the first to have opened its eyes. It was those eyes, twin orbs of chrysoprase flecked with yellow lichen, that won me over; also the delicate pink of his rose-petal nose. His markings reminded me of an Elizabethan costume, so arranged that he seemed to be wearing an iron-grey cloak flung across his shoulders. His legs were dappled like a faun's and the heart-shaped pattern on his forehead formed an almost three-dimensional head-dress recalling the bonnets worn by Mary Queen of Scots. Had he been a female, I would have so christened him. Instead, I called him Mario.

I never regretted my decision to keep him. Though still so young, he already showed the affection that I had always found absent even in adult cats (hence my previous reluctance to have one as a pet). Orphaned and separated from his brothers and sisters, he adopted me as a substitute for his own kith and kin and was as faithful as any dog. It was only at night that he left my side, and then only because I insisted on it, banishing him to a downstairs room from where he was able to set out on his nocturnal ratting excursions which I wanted to encourage. The afternoon siesta, however, he invariably shared with me, lying curled up on my stomach, his regular and singularly deep purr sending me to sleep more effectively than an opiate and giving me the same reassuring sensation that Rubio, the cat on *Memory*, had provided during those dreadful stormy nights at sea ten years before. If I overslept he would wake me with a gentle tap of a furry paw on my eyelids.

Xan, too, came round to him and even Piggy tolerated his presence. In front of us she made a point of asserting her superiority, driving him away with a show of teeth if his kittenish exuberance became too exasperating, but this was purely for our benefit. On her own, unless she knew we were looking, she seemed even to enjoy his company and from my bedroom window I would often watch them sunning themselves together on the terrace.

Any fear I still had of bad feeling between them was finally dispelled when, on coming home late one night, we found them dozing side by side in the same basket. They separated at once with a guilty start, like a couple of lovers caught red-handed, he slightly conscience-stricken at not being on the hunt out of doors, she rather sheepish at being discovered in such a compromising attitude of contentment. In a belated attempt to make amends she drove him from the room with a conventional snarl, which even to her must have sounded as half-hearted as it did to us.

Since we no longer had the interest on the mortgage to pay, we decided to engage a married couple for the housework. This was a luxury we could still ill afford, but we felt the Galerie deserved it. Besides, I hated to see the servants' quarters being wasted, especially since I knew that with such accommodation to offer we should have no difficulty in filling the post.

A single advertisement in the local paper produced over

fifty applications, which we sorted out and reduced to a short list of a dozen. But we had interviewed less than half the candidates when the student riots of May (1968) broke out, followed by the general strike. No more letters were delivered, the railway ceased to function, buses stopped running, the petrol pumps ran dry. One married couple who had come for an interview all the way from Perpignan found themselves stranded at the Galerie and unable to get home. So for the time being they moved in.

Mercifully, in this little backwater of ours, we were spared the violence and demonstrations that afflicted Paris and the larger towns during the next few weeks. The sound and fury of the outside world reached us as a muffled echo, the radio being our only means of communication. Though the whole country had been brought to a standstill, this affected us hardly at all. Everyday existence seemed simpler and more natural than before. With the banks closed, even our chronic shortage of money presented less of a problem. We merely continued to live on credit, but without being so hag-ridden by guilt. An additional advantage we derived from the circumstances was having the stranded couple on probation for so long. By the time the situation had reverted to normal we knew they would suit us even though it was clear that they had never been in service before. For we had seen how well they got on with the animals. Perhaps, for them too, what tipped the scales in our favour was having Piggy, Mario and Brillant about the house. Anyway they stayed on.

So now the Galerie was more or less adequately staffed, though we still did not have a gardener. We already had a garden, however, at least the beginnings of one. We had started with nothing, with worse than nothing in fact. What little earth there was in the courtyard had been buried inches deep in rubble and cement. Before we could plant as much as a petunia all this muck had to be removed. Xan tackled the job, single-handed, with only a pick, shovel and wheelbarrow. It was a long and arduous task, but there was a harder one to come. The whole courtyard had to be spread with gravel to prevent it from becoming a quagmire, and fresh soil had to be dug into the future flower-beds. This job too – a veritable labour of Hercules – Xan accomplished unaided. Several lorry-loads of rich brown earth and multicoloured shingle were deposited outside our front gates, forming hillocks and pyramids so huge that I felt they were bound to become permanent features in the landscape. It seemed impossible that one man would ever be able to shift them. But Xan toiled away for several weeks (stopping only long enough to allow a sprained wrist or pulled muscle to recover) by the end of which the landscape had reverted to its former contours and his own torso had assumed those of a professional strong man. But at last the courtyard was ready for planting.

We had no money for plants. To stock the garden, we begged and stole, digging up the garrigue for wild lavender, thyme and rosemary, raiding abandoned private properties for irises and bulbs. On one of our foraging expeditions I even popped over a wall and, to Xan's surprise, reappeared with a small apricot tree. To my own surprise, I won a gardening competition promoted by the magazine *Elle* and received two dozen rose bushes. Our frisky landlord from Collias gave us several creepers and three sprigs of willow cut from his own big tree, each with a grain of maize inserted into one end to encourage it to take root – a form of sorcery I had never encountered before. And whenever we went out to lunch or dinner with any of our friends, we cadged cuttings and saplings unashamedly.

A particularly rich source of supply was Jean and Lauretta

Hugo's lovely garden near Lunel. A meal at the Hugos' always included some delightful surprise. It was here I first tasted roast peacock, a gastronomic experience enhanced by the adjuncts of a huge old-fashioned dining-room and napery, plate and silver which must have been in use two generations before, in the days of Victor Hugo himself. The garden had been planned in a similar vein and on the same lavish scale as the house. Quality was not sacrificed to convenience and it was typical of our benefactors that each plant they gave us was identified not with a modern plastic label but a small enamel plate – a further legacy from bygone and better days – beautifully inscribed in Jean's own handwriting.

Another benefactor, Alan Tagg, gave us a small sack of sunflower seeds collected from the crop grown in the holiday house he owned nearby. These proved particularly successful, with heads as big as sunburst clocks. After being pricked out they lined our drive like an army of Grandville's *fleurs animées*, turning their faces daily in a wide angle to follow the course of the sun. I adopted them as our emblem.

By the autumn the Potala-like façade of the Galerie was already softened by an incipient tracery of creepers. The roses were flourishing. The looted plants had likewise thrived. The vine, saved by the Apostle of Love, had risen to the top of the arbour. The frisky landlord's magic had worked and the willows, firmly rooted, had doubled in size. Yet the courtyard still looked bare and austere, 'like the exercising yard of a prison', I complained.

So Xan planted a dozen cypresses, the cheapest trees available. 'Now it looks like a graveyard,' I told him.

Throwing caution to the winds, he then planted more trees – two pawlonias, a couple of limes, a sophora japonica, a catalpa, a mulberry platanifolia – each of which demanded a ton of fresh soil and a corresponding muscular effort. But the result was worth all the toil and expense. By the end of the following summer the courtyard was dappled with shade and we were able to eat outside without being bludgeoned by the direct rays of the sun or blinded by the glare from the gravel.

What amazed me most about this achievement was its being due entirely to Xan, who had previously shown not the faintest interest in horticulture. In Portugal he had taken the garden for granted and would hardly have known what to do with a trowel or secateurs. Now there was no holding him. Planting became his passion, pruning his vice. He assumed proprietary rights over every leaf and petal, but his enthusiasm was not supported by knowledge and experience. It was a mistake, for instance, to pinch off almost every new shoot of a Russian vine in the hope that growth would thereby be encouraged. 'One lives and learns,' was all he could say when the wretched thing died on his hands.

It was also a mistake to believe that the compost heap, his latest toy, could subsist on discarded underwear and old Wellington boots. But when my daughter Caroline tactfully pointed out his error, he went to the opposite extreme. The heap was transformed from a refuse pile into a sort of shrine, on which he deposited votive offerings of only the purest vegetable matter. I even suspected him of feeding it with fresh mushrooms from the market. This time at any rate he achieved the result he intended and I would often come across him worshipping at his odoriferous altar, sniffing the compost and running it through his fingers.

Watering became a second ritual, to which he devoted at least an hour every day, and since this coincided with a third – a drink at sundown – he performed them simultaneously, whisky-and-soda in one hand, hose-pipe in the other, slaking his own thirst and that of the flower-beds and trees at one and the same time. Long before breakfast he would be outside again, surveying the result of the previous day's activities.

One morning I found him standing in the middle of the courtyard, arms akimbo, glaring sternly at the rose-beds like a general inspecting his troops.

'Anything wrong?' I asked.

'No, I'm just seeing what buggery the plants have been up to during the night.'

By which I knew he meant, 'what buggery *your cat* has been up to', for Mario was still at a playful age and a flower nodding in the breeze was as irresistible to him as a scuttling mouse or fluttering insect.

Meanwhile I had a garden of my own indoors: on the landing which, thanks to a huge orangery window, was converted into a broad sun-deck where we sometimes had breakfast; it was too warm to sit here at any other time of the day. In this hothouse atmosphere my potted plants grew at beanstalk speed. Creepers, trained on wires, reached to the roof. Climbers spread up the stairs and over the banisters, sprouting aerial roots and suckers that dangled into the hall below. The ceiling and walls were soon well-nigh obliterated in foliage, and the floor itself was dappled with vegetation, in which Mario loved to lurk – a Douanier Rousseau panther in his own miniature jungle.

There was only one cloud in our sky, only one fly in our ointment, only one blemish on the fair face of our present existence – financial anxiety. Four years had now elapsed since we had been told that Xan's ship was coming in. Yet, despite repeated assurances, there was still no sign of it and its absence was beginning to prey on our minds.

I found myself becoming more and more superstitious,

polishing Hemingway's magic chestnut on my nose, counting the magpies in the mulberry tree and saying to them, 'Good-morning, my lords,' making wishes on the new moon according to an elaborate formula I had evolved for myself, rushing out to wave as our train went by each morning (an answering wave from the driver augured well, a toot of greeting from the engine was an even more favourable omen). And I never failed to pat the medieval stone gallows standing by the side of the path on one of our daily walks. I even exhorted our friends to do so, and most of them obliged. Larry Durrell was the only recalcitrant. 'It may bring *you* luck,' he said, 'but touching a gallows is meant to increase one's potency and I'm potent enough already, thank you very much!'

Our luck, however, remained unaltered. But not our patience. The reports from Nice now seemed an insult to our intelligence. Though still reluctant to take independent action, we realised there was no alternative. So Xan withdrew his power of attorney and engaged a lawyer of his own.

In spite of the anxiety which had plagued us ever since we moved from Portugal, we never regretted our decision to settle in this part of France. We were delighted with the landscape. delighted with the climate, delighted most of all with the people. Familiarity with Uzès had bred anything but contempt, and further afield, within a radius of fifty miles or so, we had made a number of new friends who we knew would be friends for ever.

There was one family in particular whom we never tired of seeing – the Godebskis. Jean, the head of the clan, had endeared himself to me at our very first meeting by saying, *à propos* of nothing but in perfect English, 'Cut yourself a piece of cake and make yourself at home!' I was later to discover that he had learnt this phrase from Arnold Bennett, with whom he had stayed in England as a young man, but at the time I was enchanted by its irrelevance, by the slightly theatrical quality which I already noticed was peculiar not only to himself but to his wife Mimi and their six children as well. Subsequently, whenever we lunched or dined with them, either in their lovely *hôtel particulier* at Nîmes or in their farm on the edge of the Camargue, I was amazed to find a fourth wall behind me and not an open space where the curtain comes up and down, for I felt I was in the midst of characters straight out of a Russian play.

It was not so much their appearance that created this illusion, though I was impressed by Jean's humorous features (with his twinkling eyes and horn-rimmed spectacles, he reminded me of an aristocratic version of Groucho Marx), by Mimi's physical and mental distinction (inherited from her de Bernis ancestors, as was the house at Nîmes) and by the combination of both which was apparent in each of their offspring. Nor was it the sheer size of the family (four of the children were married and the household was generally increased by two or three and sometimes all of the in-laws, several grandchildren and at least one maiden aunt). It was rather, for want of a better word, the *style* in which they lived and the attitude they adopted to the world.

We knew they were as chronically broke as ourselves. (When Mimi heard that we had paid off our mortgage her reaction was not only instinctive but also prompted by personal experience. 'Splendid!' she exclaimed, giving each of us a hug. 'Now you must arrange for another at once and so have a nice lump sum to spend.'* But they never allowed financial crises to detract from their vivacity or lower their standards.

Frequently they were servantless, as we had been, but their

* In due course we were forced to take her advice.

hospitality remained unchanged. Jean would do the shopping; Mimi would bake a cake; François, the elder son, would lay the table and act as butler; Nicolas, the younger, would do the cooking; Florence, his wife, would arrange the flowers; Pascale, the youngest daughter, would decant the wine which she herself had pressed and put in barrel; and whichever of her elder sisters – Isabelle, Ariel or Estrella – happened to be at home would volunteer for other duties. The result of this communal activity was an atmosphere of elegance and excellence that could hardly be surpassed by the richest and most leisured host and hostess.

Sometimes, when we visited them in the country, we found the house completely deserted and the family dispersed at their various occupations. As the sun set, gilding the orchards and vines and transforming each plantation into a field of cloth of gold, they would drift home one by one. Jean would trudge back with easel, paintbox and canvas after finishing one of his characteristic landscapes, or else return, booted and spurred, from the stables; François would emerge from the barn he had converted into a studio, still sweating from the heat of the blowlamp he used for his kinetic sculptures (father and son had recently had a joint exhibition of their very different work in Paris); Mimi and Pascale would appear, boiler-suited and begrimed, from the fields in which they had been toiling since dawn with their labour force of Portuguese and Spanish peasants; Nicolas and Florence would turn up in a cart laden with the firewood he had chopped and the flowers she had picked.

Within an hour they would all be transformed, the men into worldly dandies, the women into exotic butterflies, and as I glanced round the candle-lit dinner-table I would be struck once again by the illusion of ease and affluence they always managed to create. This illusion persisted even afterwards,

34 *left* Hélène

35 *below* Jean Godebski

36 *above* 'The Gods', from left to right: Pascale, Florence and Nicolas Godebski with Hélène in the background

37 *right* Jean Lafont branding his young bulls

38 *above* Diana Cooper at La Galerie des Pâtres

39 *right* Mai Zetterling and David Hughes

40 *below* Lis Frink and Ted Pool

when we sat out on the terrace flanked by bonfires of vine-shoots to ward off the mosquitoes, while the dandies strummed their guitars and the beauties lay languidly in hammocks or rose to tread a wild *sevillano*. On such occasions the abbreviated form of their surname, the Gods, which Xan and I always used when referring to them, seemed singularly appropriate.

Sometimes midsummer madness would infect us all and, with a concerted cry of '*Au bassin!*', we would find ourselves plunging fully dressed into the stone fountain on the front lawn. I remember once rising to the surface and staring at the stars overhead which seemed brighter and more numerous than I had ever remembered. 'Just look at the sky!' I said to Jean in my bad French. 'It's like a birthday cake for the whole of mankind.'

'Cut yourself a piece of sky and make yourself at home,' he replied in his perfect English.

It was through the Gods that we came to know Jean Lafont. We had heard of him before – who, in this region, had not? – but I had found it impossible to form a mental picture of him. He had been described to us in terms that seemed totally contradictory. A reference to him in connection with his herd of bulls would conjure up the image of a leathery-faced cowboy. When the word 'aesthete' was applied to him, I would find myself visualising a French version of Aubrey Beardsley. A mention of the Gothic clocks and suits of armour which he collected inevitably invoked the vision of a shrivelled old antiquarian or a foppish young one. And the accounts we had been given of memorable meals at his table suggested the aspect of a paunchy gastronome.

None of these fanciful conceptions was borne out on meeting him. The man who greeted us as we arrived for lunch at his house deep in the Camargue was a compact, sturdy figure with thick, rather unkempt hair, eyes set catlike above high Slavonic cheekbones, lines provoked by laughter or the sun etching the brown skin over forehead, jaw and temples. Puck might have looked something like this, was my immediate reflection, only he would not have had the underlying gravity of demeanour I noticed in our host. Nor, on second thoughts, could I associate Puck with such a gentle voice and diffident manner.

We were shown into a living-room lined with leather-bound books and furnished entirely with *art moderne* pieces which in their profusion and perfection reminded me of illustrations in *The Yellow Book*. Lunch was already laid in the adjoining conservatory – a semicircle walled and vaulted in glass – and as we sat down at the round table of glazed pottery with a raised design of acanthus leaves (on high-backed pottery chairs to match, which proved deceptively comfortable) our faces were dappled with the sunshine which filtered through the plants surrounding us and forming a canopy overhead.

Hare was the main course, or rather the two main courses, for the saddle was first served separately, roasted. As soon as I tasted it I realised why; it was far too delicate and delicious to be jugged with the rest of the animal which succeeded it, accompanied by freshly-picked wild leeks and globe artichokes so young and tender that we devoured them as if they were peas. The jelly that followed was the colour of champagne – not unnaturally since this was its main ingredient – and in subtle harmony with the plates off which we ate it, the preserved food which it contained echoing the wild strawberries depicted on the pale green china.

Jean – for such a convivial meal we were on Christian-name terms – revived our interest in the *course libre*, and from then on we made a point of following his bulls at whichever arena they happened to be engaged. Soon we were sufficiently conversant with the sport to be able to appreciate its finer points and assess the performance of each of the *razeteurs*. Even to an untrained eye, these white-clad figures provided an enchanting and thrilling spectacle, moving like a corps de ballet as they manoeuvred round the ring, skilfully and swiftly positioning the bull before dashing in one after the other to try to snatch the cockade attached to its brow, then leaping over the barrier with fantastic agility to avoid the horns by the fraction of an inch. Every time I watched them I was reminded of the ivory statuette in the Herakleion Museum, depicting a Minoan bull-vaulter. These men, I felt, were the direct descendants of that anonymous athlete, and perpetuating a cult infinitely more civilized than its gory Spanish counterpart.

I never ceased to be amazed by the sheer physical effort demanded of a bull-breeder as conscientious as Jean. At a *ferrade* to which he invited us in the summer – and this was only one of the many duties involved in his profession – he was in the saddle and at full gallop almost continuously from dawn until early afternoon, personally helping his troop of *gardiens* to round up each of the young bulls due for branding, dismounting only to wield the branding-iron himself and notch the animal's ear with the herd's identification mark. (As a souvenir he gave me one of these clippings, as soft and velvety as edelweiss, which I subsequently pressed between the leaves of a book.)

Afterwards, back at the farm, while the rest of the company slaked their thirst with *pastis* out in the courtyard, he put the finishing touches to the meal he had previously prepared – shrimps, chicken, sausages, pimentoes and aromatic rice gently simmering in half a dozen *paella* pans on a long row of camp-fires – to which he devoted as much care and attention as to the *haute cuisine* in which he normally indulged.

We sat down to eat, fifty of us at least, at trestle-tables under the trees through which the sky appeared all the more intensely blue, flocked with drifting clouds, heavenly siblings of the white horses grazing around us. The feast was followed by spontaneous speeches triggered off by a steady consumption of wine, some delivered in French, others in Provençal, and all in praise of our host. One of the guests, a bucolic grog-blossom of a man in a white cap and Sunday-best suit, even moved himself to tears with a recitation of an impromptu laudatory poem, and I found my own eyes prickling.

Catha Guillaume, Richard Aldington's daughter and a near-neighbour of Jean's, had once said to me, 'The local people are so fond of him that if his bulls didn't do well they might almost tear him limb from limb.' This was before we had met him and I had not quite understood what she meant. But now I did.

We knew Mai Zetterling and her husband David Hughes before they came to this part of France, but only at second hand: David through his novels and Mai from having seen her several years before on the stage, in Anouilh's *Point of Departure*, in which she had appeared with Dirk Bogarde. If anyone had told me then that these two stars would one day become close friends of ours, I would have dismissed such a prophecy as too improbable. Yet Dirk had already stepped into our hearts and subsequently Mai had followed suit, over dinner at the Durrells.

She and David captivated me at once, and when they told us they wanted to buy a house near here – 'but it must be really isolated', they insisted – we thought at once of the lovely farm near Belvezet which we had come upon by chance during our initial search of the area. We had since learnt that it was for sale, but something had prompted us to keep this to ourselves, maybe because we hated the idea of its being acquired by someone unworthy of it. Mai and David seemed destined to own it; for in her I recognised a fey, earthly quality disdainful of luxury, while to him intellectual values were clearly more important than material considerations. So we let them into the secret.

One visit was enough to persuade them to buy it. And to celebrate the purchase, Mai and I exchanged fossils (she had picked one up on the spot) like members of a primitive tribe sealing a pact of friendship.

From then on they came out as often as their work allowed, staying with us but spending all day at their own house to supervise the builders they had engaged. No sooner was their new roof on than they started living under it, indifferent to the lack of electric light and running water. Though they were virtually camping out to begin with, her energy and his ingenuity soon transformed the empty shell which, with the acquisition of a few sticks of furniture, assumed the atmosphere of a house that had been lived in for ages, indelibly marked with their personal imprint.

'You have to choose somewhere and passionately stay there,' David advocates in his lastest book.* He and Mai could not have practised more fervently what he preached.

Another young couple we knew, Ted Pool and Elisabeth Frink, had likewise given the kiss of life to a house in which the heart had ceased to beat, and revived the land round it with a transfusion of fresh stock and new husbandry. Their choice had been a whole ruined hamlet in the foothills of the Cévennes, and everything they undertook seemed to be on an equally generous scale. When Ted wanted more land to farm, he bought several hundred acres at a time. When Lis cooked a meal for six, she catered for a dozen.

* David Hughes, *The Rosewater Revolution*, soon to be published.

Her sculpture, too, had assumed similar dimensions, exemplified by the four massive bronze heads in the drive. The small winged figures, half human and half bird, which I remembered from her earlier exhibitions, were now succeeded by life-size equestrian statues. To transport each plaster model back to England for casting, a horsebox had to be specially sent out.

Her studio sometimes resembled a taxidermist's parlour and each time I entered it I used to steel myself against the possible shock of encountering whatever dead animal she happened to be drawing at the time. Once I was surprised to see a red dog fox, which reminded me at once of hunting days in England. It had in fact been killed two days before by the Mendip Hounds and brought out here by a couple of friends who had come to stay. On another occasion I was greeted by an eagle lying on the floor with wings outspread. To Lis's rage, it had been shot by a local *chasseur* after flying all the way from Norway, as the ring round one leg testified. Its mate was still circling overhead.

It was typical of the Pools' generosity to take us out to dinner as a birthday treat for me. Typical, too, of their sense of fun to choose an incongruous place for the occasion: an old-fashioned hotel in a spa which, according to the guidebook, was once famous for the treatment of syphilis and scrofula. Though none of us was suffering from either of these ailments, we agreed to go the whole hog and spend the night there.

We met in the bar, where Lis presented me with an additional gift of a painting she had picked up at a street market on the way. At an adjoining stall she had also bought herself a cheap cotton caftan, the sort of garment on which only her unerring eye would have lingered and which only her idiosyncratic style could justify. Against its chalky whiteness, her coppery brown skin gleamed like the trunk of a newly stripped cork-tree.

Ted had dressed with special care to conform to the environment: in black velvet jacket, striped trousers and dove-coloured waistcoat adorned with a heavy gold watch-chain. With his beautifully trimmed beard, he might have stepped straight out of one of the faded sepia photographs on the walls depicting clients of yesteryear having tea out on the lawn, the ghost of which, now untended, we could see through the french windows.

Dinner was of suitably Edwardian proportions, accompanied by a succession of regional wines, punctuated by an essential *trou normand* – that traditional depth-charge of Calvados to clear the way for further food – and rounded off with several glasses of the local *marc.*

Afterwards, up in our room, I rested the picture I had been given against the foot of the big brass bedstead. At first I could not see the connection between its title, *Le loup dans la bergerie*, and the characters it portrayed: a rakish elderly cavalier, sumptuously dressed in black with lace ruffles, introducing a bashful fair-haired youth to a trio of innocent girls. But the wolf we were still trying to keep from the door of our own *bergerie* at once sprang to mind, its snarling ferocity exaggerated by the evening's excesses.

I opened the window, leant out and took a deep breath. And as I inhaled the sulphur fumes rising from the ancient Roman spring, I entreated Mercury to protect our roots planted so felicitously – and, I hoped, not too precariously – in Languedoc.

Index

INDEX